# MEDICINE, LAW AND PUBLIC POLICY IN SCOTLAND c.1850–1990

T0386703

# MEDICINE, LAW AND PUBLIC POLICY IN SCOTLAND
## c.1850–1990

*Essays Presented to Anne Crowther*

*Edited by*
Mark Freeman, Eleanor Gordon and
Krista Maglen

*Foreword by*
Rick Trainor

Dundee University Press

First published in Great Britain in 2011 by
Dundee University Press

University of Dundee
Dundee DD1 4HN

http://www.dup.dundee.ac.uk/

ISBN: 978 1 84586 116 2

*British Library Cataloguing-in-Publication Data*
A catalogue record for this book is available on request from the British Library

Typeset by IDSUK (DataConnection) Ltd
Printed and bound in the UK by Bell and Bain Ltd, Glasgow

# Contents

    Scotland, 1950–1980                                              141
    *Roger Davidson*

9 'Boy' Clerks and Scottish Health Administration, 1867–1956        161
    *Ian Levitt*

10 Central Policy and Local Independence: Integration, Health
    Centres and the NHS in Scotland 1948–1990                        180
    *Marguerite Dupree*

    *Anne Crowther: List of Main Publications*                       203
    *Index*                                                          205

# Notes on Contributors

**Anne Cameron** concluded her doctoral studies at the Centre for the History of Medicine, University of Glasgow, in 2003. She then became a Research Assistant, working with Anne Crowther on 'The Scottish Way of Birth and Death: Vital Statistics, the Medical Profession and the State c.1854–1945'. She has published several articles from this research project, and is currently an Honorary Research Fellow at the Centre for the History of Medicine.

**Kenneth Collins** completed a PhD at the University of Glasgow, under the supervision of Anne Crowther, in 1987, while working as a full-time general practitioner. He is a Research Fellow at the Centre for the History of Medicine at the University of Glasgow and has published widely on various aspects of Jewish and Scottish medical history. Currently he is English language editor of *Vesalius*, the Journal of the International Society for the History of Medicine, and Visiting Professor at the Department of Medical History at the Hebrew University in Jerusalem.

**Roger Davidson** is Emeritus Professor of Social History at the University of Edinburgh and a Leverhulme Emeritus Fellow. He read History at St Catharine's College, Cambridge and received his PhD from Cambridge in 1971. He was appointed to a Lectureship in Economic and Social History at the University of Edinburgh in 1970, and was subsequently promoted to Senior Lecturer in 1984, Reader in 1996 and to a Personal Chair in 2002. He has published widely on the history of sexuality and sexual health, and is currently completing a co-authored study of 'The Sexual State: Sexuality and Scottish Governance, 1950–80', with Gayle Davis. He is a Fellow of the Royal Historical Society and a former member of the Scottish Records Advisory Council.

**Gayle Davis** completed her PhD at the University of Edinburgh in 2001, and was a Research Associate at that institution before moving to the University of Glasgow, where she worked in a research team headed by Anne Crowther. She is now Wellcome Lecturer in the History of Medicine at the University of

Edinburgh, and has published on various aspects of the social history of health, medicine and sexuality in modern Britain. She is currently working with Roger Davidson on a co-authored study of sexuality and governance in Scotland between 1950 and 1980.

**Marguerite Dupree** is Professor of Social and Medical History at the University of Glasgow and a Fellow of Wolfson College, Cambridge. She has been a core staff member of the Centre for the History of Medicine at Glasgow University since 1986. She is co-author, with Anne Crowther, of *Medical Lives in the Age of Surgical Revolution* (Cambridge, 2007) and of articles on the history of the medical profession in the *Bulletin of the History of Medicine* and *Medical History*. Among her other books and articles are publications on the history of hydropathic establishments, on medical practitioners and the business of life assurance and on issues of integration in the National Health Service 1948–74. She is also author of *Family Structure in the Staffordshire Potteries 1840–1880* (Oxford, 1995) and editor of *Lancashire and Whitehall: The Diaries of Sir Raymond Streat 1931–57* (2 vols, Manchester, 1987).

**Rosemary Elliot** completed her PhD at the University of Glasgow in 2001. She was awarded an Eileen Postan Power post-doctoral award from the Economic History Society, before taking up a position as a researcher on a team led by Anne Crowther. In 2004 she took up a Wellcome University Award at the University of Glasgow, where she is currently a Lecturer in Economic and Social History. She has published on various aspects of the history of health and gender, and oral history in twentieth-century Britain, and is currently working on a comparative study of smoking and public health in post-war East and West Germany.

**Angus H. Ferguson** read Economic and Social History and Philosophy at Queen's University Belfast, before undertaking postgraduate studies at the University of Glasgow. His PhD thesis, completed in 2005 under the co-supervision of Anne Crowther and Marguerite Dupree, examined medico-legal debates over the boundaries of medical confidentiality in Britain. In addition to expanding his work on this topic, Angus's postdoctoral research has focused on the history of infant and child nutrition and the development of medical interest in Sudden Infant Death Syndrome.

**Mark Freeman** completed a PhD at the University of Glasgow, under the supervision of Anne Crowther, in 1999. He has since worked at the Universities of York and Hull, and at the Institute of Historical Research, London. He is now a Senior Lecturer in Economic and Social History at the University of Glasgow, and has published widely on various aspects of modern British social, economic and business history. His most recent book is *St Albans: A History* (Lancaster, 2008), and he is working with Robin Pearson and James Taylor on a study of early British and Irish corporate governance.

**Eleanor Gordon** is Professor of Gender and Social History at the University of Glasgow. Her 1985 PhD was supervised by Anne Crowther and Keith Burgess and later published as *Women and the Labour Movement in Scotland 1850–1914* (Oxford, 1991). She has published widely on gender and family history. Her latest book, co-authored with Gwyneth Nair, is *Murder and Morality in Victorian Britain: The Story of Madeleine Smith* (Manchester, 2009). She is currently working on a history of the working-class family in Scotland between 1855 and 1976.

**Jacqueline Jenkinson** was a Research Assistant at the Wellcome Unit for the History of Medicine at the University of Glasgow, working with Anne Crowther and Marguerite Dupree from 1990 to 1992 on a project which led to her book *Scottish Medical Societies 1739–1939* (Edinburgh, 1993). Since then she has worked as a Lecturer in the Department of History at the University of Stirling and has published widely on the history of Scottish health and on Britain's seaport rioting in 1919.

**Ian Levitt** completed a PhD on the Scottish Poor Law (1890–1948) at the University of Edinburgh in 1982, and has published widely on aspects of the history of modern Scottish and British social policy. He is now Emeritus Professor of Social Policy at the University of Central Lancashire and is currently preparing a volume for the British Academy on 'The Treasury and the Scot, 1885–1979'.

**Krista Maglen** completed her PhD at the University of Glasgow in 2001 under the supervision of Anne Crowther and Marguerite Dupree. She has since worked at Oxford University, New York University and Santa Clara University in California. She is now an Assistant Professor at Indiana University. Her research and publications focus on issues relating to immigration and disease control in Britain, the United States, Australia and the Pacific in the nineteenth century and the present.

**John Stewart** took his first degree at Oxford Polytechnic and his MPhil at Goldsmiths' College, London. He is presently Director of the Centre for the Social History of Health and Healthcare, a collaborative venture between Glasgow Caledonian and Strathclyde Universities, and Professor of Health History, Glasgow Caledonian University. His research interests include the history of the welfare state in Britain and Europe; religion and social welfare; and the history of child psychiatry.

He is a Fellow of the Royal Historical Society and an Academician of the Academy of Social Sciences.

**David Sutton** has a particular interest in the Scottish Poor Law and home medical missions. In December 2009 he was awarded his PhD from the University of Glasgow, where he was supervised by Anne Crowther. During 2005–6 he worked as a University Teacher in the Department of Economic and Social History at the University of Glasgow.

**Rick Trainor** is Professor of Social History at, and Principal and President of, King's College London, which he joined in 2004 after four years as Vice-Chancellor of the University of Greenwich. After study at Brown, Princeton and Oxford (where he was a Rhodes Scholar and took his doctorate), he was Lecturer in Economic History (from 1979), Senior Lecturer in Economic and Social History (from 1989) and Professor of Social History (from 1995) at the University of Glasgow, where he was also Director of the Design and Implementation of Software in History project, Dean of Social Sciences and Vice-Principal. His published work has focused on nineteenth- and twentieth-century British elites, especially in industrialised urban areas; and he is currently working on a social history of the British middle class since 1850. His publications include *Black Country Elites: The Exercise of Authority in an Industrialised Area 1830–1900* (Oxford, 1993) and (with Michael Moss and Forbes Munro) *University, City and State: The University of Glasgow since 1870* (Edinburgh, 2000). He is an Academician of the Academy of the Social Sciences and a Fellow of the Royal Historical Society. He was President of Universities UK from 2007 to 2009.

# Foreword

## Anne Crowther: An Appreciation

### Rick Trainor

Anne Crowther's career is not easy to summarise because it has been characterised by both extraordinary breadth and outstanding depth. Her contribution to academic life has been so great in part because she has involved herself, energetically and productively, in a wide variety of universities, methodologies and topics of research, administrative commitments, and types of teaching and supervision. Throughout, her professionalism has been enhanced by degrees of warmth, generosity and co-operativeness that would stand out in any academic setting.

Educated as an undergraduate in her native Australia at the University of Adelaide – where she took first-class honours in English in 1964 – Anne proceeded to Somerville College, Oxford, where she took a DPhil in British history in 1968 under the supervision of Agatha Ramm. Having flourished as a student in those contrasting environments, Anne subsequently prospered as an academic not only at the new universities of Kent (1968–73) and Stirling (1973–5) but also at Cambridge (Fellow and Tutor of New Hall 1975–8). At each of these institutions her colleagues greatly lamented her departure. But it was at the University of Glasgow, a Scottish urban university of medieval origin which constituted yet another variant in her academic environment, that she spent, highly productively, the bulk of her career – as Lecturer from 1979, Senior Lecturer from 1988, Reader from 1991 and Professor (of Social History) from 1994 until her retirement (which altered the pattern of her academic endeavours without diminishing them) in 2006.

I can write most confidently of her time at Glasgow, where she and I were colleagues from 1979 to 2000, teaching a course together for thirteen of those years. I arrived in the university only nine months after Anne, but by the time of my entrance she was already a dynamic and substantial force in what was then the Department of Economic (later Economic and Social) History. Adapting without hesitation to the relatively unfamiliar task of teaching modern European economic history – a project in which, she and I, historians of Britain, in somewhat cavalier fashion divided the four leading economies between us – she also quickly became a much admired lecturer and tutor in the second-year course in

British economic and social history. Before long she had also launched a vigorous programme in third- and fourth-year (honours) teaching on topics ranging from the Poor Law and poverty, to crime, to medical history and beyond. She also undertook postgraduate teaching – in the history of industrial relations, for example – and a varied programme of postgraduate supervision.

These bare facts of Anne's teaching cannot convey the passion, dedication, expertise and co-operative spirit that she brought to these various endeavours. Even in a department noted for its diligent care for students, Anne was an outstanding teacher. None could surpass, and few could even aspire to equal, her care in course design and class preparation or, even more so, her knowledge of her students and her attention to their welfare. The especially able and the particularly diligent received appropriate encouragement, while other students received admonition when it was due but always with a kindly stimulus toward improvement. Throughout this teaching and associated pastoral care, moreover, there was constant innovation in approach and content, not least in Anne's dedicated pursuit of computer-based teaching and methods of teaching more generally. Also, while passionately devoted to undergraduate teaching, Anne played a key role in the development of the postgraduate programmes both of the department – for example, she devised the Research Resources and Skills for Historians course for all postgraduates and served as an exemplary supervisor of doctoral theses – and of the wider School of History and Archaeology. It was entirely appropriate, therefore, that she directed the departmental honours programme for many years, that she served in the 1990s as a highly effective head of department and that she proved an influential director of the university's Centre for the History of Medicine for five years from 2001. In these administrative roles, as in her teaching, Anne was not only substantively dynamic but also a very positive personal presence, always ready with a joke (often irreverent), a concerned question and an invitation to warm and lavish hospitality provided with her husband and fellow academic John Crowther at their Cambuslang home.

Anne Crowther's teaching and her administration have always been rooted in formidable research and scholarship. Here, as in her other academic pursuits, Anne's passion for scholarly discovery and her rigorous standards have proved immensely effective on a wide range of subjects using methods both quantitative and qualitative. Her doctoral research resulted in *Church Embattled: Religious Controversy in Mid-Victorian England* (1970). She then transformed herself into a major economic and social historian of modern Britain, with a particular interest in public policy, as indicated by *The Workhouse System* (1981) and *Social Policy in Britain 1914–39* (1988). Soon the academic world saw the fruits of her newly developed expertise in Scottish history and legal history, notably in *On Soul and Conscience: The Medical Expert and Crime: 150 Years of Forensic*

*Medicine in Glasgow* (1988, with Brenda White). Anne's addition of prowess in medical history gave rise to *Medical Lives in the Age of Surgical Revolution* (2007, with Marguerite Dupree) and to *A History of the Royal College of Nursing 1916–90: A Voice for Nurses* (2009, with Susan McGann and Rona Dougall). Alongside these books have been a profusion of journal articles (in periodicals such as *Historical Journal* and the *Bulletin of the History of Medicine*) and book chapters. These have been characterised, like her books, by both imaginativeness and precision, as is her current work on the Scottish way of recording births and deaths, utilising the records of the registrar general for Scotland, initially funded by a prestigious Wellcome Trust Programme Grant for five years.

Not surprisingly, Anne's research achievements have brought widespread recognition from the broader scholarly community, often in the form of invitations to serve in key roles outside the university (in which she also made significant contributions at faculty and senate level). She has been a frequent, and an especially diligent, external examiner of courses and theses. A member of the Research Assessment Exercise panel for History both in 1996 and 2001, she also served as chair of both the Scottish Records Advisory Council and the Scottish Records Association. A member of the History of Medicine Panel of the Wellcome Trust, and a board member of the Social History Society and of the Society for the Social History of Medicine, she also edited the latter's journal, *Social History of Medicine*. She is a fellow both of the Royal Society of Edinburgh and of the Royal Historical Society.

All these contributions and achievements help to explain the very high esteem in which Anne Crowther is held by colleagues at Glasgow, throughout the UK and well beyond. But that very high regard also rests on her very attractive personality and on the highly congenial approach to colleagues near and far that has characterised her whole career. She has always managed to combine with academic excellence an extraordinary warmth, liveliness and generosity. She has been a leader but, gifted with a capacity for give-and-take, also a much esteemed collaborator in teaching, administrative and research activities. Commendably critical of unpromising proposals and ideas, she has backed those she thought well of with an unselfishness also typical of her approach to the careers of her colleagues, including my own. A lively and effective debater, her infectious good humour has leavened many an encounter with superiors, equals and subordinates alike.

Academic life depends on high standards and dedication for its reputation and its usefulness. Yet academia flourishes best when professional prowess is accompanied by an extremely positive personal approach. In all these respects Anne Crowther has been, and continues to be, a model.

# Acknowledgements

The editors would like to thank the Carnegie Trust for the Universities of Scotland, and the Guthrie Trust, both of which have provided assistance with the publication of this book. We are also grateful to the publishers, Dundee University Press. A version of Roger Davidson's chapter was published in I. Goold and C. Kelly, eds, *Lawyers' Medicine: The Legislature, the Courts and Medical Practice 1760–2000* (Oxford, 2009), and appears in this collection with the permission of Hart Publishing.

# Editors' Introduction

## Mark Freeman, Eleanor Gordon and Krista Maglen

This book brings together ten essays by authors whose work has been influenced by Anne Crowther, who retired as Professor of Social History at the University of Glasgow in 2006. During an academic career lasting almost forty years, Anne Crowther worked at the Universities of Kent, Cambridge and Stirling, and then spent 27 years at Glasgow, during which time she produced most of her best-known work. Anne's DPhil thesis, carried out at the University of Oxford and completed in 1968, dealt with the internal controversies that plagued the Victorian Church of England, and was published as *Church Embattled: Religious Controversy in Mid-Victorian England* by David and Charles in 1970. Her second and probably best known book, *The Workhouse System, 1834–1929: The History of an English Social Institution*, first published by Batsford in 1981, dealt with another key institution of nineteenth-century England, and remains one of the most important contributions to the history of the English Poor Law after 1834. Turning her attention to Scotland – on which this *Festschrift* focuses – Anne wrote, in collaboration with Brenda White, a history of forensic medicine in Glasgow, which was published in 1988.[1] In the same year there appeared the sole-authored *Social Policy in Britain 1914–1939*, a contribution to the 'Studies in Economic and Social History' series of pamphlets published by the Economic History Society. More recently, in collaboration with Marguerite Dupree, Anne completed a mammoth study of medical careers and lives in the late nineteenth century, which appeared in the prestigious 'Cambridge Studies in Population, Economy and Society in Past Time' series.[2] Working with two new collaborators, Anne's sixth book was a history of the Royal College of Nursing, published in 2010.[3] Alongside these landmark books, Anne Crowther has published a range of journal articles, some sole-authored, and others with collaborators, including Brenda White, Marguerite Dupree and James Bradley. A full list of Anne's publications appears as an appendix to this book.

Many of the central themes of these contributions to historical scholarship are taken up in the essays that comprise this book. Although their subject-matter is restricted to Scotland, the thematic scope and depth of Anne Crowther's work is reflected in the array of topics that they address. Each of the contributors has brought to their work something from the expansive catalogue of Anne's scholarship, moving in varied and interesting directions. Some have been directly influenced by Anne in her role as doctoral supervisor; others have worked with her as colleagues or co-authors; and others have been more indirectly inspired by Anne's contributions to the field of social and medical history. The chapters that follow, therefore, address many of the themes that run through Anne's own scholarship; many, unsurprisingly, make direct reference to her own publications. The main exception is *Church Embattled*, which appears at first glance to lie outside the scope of the contributions to this volume. Yet even this study of religious controversy can be seen to have prefigured the dominant interests of Anne's subsequent work. As the preface noted, '[t]he arguments of the period now seem drier than the dust on the volumes which provoked them, yet, unless we can understand why so many intelligent men were roused to passionate indignation over these debates, we shall not know why the Church lacked force and leadership in its attitude towards the social evils which we now think were the chief problem of the nineteenth century'.[4]

These 'social evils', and statutory responses to them, were more fully explored in *The Workhouse System, 1834–1929*. In it she offered a challenge to the notion of the 'total institution' explored by Michel Foucault and Erving Goffman, suggesting instead that workhouses, and other such institutions, cannot be defined by 'a set of rigid definitions', but rather need to be seen as dependent upon local conditions, defying uniformity and providing 'a striking example of central policy contending against local independence'.[5] Importantly, she questioned the received model of the workhouse as simply shunned and detested by the working classes, arguing rather that the poor 'were suspicious of institutions, but nevertheless supported them: new hospital beds were filled as soon as possible; pressure on asylums and charitable homes continued to grow. Even the workhouse responded to this new belief in institutional care.'[6] Contrary to the work of the sociologists who dominated discussion of such institutions in the early 1980s, and who represented working people as objects of social control rather than as active participants in processes of institutionalisation, Anne showed that the poor, while not embracing the workhouse system, contributed to its shaping. This emphasis on what would later be widely termed the 'agency' of the working-class population, in its relationship with social institutions, was a powerful influence on future studies of the Poor Law.[7] *The Workhouse System* was seen by one influential reviewer, Michael Ignatieff, as a signpost that pointed to 'a new social history which starts from the assumption that a society is a densely woven fabric of permissions, prohibitions, obligations and rules, sustained and enforced at a thousand points rather than a neatly organized pyramid of power'.[8] The complexities of the relationships that shaped social institutions cannot be reduced to a crude calculus of 'social control'.

Some of these relationships are explored in the contributions to this book by Jacqueline Jenkinson, Kenneth Collins, David Sutton and John Stewart. Stewart considers the Poor Law in late nineteenth-century Scotland, which developed alongside the better known and perhaps more politically controversial English Poor Law that was examined in *The Workhouse System*. As K.D.M. Snell has recently reiterated, historians are 'accustomed to associate the new Poor Law with the union workhouse, both in popular and academic discussion'.[9] Scotland, however, after the reform of 1845, lacked both workhouses and Poor Law unions, although the law remained harsh in other ways, preventing (in theory) the provision of any relief to the able-bodied. As Stewart points out, one outcome of the distinct Scottish institutional arrangements was that the evolution of Poor Law medical facilities took a very different trajectory from that observed in England and Wales. This distinctiveness was also emphasised by Anne Crowther in an account of 'poverty, health and welfare' in Victorian and Edwardian Scotland.[10] However, some themes were common to both jurisdictions: notably, Stewart's chapter describes ongoing conflicts between the imperatives of localities and the central government – in the shape, here, of the Edinburgh-based Board of Supervision. Like Crowther, Stewart considers the 'consumers' viewpoint' in his assessment of the Poor Law medical services, concluding that the evolution of these services was complex and multi-faceted, and requires further detailed examination by historians.[11]

David Sutton, in his contribution to this volume, examines the relationship between charity and medical education, and specifically the history of domiciliary medical care in nineteenth-century Glasgow and Edinburgh. Based on a PhD thesis supervised by Anne Crowther and Marguerite Dupree,[12] Sutton's work makes a significant contribution to the history of education, as well as to medical history. He draws on a range of work that identifies a distinctive 'Scottish approach' to medical education, but also notes the differences *within* Scotland that can easily be obscured by too blithe an emphasis on Scottish distinctiveness. The evolution of medical education in Scotland's two largest cities followed divergent paths because of particular aspects of the institutional histories of the universities in Glasgow and Edinburgh, and the different relationships between universities, charities and local government. Although elements of the Scottish medical curriculum in the second half of the nineteenth century ensured that the 'Scottish approach' to medical education retained distinctive features that were not observed south of the Border, Sutton shows that 'stark differences of attitude are identifiable between Edinburgh and Glasgow'.[13] His discussion of the variety of institutional influences on the experience of the urban working classes and their relationship with medical services is a valuable addition to the literature on nineteenth-century welfare provision.

Both Jacqueline Jenkinson and Kenneth Collins consider specific minorities within the Scottish population, reflecting a flourishing contemporary historiography of immigrant and minority groups in modern Britain.[14] Focusing on the experience of black African and Lithuanian migrants in the early post-First World War period, Jenkinson details the inadequacy of official responses to poverty and unemployment, the hostility of the settled population – often expressed through trade unions – and the difficulties of integration experienced by the two immigrant groups. Jenkinson's chapter describes the practical relationship between immigrant groups and welfare agencies, especially the parishes, and discusses the role of arms of the state, notably the Scottish Board of Health, which we also meet in other chapters in this book. The local press is mined for vignettes of experience which bring a welcome human dimension to the history of welfare bureaucracies. Similarly, Collins, in considering the history of Glasgow's Jewish community and its rich tapestry of welfare agencies, draws on the *Jewish Chronicle* to provide the detail in which his account of organised Jewish welfare provision in the city is rich. Collins shows that the Glasgow Jewish community used a range of public welfare services in distinctive ways, while also developing its own parallel services. Beyond medical relief and welfare provision, these included boys' clubs: the Jewish Lads' Brigade, for example, was modelled on the Boys' Brigade.[15] As Collins notes, the story of the Glasgow Jewish community has many echoes in other Western European cities, and this chapter is a contribution both to the welfare history of Scotland and to the social history of immigrants and minorities more widely. Collins's interest in this area stems from a PhD on Jewish medical students supervised by Anne Crowther.[16] She has also supervised research on late nineteenth- and early twentieth-century immigration and quarantine policies, which similarly brings together medical, legal and political history in interesting and productive ways.[17]

Anne's tenure as director of the Centre for the History of Medicine at the University of Glasgow, from 2001 to 2006, reflected a long-standing interest in medical history. Only one chapter of *The Workhouse System* dealt with the history of medical relief, but in some respects this relatively brief examination of workhouse doctors and nurses prefigured the detailed consideration that some of Anne's later work gave to medical education and careers.[18] Anne's first book on the history of medicine was *On Soul and Conscience*, written with Brenda White and published in 1988. Although Crowther and White acknowledged that this was a 'celebratory history',[19] its implications ran much more widely than the relatively narrow subject-matter, the history of forensic medicine at the University of Glasgow. In particular, the book explores the relationship of forensic medicine with the evolution of the criminal law, drawing on some particularly notable and colourful cases. As one reader recognised, the

book – like forensic medicine itself – 'works on the boundaries between professions, at the interface of academic and civic institutions, and as an arm of the
social administration of disease, accidents, crime, and poverty'. As such, *On Soul
and Conscience* was 'also a history of medicine and law in Scotland, of the
University's relations with the civic interest, and of the conditions of life of the
city's police and people'.[20]

Similarly, Anne Crowther's more recent work on the history of the General
Register Office for Scotland (GROS), carried out in collaboration with Anne
Cameron, Gayle Davis and Rosemary Elliot, brings medical and legal history
together. The project on 'The Scottish Way of Birth and Death' also draws
on political and administrative history to present a rounded picture of the
development of vital statistics and civil registration north of the Border.[21] It can
be viewed as the Scottish counterpart of Edward Higgs's study of the General
Register Office, and, like Higgs's work, the exhaustive investigation of the
history of the GROS and its practices reveals many intriguing aspects of
processes of state formation in the nineteenth and twentieth centuries.[22]
The growth of what Higgs calls the 'information state' has many contemporary
resonances.[23]

In a paper presented to the annual conference of the Society for the Social
History of Medicine in 2006, Anne Crowther argued that the collection and
subsequent analysis of vital statistics were not merely a presentation of a
supposed 'reality', but rather were social constructions, reflecting the interests
and agendas of statisticians, and the local and national contexts within which
the statistics were collected.[24] Two chapters in this *Festschrift* expand upon
these themes. Anne Cameron examines the early years of civil registration in
nineteenth-century Scotland. By revealing the varied levels of education, social
standing and competence of Scotland's parish registrars, Cameron advances
Anne Crowther's argument, showing that the collection and integrity of vital
statistics was dependent on the capabilities of individual registrars and the
ability of the central authority to maintain standards among them. Cameron
reveals the difficulties experienced by the GROS in dealing with incompetent
local registrars, and, like Stewart, emphasises the importance of the relationships between the local and national state to the evolution of structures of
information-gathering. Turning to the twentieth century, Gayle Davis and
Rosemary Elliot explore the potential invasion of individual and family privacy
through governmental collection of demographic data. By examining the registration of deaths and stillbirths, Davis and Elliot also contribute to the discussion of the growing authority of the medical profession within governmental
and legal structures. Uniquely within this volume, Davis and Elliot focus on the
contribution of a single individual, Dr James Craufurd Dunlop, whose long

tenure as registrar general for Scotland saw a series of important changes in the nature and scope of vital registration. Davis and Elliot note the long-standing importance of the legal profession in the leadership of the GROS, and trace the increasing involvement of medical men as the GROS evolved into its twentieth-century form.

Returning to other aspects of the relationship between medicine and the law, two chapters in this book deal with other features of the distinctive medico-legal history of Scotland. Angus Ferguson provides a detailed account of one of the many 'Scottish myths':[25] the existence of medical privilege in Scottish courts, which some early twentieth-century observers believed to be an aspect that distinguished the Scottish legal system from its English counterpart. Ferguson's chapter – which arises from a doctoral thesis supervised by Anne Crowther and Marguerite Dupree[26] – demonstrates the doubtful grounds on which this belief was based, tracing the ambiguity of specific legal precedents to the situation north of the Border. Drawing on English and Scottish cases from the eighteenth and nineteenth centuries, and paying particular attention to the landmark case of *McEwan v Watson* in the 1900s, Ferguson shows that a 'weak form of privilege' existed, protecting medical practitioners from being sued for slander because of evidence given in the witness box, but that there was no right to decline to give evidence on the grounds of confidentiality.

A very different set of relationships between medicine and the law is explored in Roger Davidson's chapter on the treatment of homosexual offenders in Scotland between 1950 and 1980. Homosexual acts, permitted between consenting men over the age of 21 in England and Wales from 1967, remained illegal in Scotland until 1980, and Davidson draws on the evidence of Scottish witnesses to the Wolfenden Committee, and on the medical reports from a range of cases from the High Court and appeal courts, to examine the nature and extent of medical influence on the legal processes relating to homosexuality in Scotland. Reflecting Anne Crowther's concern with the complex sets of relationships that shape social institutions, Davidson concludes by emphasising the interrelationships of legal, medical and cultural developments, and the persistence of 'taxonomies of deviance' north of the Border, which delayed homosexual law reform and influenced sentencing strategies.[27] As with many other chapters in this book, Davidson's account of medical and legal responses to homosexuality makes a significant contribution in several areas, notably the histories of crime and sexuality, as well as medicine and the law.

The last two chapters in *Medicine, Law and Public Policy in Scotland* deal with the administrative history of the National Health Service (NHS), and reflect Anne Crowther's more recent interest in twentieth-century organisational history, as embodied in her history of the Royal College of Nursing, co-written with Susan McGann and Rona Dougall.[28] However, the chapters here by Ian Levitt and Marguerite Dupree focus on the statutory dimension of Scottish health services, tracing the often complex history of the institutional development of the NHS and its predecessors north of the Border. Ian Levitt navigates through the administrative structures and personnel of the boards and departments that, successively, had responsibility for Scottish health policy. Covering a period of almost a century, from 1867 to 1956, Levitt's administrative history overlaps with Stewart's chapter on the Scottish Poor Law, dealing with the Board of Supervision and its successor, the Local Government Board for Scotland, before moving on to the inter-war and post-war histories of health administration. Levitt describes the creation and workings of the Scottish Board of Health from 1919 and its successor, the Department of Health for Scotland. Anne Crowther has emphasised the weakness of Scottish welfare and health authorities in regard to oversight of local provision before the First World War;[29] and Levitt argues that this weakness was perpetuated after 1919 by the failure to reconstruct Scottish health administration along lines that would have ensured the earlier availability of effective leaders. Levitt's focus is on internal departmental politics and the recruitment and remuneration of civil servants, and complements the social and cultural history of welfare provision in some of the other chapters in this book.

Meanwhile, Marguerite Dupree takes up the theme of the relationship between central and local authorities, covering a later period but emphasising many of the same tensions that had existed a century earlier. Focusing on the development of the health centre between 1948 and 1990, Dupree asserts the value of the local study in assessing the development of health services, even in the modern era of centralisation and specialisation. She emphasises the importance of securing local co-operation and mobilising the support of local stakeholders for the creation of health centres; the varying levels of success in different regions of Scotland are evidence of this. The value of a local approach to the historical study of the National Health Service is demonstrated by Dupree's contrasting case studies of Livingston and Glasgow. Nevertheless, national support, at both Scottish and British levels, was essential to the success of health centres, and where – as in Livingston – the initiative came 'from the top', the promotion of innovation in provision was encouraged and generally successful. This chapter forms part of an ongoing study of the National Health Service in Scotland.[30]

Since her retirement from the University of Glasgow in 2006, Anne Crowther has continued to make significant contributions across her fields of interest. Most notably, 2007 saw the publication of *Medical Lives in the Age of Surgical Revolution*, in which she and Marguerite Dupree present a thorough examination of the careers of Glasgow and Edinburgh medical graduates from the late nineteenth century. In tracing the lives and careers of 'Lister's men', this prosopographical study traces the dispersal of both individuals and scientific ideas through both institutions and nations. Along with the best social histories, *Medical Lives*, in the words of one reviewer, 'reveals in the quiet force of these multiple lives a hidden, unsuspecting heroism of the ranks'.[31] The careers of 'Lister's men' were pursued in Scotland, in England and throughout the British Empire, and Crowther and Dupree demonstrate the central role played by Scottish graduates in imperial medical history. This examination of the wider international contexts of Scottish medical history remind us of the importance of international and comparative perspectives in the pursuit of the history of medicine, law and public policy, and the potential resonance of Scottish history for the world beyond its borders. It is perhaps too early to assess the legacy of *Medical Lives*, but in the breadth of its influences, the sensitivity of its treatment of individuals in their relationship to institutions, and the thoroughness of the research on which it is based, it makes a contribution to historical scholarship that will at least equal that of Anne Crowther's earlier books. The present volume, appearing in the shadow of *Medical Lives*, is gratefully offered by the contributors and editors as a token of our appreciation of Anne Crowther and her work.

## Notes

1. Crowther, M.A. and White, B., *On Soul and Conscience: The Medical Expert and Crime* (Aberdeen, 1988).
2. Crowther, M.A. and Dupree, M.W., *Medical Lives in the Age of Surgical Revolution* (Cambridge, 2007).
3. McGann, S., Crowther, A. and Dougall, R., *A History of the Royal College of Nursing 1916–90: A Voice for Nurses* (Manchester, 2010).
4. Crowther, M.A., *Church Embattled: Religious Controversy in Mid-Victorian England* (Newton Abbot, 1970), 11.
5. Crowther, M.A., *The Workhouse System, 1834–1929: The History of an English Social Institution,* (Cambridge, 1981), 6.
6. Crowther, *Workhouse System*, 66.
7. See for example Lees, L.H., *The Solidarities of Strangers: The English Poor Laws and the People 1700–1948* (Cambridge, 1998).
8. Ignatieff, M.: *History Workshop* 15 (1983), 173.
9. Snell, K.D.M., *Parish and Belonging: Community, Identity and Welfare in England and Wales 1700–1950* (Cambridge, 2006), p. 207.
10. Crowther, M.A., 'Poverty, Health and Welfare', in W.H. Fraser and R.J. Morris (eds), *People and Society in Scotland, Volume II: 1850–1914* (Edinburgh, 1990), 265–89.
11. See below, chapter 1.
12. Sutton, D.A., 'The Public-Private Interface of Domiciliary Medical Care for the Poor in Scotland c.1875–1911', PhD thesis, University of Glasgow, 2009.
13. See below, chapter 2.
14. For many examples of this literature, see the journal *Immigrants and Minorities*, which first appeared in 1982. The subject-matter is international, and by no means confined to Britain.

15. See below, chapter 4.
16. Collins, K., 'Jewish Medical Students and Graduates in Scotland 1739–1945', PhD thesis, University of Glasgow, 1987.
17. Maglen, K., 'Intercepting Infection: Quarantine, the Port Sanitary Authority and Immigration in Late Nineteenth- and Early Twentieth-Century Britain', PhD thesis, University of Glasgow, 2001.
18. Crowther, *Workhouse System*, chapter 7; Crowther and Dupree, *Medical Lives*; Bradley, J., Crowther, M.A. and Dupree, M.W., 'Mobility and Selection in Scottish University Medical Education, 1858–1886', *Medical History* 40 (1996), 1–24.
19. Crowther and White, *On Soul and Conscience*, 135.
20. Smith, R.: *Social History of Medicine* 2 (1989), 222.
21. For publications arising from this project, see Cameron, A., 'The Establishment of Civil Registration in Scotland', *Historical Journal* 50 (2007), 377–95; Elliot, R., 'An Early Experiment in National Identity Cards: The Battle over Registration in the First World War', *Twentieth Century British History* 17 (2006), 145–76; Davis, G., 'Stillbirth Registration and Perceptions of Infant Death, 1900–60: The Scottish Case in National Context', *Economic History Review* 62 (2009), 629–54.
22. Higgs, E., *Life, Death and Statistics: Civil Registration, Censuses and the Work of the General Register Office 1836–1952* (Hatfield, 2004).
23. Higgs, E., *The Information State in England: The Central Collection of Information on Citizens since 1500* (Basingstoke, 2004).
24. Crowther, A., 'By Death Divided: Scottish and English Approaches to Death Certification in the Nineteenth Century', unpublished paper, Society for the Social History of Medicine annual conference, University of Warwick, 2006.
25. See below, chapter 7.
26. Ferguson, A.H., 'Should a Doctor Tell? Medical Confidentiality in Interwar England and Scotland', PhD thesis, University of Glasgow, 2005.
27. See below, chapter 8.
28. McGann, Crowther and Dougall, *History of the Royal College of Nursing 1916–90*.
29. Crowther, 'Poverty, Health and Welfare'.
30. See also Merrick, L.A., 'Local Authorities and the Development of the National Health Service (NHS) in Scotland 1939–1974', PhD thesis, University of Glasgow, 2008.
31. Caldwell, J.M.: *Victorian Studies* 50 (2008), 697.

# 1

# The Provision and Control of Medical Relief
## Urban Central Scotland in the Late Nineteenth Century

### John Stewart

This chapter examines aspects of the provision and control of Poor Law medical relief in central Scotland – both the powerhouse of the Scottish economy and an area with increasingly identified social problems – in the last three decades of the nineteenth century. It thus seeks to build on the pioneering work of Anne Crowther in this and related fields.[1] Indeed the history of the Scottish Poor Law, particularly after reform in 1845, remains under-explored and this in itself highlights Crowther's contribution.[2] Archival material is drawn from Glasgow, Greenock, Edinburgh, Paisley, Leith and Dundee, these being among the ten largest towns in Scotland.

The first section briefly describes the dimensions of pauperism in the area. The second looks more specifically at the context of the Scottish Poor Law. We then, and thirdly, focus on the medical services which the Poor Law offered. The fourth section begins the move into the chapter's central themes, looking in more detail at the conflicts between centre and periphery, a particularly fraught issue in Scottish Poor Law history. In section five, meanwhile, we examine another difficult and contested relationship, that between local Poor Law authorities and their medical staff. Finally, some tentative conclusions are drawn. It is suggested, moreover, that historians of welfare have to be wary about over-playing normative judgements at the expense of historical accuracy.

The chronological boundaries embrace a period by whose beginning the reformed Poor Law had had time to settle down. The Scottish Poor Law, after as before reform in 1845, did not in principle allow relief to the able-bodied. This thrust medical criteria to the fore in determining an applicant's entitlement to parochial support by way of the medical test. Essentially, this placed parochial medical staff in the invidious position of having to determine whether claimants were fit enough to work. If they were, then relief was denied. None the less, in the last third of the nineteenth century at least some contemporaries identified positive improvements in Poor Law medical services. This period, furthermore, saw the replacement of one central body – the Board of Supervision for the Relief of the Poor in Scotland – by another, namely the Local

Government Board for Scotland (LGB(S)), in the mid-1890s, which preceded social policy innovations at a United Kingdom level, notably the Liberal welfare reforms.

## Pauperism in the Late Nineteenth Century

Economic expansion notwithstanding, the late nineteenth century was, for many ordinary Scots, a difficult period. As C.H. Lee puts it, 'unemployment was a frequent experience . . . and underemployment . . . endemic'.[3] In addition, and as in England and Wales, a concerted attempt was made to reduce pauperism – the campaign against outdoor relief – and in Scotland the medical test had a central role to play. At the beginning of our period the towns and cities discussed in this chapter were located on radically different points on the spectrum of pauperism. In the late 1870s the Board of Supervision began publishing data showing the percentage of paupers in towns with populations over 20,000. In 1878, a bad year for much of the Scottish economy, Paisley's rate was the highest in this category at 3.4 per cent while Greenock's was the lowest, at 1.4. Dundee was likewise at the low end of the spectrum (1.7) with Leith (2.2), Edinburgh (2.3) and Glasgow (2.4) nearer the Scottish average rate of 2.8 per cent.[4] Paisley's problems are particularly notable and were historically deep-rooted.[5]

By the mid-1890s, however, a different picture had emerged. Scottish pauperism, which reached its recorded high point in 1868, steadily declined thereafter. In 1894, for example, the proportion of paupers in the total Scottish population was 2.3 per cent; in Greenock, it was 1.9, the rate also recorded in previously problematic Paisley. The rates in Glasgow (2.3), Dundee (2.19), Edinburgh (1.97) and Leith (1.84) clustered round the Scottish average and, with the exception of Dundee, showed a reduction from the mid-1870s.[6] This suggests a more uniform Poor Law system with major towns and cities making a significant contribution to pauperism's apparent decline. As a point of comparison, English rates of pauperism also fell during this period while remaining significantly above those for Scotland: for proponents of the Scottish system, this vindicated its more rigorous approach.[7] The reduction in Scottish pauperism occurred despite socio-economic crises, although by the same token the extent to which the attempt to implement a more rigorous approach to relief actually contributed to this is unclear.[8] But for present purposes what is important is that one way in which Poor Law authorities sought to deal with 'excess' pauperism was to apply medical tests more strictly.

Audrey Paterson and Ian Levitt both point to the appointment of a new Board of Supervision chairman in 1868, and the work of the 1870 Commons

Select Committee on the Scottish Poor Law, as key factors in initiating the campaign against pauperism.[9] Towards the end of our period the Board was replaced by the LGB(S), often seen as of itself signifying a more 'professional', centralised approach to the issue of pauperism. As part of this, we see the more formal establishment of doctors' role in policy formation. Of course, medical opinion had long played a part in Scottish poor relief, not least in the run-up to reform in the 1840s.[10] But as the Scottish Secretary, Sir George Trevelyan, remarked in introducing the LGB(S) Bill in 1894, it was 'high time that on a body which superintends the public health in Scotland a representative of medical and sanitary science should find a place'.[11]

However, it was to be several years before the full impact of this change was felt.[12] It was not until 1901 that a medical inspector was appointed to the central body. One further indicator of this shift was the appointment, in 1902, of the Departmental Committee on Poor Law Medical Relief in Scotland, which, through its recommendations, offered both a critique of existing practice and suggestions of possible ways forward.[13] In short, then, the thirty years from 1870 form a relatively discrete era in the history of the Scottish Poor Law's medical services.

As to their actual delivery, the 1870 Commons Select Committee noted that the 'present condition of medical relief is not a satisfactory one'.[14] It was to be this perceived problem that both local and central authorities sought to address. So, for instance, one positive innovation came in 1885. The conditions attached to the centrally controlled medical grant were altered with respect to poorhouse nurses.[15] The aim here was to improve both the quantity and the quality – by way of required training – of nursing staff, and thereby to enhance the patient experience and medical efficiency.

**The Reformed Scottish Poor Law**

Before moving on to examine these issues in more detail it is necessary to make three general points. First, the 1845 Act required the newly created parochial boards (from the 1890s parish councils) to provide medical relief. This was due in part to the role of medical opinion in demanding change to the system. But it also derived, logically enough in its own terms, from one of the central ways in which entitlement to relief could be gained – the absence of able-bodiedness as determined by the medical test. As we have seen, this placed a considerable responsibility on the shoulders of medical staff who could either test applicants to the full, at whatever cost to the latter's immediate or long-term health; or declare eligible for medical relief applicants who were, by and large, in reason-able health, and thereby in principle flout both the law and the wishes of their lay employers. As one doctor told a Glasgow medical meeting in the mid-1870s, with respect to those not already pauperised all that 'could be said to be done at present was that when the breadwinner of the family was disabled, the inspector gave an order for medical relief'.[16] The issue was more complicated than this but it is notable that the central authority felt obliged, on a number of occasions, to remind local bodies of the law, a clear indicator that it was being broken or circumvented.

Second, the Scottish system in the late nineteenth century differed from its English counterpart in its high level of disaggregation. There were around 800 local administrations, varying enormously in population and size, compared with the 600 or so unions in England and Wales. Fragmentation made it difficult for the central authority to exercise control, a situation exacerbated by limited powers and personnel.[17] It is likewise notable that the 1870 Select Committee had disparaged the quality of Scottish local administration, noting that the 'constitution of parochial boards is not such as to secure any effective check on the increase of expenditure'. This was because of the low level of qualification needed to become a board member and the consequent close relationship of many members to pauper claimants. The temptation was, it was therefore claimed, to raise allowances at the expense of the unfortunate ratepayers.[18] Moreover, local bodies were determined to preserve their autonomy. In 1872, for instance, Paisley Parochial Board formally objected to any suggestion that impending legislation transfer to the centre certain powers 'which the Amendment Act of 1845 very properly rested in local Boards'.[19]

To focus on medical relief, the Royal Commission on the Poor Laws and Relief of Distress noted that in Scotland 'no power of initiative has been conferred on the Central Department' with respect to administering medical relief. This was especially so regarding outdoor relief, where the only means of influence was through 'the medium of the Grant'.[20] Despite the problems confronting it, the Board of Supervision increasingly sought to influence local bodies' attitudes and behaviour and indeed, and claims of local autonomy notwithstanding, its advice was often welcomed as expert opinion.[21]

Third, the Scottish system was overwhelmingly one of outdoor relief, and more so than its English counterpart. In the sphere of medical services one outcome of this, particularly when combined with the highly disaggregated nature of Poor Law administration, was that workhouse infirmaries of the English type did not develop in Scotland's (relatively few) poorhouses.[22] But, as we shall shortly see, there were local authorities that did innovate in hospital building and renovation. It is in the context of a distinctively Scottish Poor Law system that we now turn more specifically to the central issue of medical relief in the last three decades of the nineteenth century.

**The Medical Services of the Scottish Poor Law**

The 1845 Act required poorhouses to have a medical officer. Unsurprisingly, therefore, medical expenditure rose consistently thereafter. In 1870 it stood at £35,500 per annum, rising further to £53,500 in 1900. Given that pauperism was declining in the last 30 years of the nineteenth century while the total population rose, this meant that medical expenditure per pauper rose dramatically, from around 5.5 shillings in 1870 to around 10.75 shillings in 1900.[23] Superficially at least, this would appear to be an indicator of improved quality of services.

The idea of improving services was stressed by contemporaries. A prominent inspector of the poor told the 1902 Departmental Committee that 'the medical relief to the indoor poor, at least in the large poorhouses, has greatly improved of late years'. This was especially due to better hospital accommodation and the employment of trained nurses. Accommodation and treatment in the main poorhouse hospitals, he further asserted, were 'equal to those of royal and district infirmaries'.[24] On the opening of its new hospital Dundee Parochial Board claimed that it was 'quite unique in Scotland, both as regards its Architectural arrangement, and the equipment of the wards'. The 'splendid buildings' were 'fulfilling in an admirable manner the humane purpose for which they were designed', and their occupants were 'being treated under conditions' which reflected well on both the Board and the wider community.[25] Civic pride was further bolstered by the report, which noted that the Board of Supervision's medical officer, Dr Littlejohn, had remarked that 'the new buildings would stand unequalled by any of the same kind in Scotland'.[26]

Of course, it was unlikely that such individuals and bodies would publicly assert anything else. None the less, the need to claim and advertise perceived success does reveal a concern to present Poor Law medical provision in a positive and improving light. Crowther and Marguerite Dupree also note an unintended consequence of the contemporary medical market. Resident medical officer posts in Scottish Poor Law hospitals 'offered little prestige, and less hope of advancement (than in voluntary institutions)'. On the other hand, such posts did allow 'more opportunity to try out Listerian methods without the scrutiny of a critical senior'.[27] Pauper patients, in other words, might be earlier beneficiaries of the 'surgical revolution' taking place in nineteenth-century Glasgow than their voluntary hospital counterparts.

If Poor Law services were improving, they were doing so within increasingly rigid boundaries. On occasions those responsible for Poor Law medical relief articulated the beliefs on which their services were based. So, for instance, in 1876 the medical committee of Glasgow's City parish engaged in a long discussion in part inspired by a report from the reforming medical officer of

health, James Russell. 'No political economist,' the committee argued, 'has ever
maintained that it is to be desired that sickness alone should be permitted to
drive the sick into the region of pauperism.' Poor Law provision should be for
paupers alone, with others using charitable resources. Parochial medical relief
had 'a noxious quality tending to social deterioration which does not belong
essentially to sickness, but wholly accrues from the source from which it comes'.
None the less, in the period 1870–5 the parochial board had medically relieved
some 35,000 cases, over half of whom were non-paupers. This, the committee
suggested, showed that 'the Board, if it has erred at all has erred on the side of
liberality in their interpretation of the law'. Various proposals were made to
ensure that parochial aid be 'avoided as much as possible for all who, although
poor, are above the rank of paupers, being self-supporting except in the case of
personal or domestic sickness'.[28] Here we have a specific example of classification, by way of the medical test, being used as a tool to separate paupers from the
rest of the poor. All this bears out Rona Gaffney's suggestion that from around
this time the treatment of non-paupers began to be cut back.[29] More broadly,
phrases such as 'social deterioration' and 'noxious quality' point to an emerging
characteristic of the period – the pathologising of pauperism and the associated
desire to keep paupers separate from the rest of the population.

At the end of our period, the delegate from the Scottish Poor Law Medical
Officers' Association told the 1902 Departmental Committee that his organisation believed that, at least in urban areas, medical relief was now 'adequate in
all respects'. Consequently, it could not be extended without 'the danger of
pauperising the working class population'.[30] Clearly implicit here is, again, the
notion of strict boundaries in order to avoid the 'contamination' of the
respectable; and, thereby, rigorous classification by way of the medical test. By this
particular account, the campaign against pauperism was having its desired effect.

However, this was not always uncontested. In Leith in 1896 it was demanded
of one poorhouse governor that he 'get a dozen or more of the male inmates,
whom he considered to be in good health and fit for work, certified by the
Medical Officer, with a view to his discharging them'. More generally, the
committee concerned expressed 'dissatisfaction that the medical officers did
not, per se, certify as to inmates, who were well and in a condition to go out to
work'. The clerk was thus instructed to send the appropriate extract from the
minutes 'to each of the medical officers, in order to make them aware' of the
committee's views.[31] What this suggests is a reluctance on the part of medical
staff to push the medical test too far, and classification as an area of tension
between medical staff and parochial boards, an issue returned to below.

Positive views about improvements in facilities and a more efficient application of Poor Law principles and practices must, moreover, be put in their

economic context. Medical relief was a small component of total parochial spending. Paisley in the late 1870s, for instance, was devoting only around 3.5 per cent of its total expenditure to this end.[32] Of course, local bodies could also allocate resources to health matters through donations to non-statutory bodies, usually on the basis that the latter would at the very least be sympathetic to referrals of pauper patients. In 1896, for example, Edinburgh Parish Council donated £50 to Queen Victoria's Jubilee Institute for Nurses 'on the understanding that the services of the nurses are available for nursing pauper patients on the recommendation of the Inspector or Medical Officers of the Council'.[33] The central point remains, though, that medical relief was a small part of total expenditure. Similarly, although the centrally-awarded medical grant rose over the period, it remained a relatively small component of income. Again to use the example of Paisley, in the late 1870s it was £110, or around 5 per cent of non-assessable income. By the mid-1890s the grant was £125, or just over 2 per cent of non-assessable income. In both cases these percentages fall when income from the rates is included.[34]

However, this is perhaps only part of the story. In January 1900 Greenock had some 921 paupers on outdoor relief, of whom some 246 were on medical relief.[35] What these data imply is that while medical relief involved low levels of both income and expenditure, significant numbers of paupers were, nevertheless, benefiting in some way from its attentions. Evidence from elsewhere adds further dimensions to this picture. In 1891, for instance, Glasgow City parish's eight medical officers made nearly 7,000 professional visits, gave over 12,000 consultations, granted over 7,000 certificates, and wrote a staggering 15,000 prescriptions.[36] This suggests that, inter alia, the Poor Law medical services in late nineteenth-century central Scotland were more than simply residual.

### Local and Central Authorities: Conflict and (Occasionally) Consensus

We now focus on the tension between central and local authorities, looking initially at the attempts by the central authority to cajole or persuade Poor Law bodies to improve medical services. We then examine how these local bodies saw their own role by, in particular, an analysis of their relationship with the doctors and other medical staff whom they employed.

One way in which the central authority might seek to promote local action was by way of the medical grant. This had been set up in the late 1840s with the Board of Supervision having £10,000 per annum to disburse to participating local bodies. In the early 1880s this was increased to £20,000, and a new scheme was proposed whereby the Board would match local expenditure until the point where the total grant was spent. The Board made the point, however, that 'legislation would be required in order to place medical relief in Scotland on an entirely satisfactory footing', and hence that the new scheme was intended to be 'only temporary and provisional'.[37] Indeed, it was further amended in 1885 to encourage the employment of trained nurses. One half of their salary could be claimed against the medical grant, plus allowances for food, lodging and uniform. A trained nurse was defined as having had at least two years' proper training, so making her eligible for the register of trained nurses set up by the Board. Registration was a necessary requirement for any claim against the medical grant.[38]

Such improvements notwithstanding, the system was complicated and contentious. Differences between Scotland and the rest of the United Kingdom had been picked up by the 1870 Select Committee which noted that in England and Ireland 'the public Exchequer contributes one-half the actual amount expended in salaries to medical officers, and medicines'. In Scotland, by contrast, 'a fixed sum of only £10,000 is granted from the public funds, which does not meet one-third of the very limited expenditure which occurs under this head'.[39] Such issues also exercised the medical profession. The Royal College of Physicians and Surgeons of Glasgow, for example, drew up a petition in 1876 which, inter alia, asked that the 'Parliamentary Grant to Scotland in aid of Medical Relief (to the Sick Poor) in Scotland should be placed on the same footing as it is in England and Ireland'.[40]

Unsurprisingly, local bodies too were unhappy with the operation of the grant. Again in 1876, Edinburgh Parochial Board resolved to

memorialise Her Majesty's Government in favour of placing the Treasury Grant for Medical Relief in Scotland on the same footing as the Grant for Medical Relief in England, and further resolve that this Board should cooperate with other Parochial Boards in Scotland in pressing this and other questions affecting the relief of the Poor in Scotland upon the Government.[41]

The Edwardian Royal Commission, meanwhile, noted that local boards seeking access to the medical grant had to agree to central authority conditions, including the employment of nurses.[42] This was, in other words, a system of rewards and sanctions.

Paterson suggests that the Scottish medical grant involved a 'very complicated system devised by the Board of Supervision'.[43] This is certainly the case, although it is equally clear that the Board itself was not entirely happy with the prevailing situation which in certain circumstances encouraged the assertion of local autonomy. It did so because, among other things, the medical grant's limited resources and its control mechanisms could operate in such a way as to offer comparatively little reward in exchange for unacceptable degrees of central control. In a situation of both opportunities and constraints, how then did the Board of Supervision seek to exert authority and influence, and in what ways did local bodies accommodate or resist?

As well as the medical grant, attempts at central influence embraced other issues and concerns. In 1878, for example, a report on Paisley's Abbey parish by the Board of Supervision's visiting officer commented as follows:

> The pauperism of this parish continues excessive, and the Parochial Board should exert themselves to improve the Test: the two points to which attention should be specially directed are these (i) the removal of the sick and infirm to a separate building (ii) the enforcement of labour under an official separately appointed for the purpose.[44]

The clear implication here is that the proper classification and separation of the sick would reduce pauperism. It is difficult to know exactly what impact such strictures had, but it is notable that, almost immediately after the visiting officer's report, Abbey's poorhouse committee began to record regularly in its minutes that: 'The Medical Officer's report showed that after examination there was no unburdened able-bodied person in the Poorhouse.'[45] Again this is open to varying interpretations, but it is nevertheless the case that for both centre and locality increased classification could, if successful, result in a decrease in local taxation and, of course, a decrease in pauperism.

None the less, the relationship between centre and locality was fraught and complex. On occasions parochial authorities, in their general pursuit of low local taxation and high local autonomy, implicitly or explicitly rejected the cajoling or pressure that emanated from the central authority. An illustration of this difficult relationship can be found in Barony in the early 1880s. A special committee was appointed to look at the whole issue of relief, almost certainly in response to the more general campaign against pauperism and for a stricter application of the medical test. The committee extensively investigated the situation in both Scotland and parts of England. Although impressed by the impact of restrictions on outdoor relief 'and the full use of the poorhouse test', the committee argued that caution had to be exercised. There was 'some danger' in applying the test too rigorously in that 'a reaction may follow and land us in greater evils than those we are endeavouring to correct'.[46] It is possible to interpret this statement in a number of ways. Did it display genuine concern over too rigorous a use of the test which might incur resistance from doctors or result in significant health deterioration in the person being tested? Was it, perhaps, an instance of the problem identified by the 1870 Select Committee, that elected members were often too close to the paupers with whom they were dealing? Or was it simply an outcome of the desire to keep the rates down, given that outdoor relief was cheaper than the poorhouse? No doubt a combination of these factors was in some way involved.

However, we might note three contextual points that further illuminate Barony's approach. First, we have already seen that in principle Scottish paupers could be granted relief only by showing both destitution and some measure of ill-health, and that medical relief was a disproportionately large part of total outdoor relief. In essence, then, what was being rejected in Barony was a more stringent medical test. Second, there was considerable local feeling about the way in which existing legislation could push otherwise healthy individuals towards medical relief and pauperisation. We have already encountered the scepticism of a Glasgow doctor. From a lay perspective, in 1879 a report from Glasgow's unemployed relief fund noted that the current economic situation required action to meet the otherwise inevitable destitution, so preventing 'starvation and disease'. The local Poor Law authorities, however, had been instructed by the Board of Supervision not to donate to the fund. The report pointed to the anomaly that 'a body whose proper function is to grant relief to the destitute, should be prohibited from dealing with poverty-stricken workmen . . . until starvation renders them unfit for work, and thereby, in the Parochial sense, proper objects of relief'.[47]

Third, it is evident that the central authority was well aware that the rules regarding medical relief were being broken. In September 1885, for instance, it issued a circular pointing out that it had evidence of medical relief being offered to 'persons not legally entitled to it'; that this was illegal; and that parishes should not engage in this practice. As a sanction it was further pointed out that charges for medical relief 'given to persons who are not paupers will not be allowed to form a valid claim to participation in the Medical Relief Grant'.[48] The use of the medical grant as a threatened sanction is notable here; however, the very fact that the Board had to issue such a reminder is eloquent testimony to the gap between Poor Law principles and practice, particularly as pertaining to medical relief.

### Local Bodies and Medical Staff

Another way in which local boards could exert their own authority, and also keep down the rates, was through their relationships with their medical staff. To focus initially on outdoor medical officers, these had their posts renewed annually, and while this was generally a formality it was not always so. In

Greenock in 1890, for instance, the committee of management voted not to reappoint the three medical incumbents and to have the posts publicly advertised. Seven applications were received, including three from those originally in place and it was they who were duly, and unanimously, appointed at a salary of £50 per annum each.[49] It is hard to see in this somewhat farcical episode anything other than lay representatives flexing their muscles and doctors being rather humiliatingly kept in line. It is notable, too, in this particular context that parochial authorities frequently raised objections to attempts by the Board of Supervision to gain more control over the employment of medical staff – for example in Paisley in 1879.[50]

Lay local control could also exert itself in other ways. In 1883 City's medical committee investigated the case of the pauper Ann Cassidy Thomson. Mrs Thomson had complained that the medical officer, Dr Orr, had failed to attend on her children, although called upon to do so on four occasions. The doctor expressed regret and acknowledged that Mrs Thomson had a right to complain. He also pointed to his 15 years of service. Nevertheless, the medical committee dismissed him, and although this decision was later reversed, the central point remains – that lay bodies felt that they could act in this sort of way towards their medical officers.[51]

Notwithstanding the Board of Supervision's various attempts to gain more control over medical officers, local bodies clearly had strong views about their own right to discipline such personnel. As Stephanie Blackden remarks, 'the outdoor medical service was by far the most important provided by the parish', and paupers themselves 'came near to accepting this as a right and were quick to complain' if doctors behaved in what was deemed an unsatisfactory manner.[52] Indeed, a further characteristic of the Scottish Poor Law was paupers' right to complain directly to the central authority regarding issues of inadequate relief. Crowther is sceptical about the efficacy of this apparent 'right' of the poor.[53] None the less, the Board of Supervision and its successor would act if necessary against failing doctors. In 1890, for example, it recorded that, during the preceding year,

> we have been called upon to investigate charges against 7 Medical Officers. In one of these cases we permitted the Medical Officer to resign, in two cases we found it necessary to censure the Officers concerned, and the remaining 4 instances we found the complaints groundless.[54]

The terms and conditions of medical practitioners' employment was thus a contested area between doctors themselves, local bodies and the central authority. In the mid-1890s City's medical officers petitioned for a salary increase which they justified on a range of grounds. The work itself was 'not only of an arduous and exacting nature' but was also more than 'ordinarily dangerous' because of the unsanitary state of the dwellings visited. Salaries had not uniformly risen since the introduction of the current system in the 1840s – some medical officers were receiving £55 per annum, the rate fixed at the outset – and indeed the parish's salary bill had actually decreased due to administrative reorganisation. Neighbouring Barony and Govan, meanwhile, paid medical staff significantly better. After some deliberation it was duly agreed to raise salaries by £10 per annum.[55] What is revealing here are the issues of increasing work-loads for, at least in some cases, unchanging remuneration; and inequities between even neighbouring parishes – a clear sign of a medical marketplace being in operation. Moreover, local bodies sought to garner as much informa-tion as possible on what their doctors actually did. In Paisley in the early 1870s, for example, data was compiled on the number of cases and the number of visits carried out by its four medical officers which showed, inter alia, a huge variation in cost per visit.[56] Such analyses were common and intended not only as impor-tant sources of information in themselves, but also as a means of surveillance and of ensuring value for ratepayers' money.

Looking across urban central Scotland, disparities in remuneration become even more evident. In Leith, for instance, two medical officers were appointed in 1895 at a salary of £140 each.[57] In Dundee a few years earlier, meanwhile, medical officers were receiving £70, or in one case £60, per annum.[58] The problem here is, of course, attempting to compare like with like. Given the system's high level of disaggregation, the emphasis on local autonomy, and the huge variations in parishes and their circumstances, it is unsurprising that local practices and salaries varied. So, for example, the Leith appointees mentioned above were required to undertake tasks that would not have been expected of their counter-parts elsewhere, albeit for greater remuneration. This is not to say, though, that all local bodies were unswervingly determined to keep down financial outlay at all costs or to treat their staff in a particularly unsympathetic manner. The City case shows both long-term 'neglect' of Poor Law doctors alongside a willing-ness to acknowledge legitimate demands, albeit after a considerable period of doctors' agitation.

The economic realities of providing improved services were also on occasion recognised, and here we can draw on evidence pertaining to another group of parochial medical staff, nurses. In Greenock in the mid-1890s, for instance, the poorhouse committee agreed that the salary level previously set for nurses had been inadequate, not least when compared with conditions in other districts, and immediately and unanimously raised the rate.[59] In Barony in 1879, a sub-committee on sick nursing was set up. In a comment that reveals much about contemporary local attitudes towards the centre, this committee's brief was to 'investigate and report what are our present arrangements what they would suggest as an improvement and how far the suggestions of the Board of Supervision should be adopted or avoided'. None the less, the sub-committee took its work seriously and after investigation of organisation and practices in other Scottish and English hospitals, it proposed, among other things, a significant expansion in the number of trained nurses, the creation of the post of lady superintendent to oversee nursing and nurse training, and payment and subsistence at a relatively generous rate.[60] It is worth noting that all this activity took place ahead of the changes in the medical grant aimed at encouraging better quality nursing. More positively, both Greenock and Barony were clearly responding to labour market pressures alongside a perceived need to improve nursing standards.

**Conclusion**

What, then, does all this tell us? First, it is clear that there could be both commonality of purpose and tensions between centre and periphery over Poor Law medical relief. There was still a considerable emphasis on local autonomy and one way in which this manifested itself was through direct control of medical and nursing staff. Local bodies appear to have had few qualms about calling their medical staff to heel and even, if evidence of neglect was forthcoming, in dispensing with their services. This is not to say that they were necessarily bad employers. On occasions, parochial authorities could be sensitive to staff demands and concerns if only for pragmatic reasons. A further complicating factor here is the apparent willingness of Scottish paupers to complain about their medical treatment, or neglect, and for this to result in some form of disciplinary action against an individual doctor. Local bodies were concerned about legal actions, of course, but whatever the cause of their concern their actions on behalf of their pauper 'clients' can be seen as a form of pressure from below. On the other hand, it is clear that both the localities and the Edinburgh authorities realised that better and more efficient health services could contribute to the ongoing decline in pauperism, as well as being a social and economic good in itself.

Second, we have seen that alongside a general decline in pauperism there was a significant increase in medical expenditure, and that this in turn formed a disproportionately large component of outdoor relief. Other constituents of medical expenditure included new buildings – as in Dundee – and increased quantity and quality of nursing staff. All this led to some contemporaries claiming significant improvement in services. Whether such perceptions and claims are justified is another matter, and counter-arguments and evidence are certainly available. Crowther, for instance, suggests that the development of Scottish Poor Law hospitals may have been delayed by the strength of the voluntary system, which 'continued until relatively late in the century to take in patients who in England would have been consigned to the Poor Law'.[61] Subscriptions by local Poor Law bodies themselves may have further solidified this situation. Gaffney, meanwhile, draws attention to the poor quality of Glasgow's Poor Law hospital accommodation and service, arguing that it was only with the merger of the Barony and City parishes towards the end of the century that this situation began to change with the construction of new, purpose-built hospitals.[62] The Royal Commission on the Poor Laws confirmed what the Select Committee had argued some forty years earlier, that the provision of Poor Law medical relief was problematic. Pauper nursing, which had been prohibited in England and Ireland in the mid-1890s, was still permissible in Scotland and practised in over one-third of its poorhouses. Poor Law medical provision in the large towns was 'perhaps fairly adequate', but this was due in large part to the existence of medical charities and the individual generosity of private practitioners.[63]

However, and finally, it may be possible to put a more positive interpretation on what was being offered by the Poor Law medical services in late nineteenth-century urban central Scotland. We have noted that this period saw rising medical expenditure and provision, and rising expenditure per pauper. We have also encountered local data which illustrates two points in particular: first, that medical relief was a small component of both income and expenditure; and, second, that medical relief was a large component of outdoor relief. One way of interpreting this material is that the Poor Law medical services were, in fact, economically efficient in the fairly straightforward sense that they increasingly provided a lot for comparatively little. So, from the providers' point of view, investing a relatively small amount was a way of dealing – at least in the short term but also with the possibility of long-term improvement – with a fairly large proportion of the pauper population. Moreover, were medical criteria to be rigorously applied, this in itself could bring down pauperism and stop its deleterious spread to more 'respectable' parts of the population.

From the consumers' viewpoint, outdoor medical relief was a way of both avoiding the poorhouse and gaining some form of healthcare, however primitive and rushed. In this sense it could circumvent the disqualification of the able-bodied in an era when the underlying cause of destitution had as much to do with the labour market as with individual health circumstances. For those who had to seek the services of the Poor Law hospital service, meanwhile, this was undoubtedly not a pleasant experience. Having said that, however, efforts were clearly being made by the authorities we have examined to improve the situation through, for instance, the provision of better-trained nurses. As suggested earlier, it is thus possible to see these Poor Law medical services as more than simply residual, or indeed static.

Historians of welfare should not shy away from normative judgements about the quality and equity of services offered by, to use the present instance, the new Scottish Poor Law. None the less, we also need to recognise that 'quality' and 'equity' are concepts which, precisely because of their relative nature, can be used ahistorically. They are also, of course, concepts which of themselves have no exact definition and remain highly contested in contemporary social policy debates. What was being offered by the medical services in the period and area discussed above needs to be analysed and viewed in its own terms, and not against standards which might be deemed acceptable or unacceptable today. Instead, we should seek an understanding of how limited resources were distributed and controlled in a system of constraints and blockages, albeit constraints and blockages that were in some instances self-imposed and self-perpetuating. Work on the still under-researched Scottish Poor Law is therefore necessary, and has the potential to open up much wider debates in welfare history.

### Acknowledgements

I am grateful to the Carnegie Trust for the Universities of Scotland for a grant in support of my research on the Scottish Poor Law; and to Mark Freeman, Eleanor Gordon and Krista Maglen for their comments on an earlier draft.

### Notes

1. See, for example, Crowther, M.A., 'Poverty, Health and Welfare', in Fraser, W.H. and Morris, R.J., eds, *People and Society in Scotland, Volume II: 1830–1914* (Edinburgh, 1990), 265–89.
2. On the Old Scottish Poor Law, see Mitchison, R., *The Old Poor Law in Scotland: The Experience of Poverty* (Edinburgh, 2000). The context of reform, from a medical perspective, is dealt with in Hamlin, C., 'William Pulteney Alison, the Scottish Philosophy, and the Making of a Political Medicine', *Journal of the History of Medicine and Allied Sciences* 61 (2006), 144–86. Important contributions to the history of the medical services of the reformed Poor Law are Blackden, S., 'The Poor Law and Wealth: A Survey of Parochial Medical Aid in Glasgow, 1845–1900', in Smout, T.C., ed., *The Search for Wealth and Stability* (London, 1979); Blackden, S., 'The Board of Supervision and the Scottish Parochial Medical Service, 1845–95', *Medical History* 30 (1986), 145–72. Gestrich, A. and Stewart, J., 'Unemployment and Poor Relief in the West of Scotland', in King, S. and Stewart, J., eds, *Welfare Peripheries: The Development of Welfare States in Nineteenth and Twentieth Century Europe* (Bern, 2007) is pertinent to the present chapter and contains references to the literature on the reformed Scottish Poor Law.
3. Lee, C.H., 'Economic Progress: Wealth and Poverty', in Devine, T.M., Lee, C.H. and Peden, G.C., eds, *The Transformation of Scotland: The Economy since 1700* (Edinburgh, 2005), 128–56, at 142.

4.  *Thirty-Fourth Annual Report of the Board of Supervision for the Relief of the Poor in Scotland* (Edinburgh, 1879), appendix A, document 8, tables 1 and 2.
5.  Mitchison, *Old Poor Law*, chapter 9.
6.  *Forty-Ninth Annual Report of the Board of Supervision for the Relief of the Poor in Scotland* (Edinburgh, 1895), appendix A, document 7, tables 1 and 2.
7.  Crowther, 'Poverty', 269.
8.  Englander, D., *Poverty and Poor Law Reform in Nineteenth-Century Britain* (London, 1998), 52.
9.  Paterson, A., 'The Poor Law in Nineteenth-Century Scotland', in Fraser, D., ed., *The New Poor Law in the Nineteenth Century* (London, 1976), 171–93, at 190–1; Levitt, I., *Poverty and Welfare in Scotland* (Edinburgh, 1988), 16–17.
10. Hamlin, 'William Pulteney Alison'.
11. Hansard (Commons) 4th series, xxiii, 27 April 1894, col. 1616.
12. Crowther, 'Poverty', 273, 285; Levitt, I., *Government and Social Conditions in Scotland* (Edinburgh, 1988), xvi–xviii.
13. *Report of the Departmental Committee on Poor Law Medical Relief (Scotland): Volume I*, Parliamentary Papers, Cd. 2008 (1904), Part VII: Summary of Recommendations.
14. *Report from the Select Committee on the Poor Law (Scotland), Together with the Proceedings of the Committee, Minutes of Evidence, and Appendix*, Parliamentary Papers, C. 357 (1870), xvii.
15. *Royal Commission on the Poor Laws and Relief of Distress: Report on Scotland*, Parliamentary Papers, Cd. 4922 (1909), 144.
16. *Glasgow Medical Journal* 5 (1876), 273.
17. Crowther, 'Poverty', 272–3; Brundage, A., *The English Poor Laws*, (Basingstoke, 2002), 111.
18. *Report from the Select Committee on the Poor Law (Scotland)*, xii.
19. Paisley Central Library: Reference and Local Studies Library (PCL), B.57 7/29, minutes of the Poor Law Amendment Bill (Scotland) Committee of Paisley Parochial Board, 3 April 1872.
20. *Royal Commission on the Poor Laws and Relief of Distress*, 145.
21. Levitt, *Poverty*, 8.
22. Levitt, *Poverty*, 12.
23. *Report of the Departmental Committee on Poor Law Medical Relief (Scotland): Volume II*, Parliamentary Papers, Cd. 2022 (1904), appendix LVI.
24. *Report of the Departmental Committee on Poor Law Medical Relief (Scotland): Volume II*, minutes of evidence, q. 2257.
25. Dundee City Archives (DCA), P/D/1/19, minutes of the Statutory Meeting of the Parochial Board of the Dundee Combination, 1 August 1894.
26. *The Dundee Year Book: Facts and Figures for 1893* (Dundee, 1894), 156.
27. Crowther, M.A. and Dupree, M.W., *Medical Lives in the Age of Surgical Revolution* (Cambridge, 2007), 132.
28. Glasgow City Archives (GCA), D-HEW 1/5/3, minutes of the Medical Committee, City Parish, 1 May 1876.
29. Gaffney, R., 'Poor Law Hospitals 1845–1914', in Checkland, O. and Lamb, M., eds, *Health Care as Social History: The Glasgow Case* (Aberdeen, 1982), 44–58, at 57.
30. *Report of the Departmental Committee on Poor Law Medical Relief (Scotland) Volume II: Minutes of Evidence*, q. 995.
31. Edinburgh City Archives (ECA), SL 21/2/1, minutes of a sub-committee of the House Committee, 25 June 1896.
32. PCL, B.57 7/30, minutes of the Finance Committee, Paisley Parochial Board, 24 June 1878.
33. ECA, SL 14/1/1, minutes of the Half-Yearly Statutory Meeting of Edinburgh Parish Council, 4 February 1896.
34. PCL, B.57 7/30, minutes of the Finance Committee, Paisley Parochial Board, 24 June 1878; B.57 7/31, minutes of the Finance Committee, Paisley Parochial Board, 14 June 1893.
35. GCA, CO 2/22/18, minutes of Greenock Parish Council, 30 January 1900.
36. GCA, D-HEW 1/5/4, minutes of the Medical Committee, City Parish, 19 November 1891.

37. National Archives of Scotland (NAS), HH 23/19, Board of Supervision, minutes of the General Half Yearly Statutory Meeting, 3 August 1882; Board of Supervision, minutes 10 August 1882.
38. NAS, HH 23/20, Board of Supervision, minutes 26 March 1885, circular *Trained Sick Nursing in Poorhouses.*
39. *Report from the Select Committee on the Poor Law (Scotland),* xvii.
40. Archives of the Royal College of Physicians and Surgeons of Glasgow, RCPSG 1/1/1/10, minutes of a meeting of the RCPSG 3 April 1876.
41. ECA, SL8/1/7, minutes of a meeting of the Parochial Board of Edinburgh, 21 February 1876.
42. *Royal Commission on the Poor Laws and Relief of Distress,* 144.
43. Paterson, 'Poor Law', 181.
44. PCL, B.57 7/5, minutes of Abbey Parochial Board, 21 February 1878.
45. For example, at PCL, B.57 7/10, minutes of Abbey Parochial Board Poorhouse Committee, 2 September 1879.
46. GCA, D-HEW 2/15/2, minutes of the Special Committee on Out- and In-Door Relief, Barony Parish, 7 May 1883.
47. [Kenneth M. Macleod,] *Report of the Administration of the Glasgow Unemployed Relief Fund during the Winter of 1878–9* (Glasgow, 1879), 8–9, 31.
48. NAS HH 23/20, Board of Supervision, minutes 9 September 1885, circular *Medical Relief to Persons not Paupers.*
49. GCA, CO 2/22/9, minutes of the Committee of Management, Greenock Parochial Board, 24 June 1890, 29 July 1890.
50. PCL, B.57 7/20, Paisley Parochial Board, minutes 25 June 1879, 27 August 1879.
51. GCA, D-HEW 1/5/3, minutes of the Medical Committee, City Parish, 5 July 1883, 19 July 1883. I owe the point about Dr Orr's reprieve to David Sutton, University of Glasgow.
52. Blackden, 'Poor Law', 249.
53. Crowther, 'Poverty', 273.
54. *Forty-Fifth Annual Report of the Board of Supervision for the Relief of the Poor and of Public Health in Scotland, 1889–90* (Edinburgh, 1890), iv.
55. GCA, D-HEW 1/5/4, minutes of the Medical Committee, City Parish, 22 November 1894, 18 April 1895, 24 April 1895.
56. PCL, B.57 7/29, minutes of the Relief Committee, Paisley Parochial Board, 25 September 1874.
57. ECA, SL 21/2/1, minutes of a sub-committee of the Relieving Committee, 3 June 1895.
58. DCA, P/D/1/4, minutes of Sub-Committee Appointed to Inquire and Report as to the Arrangements for Affording Medical Relief to the Poor, 28 April 1879.
59. GCA, CO 2/22/12, minutes of the Poorhouse Committee, Greenock Parochial Board, 13 February 1894.
60. GCA, D-HEW 2/15/1, minutes of the Sub-Committee of the House on Sick Nursing, Barony Parish, 8 September 1879, 16 September 1879, 31 October 1879.
61. Crowther, 'Poverty', 276.
62. Gaffney, 'Poor Law', 53.
63. *Royal Commission on the Poor Laws and Relief of Distress,* 148, 152.

# 2

# Charity Dispensaries, Medical Education and Domiciliary Medical Care for the Poor in Edinburgh and Glasgow, c.1870–1914

**David Sutton**

Writing in 1969 – two decades after the advent of the NHS – Sir Vincent Zachary Cope pointed out the very close relationship that formerly existed between charity dispensary work and medical education north of the Border in Britain. This relationship, he said, had lasted in Scotland until the reorganisation of medical services and the close of the private dispensaries in 1948. He argued that '[t]he part played by the free dispensaries in the evolution of medical education in Britain has not yet been adequately appreciated', and that 'in Scotland the dispensaries [had an] education[al] function', noting that 'dispensary work became part of the normal curriculum of the medical student'.[1] Regarding the work of these charity dispensaries, this chapter seeks to explore this 'Scottish system' of medical education by building upon an interest in agencies of domiciliary medical care of the poor. The poor here are understood simply as those unable to pay the doctor for the services they received.[2] A central conundrum is identified and resolved: why was it that, within Scotland, the two key cities and main centres of medical education differed in their attitude and approach to utilising medical students to treat poor patients in their homes? Themes explored include domiciliary care, medical provision for the poor, the training of doctors in Scotland, changing curricular arrangements, and the intersection of institutional medical care with issues of medico-legal responsibility.

In a commemorative history of the Royal College of Physicians of Edinburgh published 1976, Stuart Craig noted with sadness how, 'from the teaching angle, and more especially from the viewpoint of what is now commonly referred to as Community Medicine, the gradual disappearance of public dispensaries is an irreplaceable loss'.[3] This was a link, he identified, that had its roots in Edinburgh in the eighteenth century; survived, flourished and strengthened over the nineteenth century, as the range of medical dispensaries expanded; and held until after the First World War. Although it remained a strong influence on men trained under that system – men like Britain's first Chief Medical Officer of the Ministry of Health, Sir George Newman – by the 1920s the Edinburgh dispensary and domiciliary training tradition had given way. At this time, the reorganisation of academic priorities promoted by new forms of university funding pushed students towards a greater grounding in laboratory science.[4]


**The Scottish Approach**

An intrinsic aspect of the work of free dispensaries, home visitation was not just an important element of the range of medical provision made available for the poor during the late nineteenth and early twentieth century in Scotland; within a broader British context – as Cope makes clear – it was an essentially and intrinsically 'Scottish' approach to a recognised set of additional problems. The use of senior medical students, organised under supervision to visit and treat selected cases at home, was both a pragmatic response to issues of manpower and funding, and a strategic response to the challenge of how to bring those same medical students, as Britain's future general practitioners, out of the lecture room during their studies. Scotland has long been a major international centre of medical education. In terms of its broader appeal, Scottish medical education was at its zenith during the period of interest here. Recovering from a slump in reputation, medical enrolments across Scotland more than tripled in thirty years after the Medical Act of 1858.[5] The Students' Representative Council estimated that there were around 2,000 medical students in Edinburgh alone by the mid-1880s. Medical student numbers had expanded rapidly from the 1870s and were, as R.D. Anderson has previously shown, at a peak by 1890 in both Glasgow and Edinburgh.[6] Those numbers at this time were boosted by a number of factors, including the general expansion of the middle classes across Britain; educational arrangements after the Medical Act that were supportive of Scottish institutions; and, latterly, by the acceptance of female students to the study of medicine. Of Scottish medical schools, it was formally if grudgingly acknowledged from London that students came to 'recognise [both] the cheapness and excellence of their education'. The cost of a medical education could be as little as half the equivalent cost in Glasgow or Edinburgh compared to London.[7]

Across the second half of the nineteenth century surgical advances had put Scottish medicine at the forefront of hospital treatment. However, within Scotland, there was also wide recognition amongst prominent figures in the academic medical community of the fundamental importance of providing arenas for the acquisition of practical outdoor treatment experience as part of the routine curriculum of medical education. Thus whilst in 1875, for example, there were 21 different courses of study within Britain providing a prospective route to qualification and legal registration as a medical practitioner, only the eight specifically Scottish routes stipulated as a mandatory requirement that all students before qualification needed to demonstrate and certify that they had undertaken six months' dispensary or outdoor practice.[8] Home visits to patients were understood best to provide the hands-on practical clinical experience that it was deemed they required for their future careers. Medical students who undertook visitation of the poor were said to graduate with a greater under-standing of poverty and a more realistic expectation of general private practice. Thus in September 1901, reflecting the spirit of 'consciousness of sin', the *Lancet* published reflections on 'Medical Students and the Poor', in which it was argued that solely hospital-trained students entered the profession at a distinct disadvantage, with unrealistic expectations, and no real understanding of, or empathy with, the problems of poverty.[9] Echoing these thoughts, one who had been a medical student in Edinburgh in the 1890s and who rose to become superintendent of the Edinburgh Medical Missionary Society, noted how only students exposed to home visitation rounds learned at close quarters 'the evils attendant on poverty, overcrowding and squalor'. They also learned the 'disci-pline', 'disappointments and heartbreaks' that were mainstays of medical prac-tice. The medical mission, sited at the head of the most notorious thoroughfare in the city, had provided an important medical charity dispensary in Edinburgh from the mid-1850s. Home visits were a test bed. Treatment in the difficult and disadvantaged conditions of the poor man's home required patience and calm-ness to deal with variable, strained and sometimes outright dangerous circum-stances. It required fortitude and flexibility, and the adeptness to adapt treatments to prevailing conditions. Essentially therefore, it was during domicil-iary visits amongst the poor, Lechmere Taylor argued, that the would-be practi-tioners and medical missionaries of his generation learnt the three g's necessary for a successful career: 'grit, grace and gumption'.[10]

This 'Scottish approach', of sending students into the homes of the poor, came to be admired. Indeed, by the end of the 1880s, it was held up for emula-tion elsewhere in Britain.[11] However, whilst this was recognised to be a 'Scottish' approach and referred to as such, the comparison between Edinburgh and Glasgow medical charity services shows that there were, in fact, stark differences within Scotland. The rest of this chapter explores these differences. Tables 2.1 and 2.2 give a clear indication of the extent of these differences. As will be shown, differences in approaches to domiciliary treatment in Edinburgh and Glasgow were due to differing local educational arrangements, institutional contexts and concerns, and traditions of care.

## Outdoor Medical Charity in Glasgow and Edinburgh

Outwith the service of the Poor Law, tables 2.1 and 2.2 demonstrate that Glasgow and Edinburgh both saw a noticeable expansion of outdoor private

**Table 2.1 Total reported annual dispensary and domiciliary medical charity cases treated in Glasgow (and Govan), mid-1870s to mid-1900s**

| | c. mid-1870s | c. mid-1880s | c. mid-1890s | c. mid-1900s |
|---|---|---|---|---|
| **Dispensary patients** | | | | |
| Hospital out-patients | 28,970 | 56,487 | 72,743 | 128,379 |
| Charity dispensary | 3,771+ | 17,050+ | 15,987+ | 17,522+ |
| Medical missions | 15,833 | 20,450+ | 25,000+ | 24,000+ |
| **Total treated at dispensary** | **48,574+** | **93,987+** | **113,730+** | **169,901+** |
| **Domiciliary patients** | | | | |
| Hospital out-patients | 927 | 1,560 | 2,100 | 2,100 |
| Charity dispensary | 0+ | 1,500+ | 0+ | 0+ |
| Medical missions | 1,266 | 1,886+ | 2,793+ | 2,073+ |
| Welfare charity medical visits | unknown | unknown | 80+ | 500+ |
| **Total cases treated at home** | **2,193+** | **4,946+** | **4,973+** | **4,673+** |
| **Annual out-patient cases** | **50,767+** | **98,933+** | **118,703+** | **174,574+** |
| Out-patients per pop. est. (%) | 9.1% | 14.8% | 15.7% | 19.3% |
| Home patients per pop. est. (%) | 0.4% | 0.7% | 0.7% | 0.5% |

**Note:** Totals given represent *a minimal estimate*, with data for various smaller medical charities unknown or unidentified (indicated by a + sign next to numbers)
**Source:** Various, including extant charity reports, centenaries, historical texts, medical directories, newspaper and journal reports

medical charity before 1911. Providing evidence to the Royal Commission on the Poor Laws in 1909, A.C. Kay and H.V. Toynbee noted, for example, a direct correlation between the relative lack of provident and friendly society provision in Edinburgh and 'the very great amount of competition which would have to be

**Table 2.2  Total reported annual dispensary and domiciliary medical charity cases treated in Edinburgh (and Leith), mid-1870s to mid-1900s**

|  | c. mid-1870s | c. mid-1880s | c. mid-1890s | c. mid-1900s |
|---|---|---|---|---|
| **Dispensary patients** | | | | |
| Hospital out-patients | 23,962 | 40,742 | 51,530 | 73,081 |
| Charity dispensary | 21,175 | 26,276 | 27,532+ | 28,807+ |
| Medical missions | 12,914+ | 10,169+ | 10,360+ | 11,798+ |
| **Total treated at dispensary** | **58,051+** | **77,187+** | **89,422+** | **113,686+** |
| **Domiciliary patients** | | | | |
| Hospital out-patients | 2,699 | 4,561 | 5,067 | 7,861 |
| Charity dispensary | 5,907 | 9,116+ | 9,002+ | 8,844+ |
| Medical missions | 3,272+ | 3,201+ | 3,512+ | 3,211+ |
| Welfare charity medical visits | unknown | unknown | unknown | unknown |
| **Total cases treated at home** | **11,878+** | **16,878+** | **17,581+** | **19,916+** |
| **Annual out-patient cases** | **69,929+** | **94,065+** | **107,003+** | **133,602+** |
| Out-patients per pop. est. (%) | 28.3% | 31.6% | 31.6% | 34.0% |
| Home patients per pop. est.(%) | 4.8% | 5.7% | 5.2% | 5.1% |

Note/Source: See Table 2.1

encountered from the out-patient departments of the numerous hospitals and dispensaries'. Also giving evidence, Hugh Barrie of the Free Gardeners Friendly Society noted of 'the various charitable institutions in the city of Glasgow' that they were 'so numerous that one could not enumerate them without referring to the Glasgow Post Office Directory'.[12]

The aggregated annual number of dispensary and domiciliary patients given free treatment by medical charities in Edinburgh and Leith between the mid-1870s and mid-1900s demonstrates the sustained importance of dispensary and domiciliary medical services in that city at this time. As table 2.2 shows, the proportion of the population of Edinburgh accessing outdoor charity each year was extremely high, perhaps in excess of one in four people in the city.[13] The number of poor recorded as being visited at home by one or other of the different medical charity dispensaries, infirmary outpatients or medical missions – shown in the row headed 'total cases treated at home' – was also high, between 15,000 and 20,000 each year in the decades around the beginning of the twentieth century. This is equivalent to around 5 or 6 per cent of the population of the city. Whilst substantial, this total overlooks additional family members who might also have been attended to, or given medical advice, as an offshoot of each visit. Each of these patients could be seen several times over the course of a bout of illness, with approximately three visits per patient a typical mean reported for each case. In conducting these services the use of medical students was paramount. Thus the Edinburgh Provident Dispensary (founded in 1878), which recorded the second highest number of home visits by medical students in Edinburgh most years to 1911, declared that its objective was not only to provide medical assistance to the poor, but also to encourage the poor in the ethos of self-help; to provide a public health surveillance service and a localised medical service; and to give the city a medical training institution.

The pattern of development of private institution, charity dispensary domiciliary services in Glasgow was very different from that in Edinburgh (table 2.1). In Glasgow, between 1875 and 1914, only Anderson's Medical College provided a charity dispensary domiciliary care service for the poor.[14] Medical Officer of Health (MOH) James Burn Russell noted in 1874 that of the city's non-parochial medical services, only the Glasgow Medical Missionary Society (founded in 1868) and the Maternity Hospital (1834) had conducted home visits in the city before that point. As an evangelical and a public health official, Russell was an advocate of treating the poor at home. Playing on traditional rivalry by drawing a deliberate comparison between Glasgow and Edinburgh, Russell suggested that the lack of emphasis on domiciliary services compared to Edinburgh was a key factor in explaining the relatively high number of uncertified deaths in Glasgow.[15]

### Charity Dispensaries and Medical Education in Edinburgh

The oldest of the network of medical charities active in Edinburgh was the Royal Public Dispensary (ERPD). Building upon the example of patient-centred clinical teaching methods developed at Leyden by Herman Boerhaave, but taking their teaching out of the ward, the founders of the ERPD pioneered the use of medical students in the supervised visitation of sick-poor persons at home. Richard Scott became Britain's first professor of general practice when appointed in Edinburgh in 1963, and like Craig and Cope he also noted that, before the NHS, '[i]n Edinburgh the role of the dispensary in the provision of medical care and in the education of medical students was a particularly prominent feature'. With reference to the influence of the ERPD, Scott also noted that '[t]he deliberate establishment of dispensaries for undergraduate teaching purposes [in Edinburgh] was probably unique'.[16] As noted in the *Scotsman* in 1904,

> It [the ERPD] helped in medical education by training students and by sending them to visit the poor at their own homes, under supervision. This was a very useful part of medical education, because it enabled the student to see patients in their ordinary surroundings, and he had to treat them with the difficulties which encumbered the ordinary medical attendant.[17]

At the ERPD, the domiciliary service was organised under the various physicians and surgeons employed, without pay, as honorary medical officers. Assigned charge of a unique visitation district, each medical officer was allowed to deploy two senior students of his choice for individual visitation assignments. These students paid fees to the ERPD for the privilege. They were rewarded with a testimonial that could be used to satisfy examination requirements. Regulations at the dispensary stipulated that each student selected 'must have attended medical cases for at least two winter sessions and an hospital for at least one year' prior to being allowed to undertake visits. Duties included certain latitude to act independently in emergencies, and were:

> To assist him [the medical officer] in registering the Patients, to visit at their own houses, and prescribe for such Patients as the Medical Officers may direct; and to perform the dressings and lesser operations which may be required. If called to any case of emergency in the course of their visits, the Pupils may prescribe for it what may be immediately required. They shall afterwards report the case to the Medical Officer under whom they act . . .[18]

The ERPD provided a model that other dispensaries subsequently followed for different parts of the city. One can explore the links between medical charity, medical education and domiciliary care of the poor in Edinburgh in a number of ways. The student graduation records for Edinburgh University are thorough and well preserved.[19] These confirm the extent to which charity dispensaries in Edinburgh provided an outlet for the training of students.

Both university and extramural teaching school students were required to attend at either charity dispensaries or outpatient departments in order to satisfy requirements across four separate statutory strands of the medical curriculum after 1858. Students attended charity dispensaries across Edinburgh for practical pharmacy instruction (or materia medica); in order to gain practical midwifery experience; for courses of vaccination instruction; and (most essentially) to acquire the required amount of dispensary, outpatient or general practice training. Taking one sample year selected at random (see table 2.3), from amongst the 198 students graduating with an ordinary medical degree at Edinburgh University in 1896, 90 per cent of the 179 students for which details are recorded had undertaken their six-month training at one of the city's seven leading charity dispensaries. The ERPD is shown as marginally the most popular venue, with around one-quarter of all graduating students attending. Students were a vital resource. They brought to the charities both manpower and much needed revenue in terms of fees. The importance of the revenue that students brought to the dispensaries increased as the decades passed. A growing dependency on such revenues lay behind the dispute that arose in October 1882, in Edinburgh, between the university and the medical charities. The university had just introduced a new in-house materia medica course that threatened to

**Table 2.3 Site at which was acquired the six month out-patient experience required by each graduating student, per graduation records of Edinburgh University [sample year: 1896]**

Total medical graduates in 1896: 198

| Recorded site of out-patient training | No. of students | Percentage of total |
| --- | --- | --- |
| Royal Public Dispensary (ERPD) | 45 | 22.7% |
| Western Dispensary> | 43 | 21.7% |
| Edinburgh Provident Dispensary | 30 | 15.2% |
| Medical Mission Dispensary | 22 | 11.1% |
| New Town Dispensary (ENTD) | 16 | 8.1% |
| at General Practitioners | 9 | 4.5% |
| ERPD & Royal Infirmary out-patients | 2 | 1.0% |
| Disp. Women and Children, Grove St | 1 | 0.5% |
| ERPD & St Anne's Dispensary | 1 | 0.5% |
| Western Dispensary & Royal Infirmary | 1 | 0.5% |
| Other (outside Edinburgh) | 9 | 4.5% |
| Unspecified/unclear | 19 | 9.6% |

**Source:** Graduation records, University of Edinburgh (1896): University Archives Ref: Da 43

monopolise the discipline. In response, the University Court was sent memorials by the directors of the four main Edinburgh dispensaries, complaining that '[t]he effect of the proposed change would be, in their view, seriously to cripple the resources of the dispensaries by depriving them of the students' fees for these classes, and also seriously to effect [sic] their power to relieve the sick poor who came to them for advice and treatment'.[20]

Another way the relationship between medical charity, medical education and domiciliary care of the poor in Edinburgh can be explored is by looking at the advice given to students by their medical professors during inauguration and graduation addresses. As the top and tail to training, philosophically speaking, these addresses set the tone for classes. Regularly, in Edinburgh, an emphasis was put, in formal public addresses, on the unique advantage of pursuing a medical education in that city. Thus in his opening address to the medical students in 1889, John Chiene, professor of surgery, commended 'dispensary work', by noting how it 'readied the student[s] for private practice . . . [teaching them] the need for courtesy and gentleness, more especially in their dealing with the poor'. In 1889, the strength of dispensary work in Edinburgh had gained recent national approval. The theme, however, was not a new one. Ten years earlier, at the opening of classes in November 1879, Professor Douglas Maclagan had similarly claimed to the students that the dispensary 'was invaluable as giving him [the student] that self-reliance without which he could never succeed in practice'. Addressing the university graduating class in 1893, Professor Thomas Grainger Stewart advised the students that Edinburgh medical charity dispensary work – with which he, like the other professors mentioned, was closely associated – enabled earliest access to 'study cases'. It was only through such study of cases that the students could hope to acquire what he referred to as the 'mens medica': this he described as the moral, observant, attentive, discriminating, sympathetic, analytic, synthetic and well-balanced mind necessary for independent medical judgement.[21] Giving the inaugural address to students of the Edinburgh School of Medicine in October 1879, Professor John Batty Tuke, then the General Medical Council (GMC) representative of the Royal College of Physicians of Edinburgh, sparked a heated exchange with the retiring president of the Edinburgh Botanical Society by proclaiming:

The practical knowledge he spoke of was not to be obtained by merely walking the hospital. There they would only meet with the more grave forms of disease. It was in the dispensary where they could acquire an insight into those minor complaints which formed the staple of everyday practice, and in the proper diagnosis of which mainly depended their position in their profession. Speaking for himself, he would rather choose a man for an assistant who could show his dispensary book well and truly filled with the names of patients whom he had personally attended in the Cowgate and Canongate than the holder of a gold medal for natural history . . .[22]

Although much is made here of the support within the Edinburgh medical elites for the involvement of students in home visitation, there were stray voices. Pre-empting later incredulity (detailed below), some disquiet was felt by at least one prominent Edinburgh surgeon of the period. Joseph Bell MD had been editor of the *Edinburgh Medical Journal*, was a long-serving consultant surgeon at the Royal Infirmary, and was director of the Edinburgh Medical Missionary Society from the 1860s. Despite these allegiances, in his written evidence to the Poor Law Commission in 1907, Bell argued that whilst Edinburgh's voluntary charity dispensaries generally in his opinion 'fairly met the case of slight ailments in patients who can walk to the dispensary . . . sudden illness in children and the aged requiring attention at their own homes are not I fear adequately met'. This inadequacy, Bell claimed, was because 'visits are often delayed' and, most tellingly, 'many cases are attended to by students of medicine'.[23]

### The Historical Account

Strangely, the special relationship described here, between medical education and the home visitation work of charity dispensaries in Edinburgh, is absent from most specialised accounts of medical education in Scotland for this period. Given the emphasis put on it at the time, this is a significant omission. One prominent recent example is Christopher Lawrence's study of 'Scottish Medical Education, 1700–1939'.[24] Lawrence makes much of what he refers to as the special environment of a Scottish education. He emphasises the aim of medical education in both Glasgow and Edinburgh in the nineteenth century, which he says was to produce rounded, generalist practitioners with a surgical and public service bent. Lawrence describes 'a commitment among Scottish teachers to present medicine as a practical art'. For the later nineteenth century he points to a move towards what he describes as a scientific 'pre-clinical curriculum'. He identifies this move with the particular role played in the training of students, after the mid-1870s, by the rebuilt Edinburgh Royal Infirmary and the newly founded Glasgow Western Infirmary, which became the central focal point of teaching in Glasgow. However, Lawrence's account does not mention one of the key factors that drove the expansion of the medical curriculum at the end of the 1880s: home visitation. Lawrence also makes no mention of the role of charity dispensaries in Edinburgh, and no mention therefore of just how it was that Edinburgh students in particular acquired important elements of this rounded, generalist, practical training. This omission is made all the more strange by the fact that from other writings it is clear that Lawrence is not unaware of the vital and peculiar role of home visits in the Edinburgh training tradition. In an earlier publication – detailing the role played by Rockefeller money in transforming Edinburgh medicine from the 1920s – Lawrence makes much of the incredulity of the dean of Harvard, David Edsall, who, during visits to Edinburgh in 1922, had critically commented that 'the most extraordinary thing about this school is the dispensary system . . . [where] the students are assigned to them [the patients] and actually take charge of them in their homes'.[25]

In *The Healers*, David Hamilton mentions 'the first Scottish dispensary', the ERPD, noting how it 'even extended to home visits'. However, in describing the evolution of medical education from the mid-nineteenth century he makes nothing further of this link, and instead concentrates on more familiar issues: battles with London over the value and legitimacy of a Scottish medical education; the impact of the growth of medical research and laboratory science on the curriculum; and the opening of medical schools to women.[26] Helen M. Dingwall's recent study, *A History of Scottish Medicine*, focuses on the evolution of the hospital rather than on what she describes as its corollary, the decline in 'aspects of medicine . . . practised or influenced wholly in the home'. She therefore completely overlooks the continuing role of dispensary charity in medical education, arguing simply that as the nineteenth century progressed it was 'the hospital [that] became . . . the focus of professional medicine and surgery, medical and surgical training' in Scotland.[27]

Recent Glasgow-centric studies of Scottish medical education across the second half of the nineteenth century have also largely missed the connection, having chosen to concentrate on the period between Medical Acts, 1858 to 1886. This was a time when Scottish medical education was largely looked down upon from London.[28] However, the gradual wider diffusion of Scottish surgical breakthroughs; the successful defence of the integrity of plural Scottish medical education traditions against criticisms from London (typified in the Royal Commission into the Medical Acts, 1882); and the increasing colonisation of positions of political prominence south of the Border by more Scotland-trained medics: these developments mean that the years immediately *after* 1886 are, in fact, also of much interest.[29] A number of additional factors made the period of half a decade following the passage of the 'safe generalist practitioner' legislation – the Medical Act of 1886 – of specific significance for both Scottish medical education and, ultimately too, for the 'Scottish system' of home visitation services.[30] First, as already noted, 1889–91 coincided with the peak in medical student numbers in Scotland. Second, the Universities (Scotland) Act of 1889 opened the way, formally at least, for women to pursue the study of medicine in

Scottish universities on a par with men. Third, after 1890, the standard medical curriculum across Britain was lengthened, to a modern format of five years. Over and above these changes, three separate decisions taken during the course of Glasgow's International Exhibition year of 1888, explored next, were to have particular ramifications for the use of medical students in domiciliary work amongst the poor, at once strengthening the use of them in Edinburgh, whilst dissolving the case for them in Glasgow.[31]

### Meetings of the GMC in May 1888

Historians have mainly accounted for the increase in the medical curriculum after 1890 in a progressive vein, by pointing to the failure of the four-year system to keep pace with new developments in medicine. W.F. Bynum, for example, has argued that, in Britain over the nineteenth century, 'the minimum course lengthened, first from three to four years, and then from four to five, to take account of the newer demands of science (especially practical work in histology, physiology, and bacteriology) and introductory teaching in specialist clinical subjects'.[32] Whilst the needs of science and of competing strands of specialist medicine may explain *what* happened after the curriculum expanded after 1891, it does not, in fact, explain *why* it was expanded at this time. To understand the true cause of change one needs explore the intentions of those who engineered the change. The key moments in the decision to extend the medical curriculum by one year occurred during meetings of the GMC.

The GMC was created under the Medical Act of 1858. It had two main functions: monitoring medical educational standards across Britain, and determining who should be on the medical register. A newly-arrived-at complement of 30 members of the GMC gathered for the first time, in London, in May 1888. It was over five days of these meetings that the GMC agreed the case for extending the medical curriculum.[33] Whilst nine members of the new complement represented Scotland directly, fully half of the members held some form of Scottish qualification: eight had undergraduate experience in Edinburgh, and three had undergraduate experience in Glasgow (table 2.4). A kindly disposition towards Scottish educational interests amongst the new leaders of the profession was natural.

On the first day of meetings in 1888, the executive committee of the GMC presented findings on the question of the improper use of 'unqualified assistants'. The issue came to national attention in March 1868, and had vexed the GMC from the 1870s.[34] Cases investigated gathered pace in the 1880s, and in 1887 the GMC advised through the medical press that it would henceforth take steps against all practitioners found guilty of using unqualified assistants. The resolutions agreed upon in 1888 had important ramifications for the future deployment

**Table 2.4   Qualifications of the 30 GMC members meeting in May 1888**

| Direct Representatives | Area or Institution | Education |
|---|---|---|
| C.G. Wheelhouse | England | London |
| Sir Walter Foster | England | Not known |
| James Grey Glover | England | **Edinburgh, MD Edinburgh** |
| William Bruce | Scotland | **Edinburgh, MD Aberdeen** |
| George Hugh Kidd | Ireland | **Ireland, MD Edinburgh** |

**Elected**

| | | |
|---|---|---|
| Sir Dyce Duckworth | RCP London | **MD Edinburgh** |
| John Marshall (pres.) | RCS London | London |
| R. Brudenell Carter | Apothecaries Soc. London | London |
| T.K. Chambers | Univ. Oxford | London, Oxford |
| G. Murray Humphry | Univ. Cambridge | London, Cambridge |
| G. Yeoman Heath | Univ. Durham | **LRCP Edinburgh** |
| Samuel Wilks | Univ. London | **London, LLD Edinburgh** |
| W. Mitchell Banks | Victoria Univ. Manchester | **Edinburgh, MD Edinburgh** |
| John Batty Tuke | RCP Edinburgh | **Edinburgh, MD Edinburgh** |
| Patrick Heron Watson | RCS Edinburgh | **MD Edinburgh** |
| Hector Clare Cameron | FPS Glasgow | **Glasgow, MD Glasgow** |
| Sir William Turner | Univ. Edinburgh | **London, FRCS Edinburgh** |
| John Struthers | Univ. Aberdeen | **Edinburgh, MD Edinburgh** |
| William Leishman | Univ. Glasgow | **Glasgow, MD Glasgow** |
| James Bell Pettigrew | Univ. St. Andrews | **MD Edinburgh** |
| Aquilla Smith | King & Queens Ireland | Dublin |
| Rawdon Macnamara | RCS Ireland | Dublin |
| Thomas Collins | Apothecaries Ireland | Dublin, London |
| Rev. Samuel Haughton | Univ. Dublin | Dublin |
| John Thomas Banks | Royal Univ. Ireland | Dublin |

**Crown Nominations**

| | | |
|---|---|---|
| Richard Quain | | London |
| Sir John Simon | | London |
| T. Pridgin Teale | | Oxford |
| Sir G.H.B. McLeod | | **MD Glasgow** |
| William Moore | | Dublin |

**Source:** Medical Directory and Medical Register (1888)

of medical students whilst under training, particularly regarding locum positions. It was determined by the GMC that the key issue was whether or not a practitioner was using a student 'either in complete substitution for his own services or under circumstances in which due supervision and control are not . . . exercised'. The key issue was what constituted 'due supervision and control'. The year 1888 was the first to see a medical practitioner stuck off for using an unqualified assistant.[35]

On the final two days of meetings discussion was given over to the issue of how best to incorporate the fresh demands of a host of competing specialist strands of medicine into the standard undergraduate curriculum. The requirement that students be given more opportunity to become acquainted with fevers and infectious diseases, with a greater number of midwifery cases, and with the study of insanity were all issues discussed; but at this stage proposals that the curriculum be altered to accommodate more study of different specialisms faced significant opposition from within the ranks of the central authority regulating British medical education. The reluctance was summed up by Professor Humphry, member for the University of Cambridge, who argued: 'Specialisation was all very well when a man had obtained the general knowledge necessary for practice of his profession, but to introduce it into the studies by which he was to secure his qualification was a new and objectionable principle.'[36]

The key decision to alter the medical curriculum was not, therefore, made in order to accommodate specialist strands. The decision was actually taken on day two of the meeting. It was on this day, under the chairmanship of the professor of anatomy at Aberdeen University, John Struthers, that the education sub-committee of the GMC presented its recommendations for change to the standard undergraduate curriculum: these were accepted.[37] With Struthers on the sub-committee were two other Scottish GMC representatives: Glasgow's Professor William Leishman and John Batty Tuke, representative of the Royal College of Physicians of Edinburgh (RCPE). Realising that return to a system of medical apprenticeship was a non-starter, and desirous none the less that students across Britain should routinely undertake far more outdoor practical and home visitation work during training, the committee put forward the following recommendation for all British medical students (which was agreed to): 'That all candidates for the final examination be required to produce evidence that they have attended for six months the practice of a public dispensary, or the outdoor practice of an hospital, or have acted for six months as assistant to a registered practitioner.'[38]

Supporting the motion to alter the curriculum, as well as the intentions behind it, and expanding on the principles that guided the decision, Dr William Mitchell Banks, surgeon to the Liverpool Royal Infirmary and member of the GMC for Manchester, noted:

With regard to the practice of a public dispensary, or the out-door practice of a hospital, the idea had been taken from an existing practice in Scotland ... It consisted, under proper supervision, on [sic] the out-door practice of a dispensary or hospital. When he was himself a student [in Edinburgh] he went over to one of the dispensaries, visited the patients at their homes, and prescribed for them. He was generally accompanied by a senior student ... and in case of any special difficulty or trouble he fell back upon his superior at the dispensary. In that way he taught himself a certain amount of private practice, learning to recognise measles, whooping-cough, and other minor ailments ... [Banks went on to clarify:] What the committee meant was not a mere attendance on the outdoor practice [for six months] ... but attendance on the patients at their homes.[39]

Dr Patrick Heron Watson of the RCPE supported the adoption of his home-town system, noting further that, '[i]f a student had the opportunity of going into the house[s] of patients and seeing the wretched circumstances in which they were placed, he would have the opportunity of learning a lesson that he would never forget, and that would fit him for practice in any sphere of life.'[40] In also supporting the proposal, the London-based English representative James Grey Glover saw the shift towards outdoor work as desirable in that it met a gap in educational provision. Glover argued (in the face of much modern historical analysis): 'There was a growing objection to hospitals being used for anything but the graver class of cases, and the teaching required by the student could not be learned in the out-patient department of a hospital; he could only learn it properly at the homes of the patients.'[41]

The motion to alter the medical curriculum passed, as stated, but with compromises that ultimately defeated the central call for more visitation nation-wide. Compromises were put in place to accommodate the existing systems in place both in London and Ireland. Ireland had its own flourishing public dispensary system and methods of training. In London, with its array of teaching hospitals, the stipulation became instead that the six months' outdoor practice could be spent in the outpatients department of a hospital rather than at a dispensary. In summing up the changes initiated, Struthers noted with satisfaction that the passing of the recommendation was a significant validation for Scottish educational methods. Scottish medical institutions previously had been 'very much criticised on the ground of their great deficiency in practical education ... [Yet] today they were congratulated by English members of the Council!'[42]

Given then, the decision by the GMC in May 1888 to endorse what it referred to as the 'Scottish system' whereby charities utilised students under training to visit the poor, and the decision to expand the medical curriculum as a consequence, why was such a system absent in Glasgow in the years after 1888? A clue to this puzzle is provided in the reaction of University of Glasgow member William Leishman to the curriculum changes. Whilst 'rejoicing' at seeing the support of fellow GMC members for the wider adoption of student visitation, Leishman also noted that, to his regret, 'an attempt had recently been made in Glasgow to establish a visiting department in connection with the dispensary of one of the large hospitals, but that the governing body of the hospital were *afraid of the responsibility*, and declined to give their sanction'.[43]

### The Fate of Student-led Domiciliary Care in Glasgow

Two distinct events that occurred around the time of the GMC meeting in 1888 had sealed the fate of student-led home visitation services in Glasgow. Both were connected with the relocation of the university in 1870, and with the associated drift to the western outskirts of Glasgow of the main focus of medical teaching in the city. First, in 1888, Anderson's Medical College relocated nearer Glasgow University. This forced the abandonment of its dispensary, previously the only general dispensary in Glasgow on the Edinburgh model. Second, also at the start of 1888, the managers of the recently built Western Infirmary came to the decision that it was prudent to abandon hope of implementing a similar home visitation scheme.

Whilst the teaching staff of Anderson's did not open a new dispensary when they moved to their new site, the older dispensary that the college had established in the city centre did not disappear altogether. The directors of the old college dispensary had been made up of a number of elite persons, from the world of Glasgow business, industry, Church and medicine. As a group they expressed collective concern that the relocation and the prospective closure of the dispensary would leave a large void in Glasgow's network of medical services. Meeting under James Burn Russell, in September 1889, it was resolved that the dispensary should be refounded as an independent entity. This new charity became Glasgow Central Dispensary.[44] Although refounded, the dispensary quickly resumed an equivalent volume of cases, but the staffing and focus of the dispensary entirely shifted. In particular, home visitation was abandoned and never reintroduced. Financial restrictions rather than managerial preference were blamed for this. An application for financial assistance to the Bellahouston Fund noted that with the loss of students previously used to underpin the service, any re-establishment of the home visitation service would require the appointment of a new staff member on 'a salary which we cannot presently afford'.[45]

Glasgow Western Infirmary (GWI) was the adjunct of the newly rebuilt university. Given its acquired importance in fashioning medical education in the city, hopes that the gap in student home visitation services might be filled passed to the GWI. Thus when Professor Leishman claimed at the GMC meeting that in Glasgow some had been 'afraid of the responsibility' of providing student visitation services, what he was referring to was not the abandonment of the Anderson's scheme but rather to the fears of the directors and managers of Glasgow's new showpiece infirmary. Surviving archival records for the GWI reveal the cause of this fear.

William Leishman was appointed to head a new department at the GWI in 1877, becoming the physician for diseases of women. Previously he had served as professor of midwifery at Glasgow University since 1868. Some years before this he had also taken control of an institution in the neighbourhood of the old university site called the Glasgow University Lying-In Hospital and Dispensary for Diseases of Women. This had long been used to instruct students, being formerly under the direction of Leishman's predecessor as professor of midwifery, John M. Pagan. Following a puerperal fever crisis in the mid-1850s, Pagan had decided to take the work of the training institution out of the ward and into the homes of the poor; and here it had stayed.[46] Following Leishman's appointment in 1877, negotiations began to amalgamate this Lying-In Hospital with the GWI dispensary. The managers of the GWI, lukewarm to the idea at first, eventually agreed to allow a system of what was referred to as 'professional attendance to poor women in their homes, at their confinement'. This was agreed to on two conditions. Leishman agreed to take personal control and responsibility of the new department. Crucially, he also had to agree to transfer to the GWI the £1,000 in funds that it was known was being held by him in the name of the Lying-In Hospital. The main broker in the arrangement was Professor John Gray McKendrick. McKendrick was relatively new to the Glasgow medical scene and a link to affairs in the capital, having only a year earlier transferred his practice from Edinburgh to Glasgow.[47]

Regulations for the new adjunct to the GWI dispensary, the midwifery visitation department, were established in 1878. Two 'outdoor physicians-accoucheur' were appointed: Robert Kirk and William Loudon Reid. A year later they were joined by a third, Murdoch Cameron. Kirk, Reid and Cameron took charge of Partick, Anderston and 'the Northern district' respectively; and together they oversaw the organisation of student visits, thus satisfying examination requirements. Although over the coming years the service remained small – with fewer than 400 cases recorded during the next nine years – the scheme ran largely without reported hiccups, save occasional issues, quickly resolved, relating to the dependability of certain students.

Gradually proposals were mooted from different quarters to the effect that, given the recognised general absence of non-midwifery home visitation services in Glasgow compared to Edinburgh, the GWI might pick up the slack. In 1884, for example, Professor McKendrick chose to speak on the issue of the efficacy of domiciliary services when addressing a meeting of the directors of the Glasgow Medical Missionary Society. More pointedly, in the same year, John Young, professor of natural history, raised the topic at the graduation address of Glasgow University students. Here he argued: 'If dispensary visitation was – and there could be no doubt of the fact – a very valuable means of future education for the practitioner, it ought to be provided.' Young then asserted that 'it ought to be enforced by ordinance, as was attendance on midwifery cases', noting further that 'domestic visitation under the auspices of a Dispensary was the natural complement of clinical teaching'.[48]

Using his appointment to the GWI house committee in 1887, John Cleland, professor of anatomy at Glasgow University, finally persuaded the management to agree to consider the matter of student home visitation in full. A sub-committee of six was elected to weigh the issues. It included four men who together were representative of the major medical institutions of the city: Professor Cleland; Cleland's fellow Glasgow University professor, Dr Matthew Charteris; Glasgow MOH James Burn Russell; and Thomas Lapraik, the nominated board member of the Faculty of Physicians and Surgeons, Glasgow. In November 1887, the sub-committee reported. It unanimously recommended that 'no obstacle [should be put] in the way of the speedy consideration of the institution of a Home Visitation Department by means of students under the supervision of the staff'. With this green light, Professors Charteris and Cleland set about drawing up (what they entitled) a new 'scheme for managing the medical and surgical dispensary of the Western Infirmary'. This put supervised student visits to patients right at the centre of the proposal. Rule IV of the scheme stated: 'The Physicians shall, in the case of Patients who are not considered suitable for admission into the Infirmary, but are too ill to attend at the Dispensary, appoint a Student to visit them at their homes.'[49]

All seemed well. However, given that it was already late in the financial year, the GWI house committee proposed to leave the implementation of the mooted new scheme for a new board, with elections due within weeks. Initially the new board of managers of the GWI also expressed approval of the scheme. Then, at the monthly meeting in December 1887, the scheme hit another delay. The matter was returned once more to the medical committee by the managers, who were again instructed 'to look carefully into the matter and report'.[50] At this juncture the plans were passed to the GWI lawyers. And it was at this moment the scheme finally hit the rocks. On 31 January 1888 the law agent, a Mr Hill, was instructed

> to advise as to the nature and extent of the responsibility . . . which would attach to the managers in connection with such a scheme, involving the attendance of students upon out-door patients; also to the visiting physicians and surgeons and dispensary physicians and surgeons . . .[51]

Hill's response confirmed the worst fears of some of the managers. After considering the matter, Hill reported back that, in his legal opinion, the scheme involved immeasurable financial risk to all involved in management at the GWI. He stated that any responsibility for the practice of unqualified medical students 'would attach to the managers' for their part in sanctioning the scheme. 'The nature of the responsibility', Hill ruled, 'would be damages for want of professional knowledge, or skill, carelessness or neglect on the part of student as pupil practitioner, and the extent would depend on the measure of the default and amount of damages which might be awarded.'[52]

This judgement proved final for the future of medical charity, medical education and domiciliary care in Glasgow. On the say-so of Mr Hill and the infirmary's legal department, the new scheme and the existing midwifery service were both hastily abandoned. The three physicians-accoucheur involved were all redeployed to in-house duties. Despite the resolution of the GMC three months later in favour of promotion of home visits by students, and despite, too, the seemingly litigation-free success of ongoing equivalent services operating in Edinburgh, the idea of using medical students at the GWI dispensary to visit patients was not returned to. The 'Scottish system', championed by the GMC in May 1888, had already been disowned by the major medical charities of Glasgow.

## Conclusion

This chapter has sought to explore the close links in Scotland, before the First World War, between the education of medical students, charity dispensary and the provision of domiciliary medical care for the poor. It is shown that whilst a Scottish approach is identified in previous literature and accounts, in fact stark differences of attitude are identifiable between Edinburgh and Glasgow. This is clearly indicated in comparative reported case numbers (tables 2.1 and 2.2). And whilst the GMC meeting in 1888 saw an extension of the medical curriculum within Britain to five years distinctly in order to accommodate greater opportunity for practical home visitation experience amongst medical students before graduation, the same year also saw the effective abandonment of student visitation of the poor in Glasgow. One key factor in terms of difference between educational provision and the development of dispensary services in Edinburgh and Glasgow was the greater 'collegiate' culture that existed between institutions in Edinburgh. In Edinburgh, the town council recognised the strategic importance of the medical school, and there was distinct encouragement for the spread of medical charities because it was recognised that they served as valuable training sites in an overcrowded student centre. This relationship was eventually under-mined in the 1910s, when, following the advent of national insurance, patients' use of medical charity changed, and 1920s, when new sources of revenue began to take the focus of medical training in new directions. In Glasgow, over the nine-teenth century, the different institutions rarely saw eye-to-eye in the same way. There were on-going territorial disputes, for example, between the Royal College and the university, and between the relocated university and the abandoned Royal Infirmary. As Christopher Lawrence has argued, from the mid-1870s the Western Infirmary became of over-arching importance in Glasgow in terms of the training of the majority of the medical students in the city; and the decision by its managers to steer clear of using students to visit patients at home for legal reasons was deci-sive in terms of the subsequent provision of such services in the town.

## Notes

1.  Cope, Z., 'The Influence of the Free Dispensaries upon Medical Education', *Medical History* 13 (1969), 29–36, at 29, 36.
2.  This chapter is based on Sutton, D.A., 'The Public–Private Interface of Domiciliary Medical Care for the Poor in Scotland, c.1875–1911', PhD thesis, University of Glasgow, 2009, esp. chapter 14.
3.  Craig, W.S., *History of the Royal College of Physicians of Edinburgh* (Oxford, 1976), 499.
4.  See, for example, Newman, G., *Some Notes on Medical Education in England*, Parliamentary Papers, Cd. 9124 (1918). On the usurpation of traditional Edinburgh approaches to medical education in the 1920s with the advent of Rockefeller funding of laboratory clinical science university posts see Lawrence, C., *Rockefeller Money, the Laboratory, and Medicine in Edinburgh, 1919–1930* (New York, 2005), esp. chapter 4.
5.  On the impact of the Medical Act of 1858 on Scottish university medical education see Bradley, J., Crowther, A. and Dupree, M., 'Mobility and Selection in Scottish University Medical Education, 1858–1886', *Medical History* 40 (1996), 1–24, at 1.
6.  Anderson, R.D., *Education and Opportunity in Victorian Scotland* (Oxford, 1983).
7.  *Report of the Royal Commission Appointed to Inquire into the Medical Acts*, Parliamentary Papers, C.3259-1 (1882), paragraph 44. Bradley et al., 'Mobility and Selection', 18–19.
8.  *Edinburgh Medical Journal* 20 (1875), 349
9.  *Lancet*, 14 September 1901, 745.
10. Lechmere Taylor, H.F., *A Century of Service, 1841–1941* (Edinburgh, 1941), 16–18.
11. *Scotsman*, 24 May 1888.
12. Kay, A.C. and Toynbee, H.V., *Report to the Royal Commission on the Poor Laws and Relief of Distress on Endowed and Voluntary Charities in Certain Places, and the Administrative Relations*

of Charity and the Poor Law, Parliamentary Papers, Cd. 4593 (1909), appendix, vol. 15, sections on Edinburgh; Hugh Barrie, in *Royal Commission on the Poor Laws and Relief of Distress: Scottish Evidence*, Parliamentary Papers, Cd. 4978 (1910), appendix 17.

13. The amount of 'doubling-up' is difficult to determine. Making allowance for those who came into Edinburgh to use its charities from the hinterland, Kay and Toynbee estimated that, in 1907, 28 per cent of the population of Edinburgh had accessed free dispensary services: Kay and Toynbee, *Report on Endowed and Voluntary Charities*, appendix, vol. 15.

14. On domiciliary care arrangements at Anderson's Medical College Dispensary in Glasgow see Christie, J., *The Medical Institutions of Glasgow: A Handbook, Prepared for the Annual Meeting of the British Medical Association Held in Glasgow* (Glasgow, 1888), partly quoted in Cope, 'Influence of the Free Dispensaries', 36.

15. Russell, J.B., 'Report on Uncertified Deaths' (1874), quoted in Ferguson, T., *Scottish Social Welfare, 1864–1914* (Edinburgh, 1958), 443–4.

16. Scott, R., 'Edinburgh and General Practice,' in McLachlan, G., ed., *Medical Education and Medical Care: A Scottish-American Symposium* (London, 1977), 57–69, at 59.

17. *Scotsman*, 1 February 1904.

18. Edinburgh Public Dispensary Royal Warrant: Edinburgh City Archives, SL73/1/1.

19. Bradley et al., 'Mobility and Selection', 6.

20. *Scotsman*, 25 October 1882. On the growing dependence of Edinburgh medical charity dispensaries on student fees see the speech by Edinburgh's then lord provost, the general practitioner James Alexander Russell, in the *Scotsman*, 1 February 1892.

21. Chiene, Maclagan and Grainger-Stewart, quoted from the *Scotsman*, 5 November 1879; 16 October 1889; 2 August 1893.

22. *Scotsman*, 29 October 1879; 14 November 1879.

23. Joseph Bell, in *Royal Commission on the Poor Laws and Relief of Distress: Scottish Evidence*, appendix 15.

24. Lawrence, C., 'The Shaping of Things to Come: Scottish Medical Education, 1700–1939', *Medical Education* 40 (2006), 212–18.

25. Lawrence, *Rockefeller Money*, 96.

26. Hamilton, D., *The Healers: A History of Medicine in Scotland* (Edinburgh, 1981, repr. 2003), 107, 207ff.

27. Dingwall, H.M., *A History of Scottish Medicine* (Edinburgh, 2003), 178

28. See, for example, Bradley et al., 'Mobility and Selection'; Hull, A. and Geyer-Kordesch, J., *The Shaping of the Medical Profession: The History of the Royal College of Physicians and Surgeons of Glasgow, 1858–1999* (London, 1999), chapter 1. Hull and Geyer-Kordesch have little to say of the years immediately after 1886 in terms of the development of medical education in Scotland except that they were 'momentous . . . for the growth of scientific medical disciplines' (52).

29. The first is the subject matter of the more recent Crowther, M.A. and Dupree, M.W., *Medical Lives in the Age of Surgical Revolution* (Cambridge, 2007).

30. Newman, C., *The Evolution of Medical Education in the Nineteenth Century* (London, 1957), 194: the aim of medical education in Britain, as recorded in the Medical Act of 1886 was: 'to produce a doctor who, on the day he was registered, would be a safe man to let loose on the public, competent to practise all branches of his profession'.

31. The extension of standard undergraduate study from four years to five years after 1890 was a crucial development. It set medical training in Britain on a course that remained little changed for the next hundred years. On this see Waterson, S.W., Laing, M.R. and Hutchinson, J.D., 'Nineteenth-Century Medical Education for Tomorrow's Doctors', *Scottish Medical Journal* 51 (2006), 45–9.

32. Bynum, W.F., *Science and the Practice of Medicine in the Nineteenth Century* (Cambridge, 1994), 219; Newman, *Evolution of Medical Education*, 217–18: 'The latter part of the [nine-

teenth] century saw the beginnings of the development of specialism, and as one special subject after another was elaborated as soon as it had achieved an independent status, its exponents began to clamour for its inclusion in the basic curriculum required for all doctors.'

33. For press coverage of the debates of the GMC debates during the meetings in May 1888 see *Lancet*, May 1888, 1030–6; *Scotsman*, 22 to 26 May 1888.

34. *British Medical Journal* 1 (1868), 226ff.

35. Smith, R., 'The Development of Ethical Guidance for Medical Practitioners by the General Medical Council', *Medical History* 37 (1993), 56–67; *Scotsman*, 25 May 1888.

36. *Scotsman*, 23 May 1888.

37. For a recent assessment of the significance of John Struthers on British medical education reform during the later nineteenth century see Waterson, S.W. and Hutchison, J.D., 'Sir John Struthers MD FRCS Edin LLD Glasg: Anatomist, Zoologist and Pioneer in Medical Education', *Surgeon* 2 (2004), 347–51.

38. *Scotsman*, 24 May 1888.

39. *Lancet*, May 1888, 1034; also quoted in *Scotsman*, 24 May 1888.

40. *Lancet*, May 1888, 1036.

41. *Lancet*, May 1888, 1035.

42. *Scotsman*, 24 May 1888.

43. *Scotsman*, 24 May 1888. Emphasis added.

44. Glasgow Central Dispensary minutes, 30 September 1889: Greater Glasgow Health Board archives (GGHB), HB48/1/1.

45. Glasgow Central Dispensary minutes, 2 March, 1892.

46. I am grateful to Mark Skippen, University of Glasgow, for pointing this out. See Pagan, J.M., 'Contributions to Midwifery and Practice', *Glasgow Medical Journal* 1 (1854), 207–16, at 207f, and Pagan, J.M., 'Statistics of the Glasgow University Lying-In Hospital', *Glasgow Medical Journal* 8 (1860), 198–203, at 198f.

47. Glasgow Western Infirmary (GWI) minutes, 21 December 1877, house sub-committee report: GGHB HB 6/1/1.

48. *Scotsman*, 1 August 1884.

49. GWI minutes, 12 November 1887: medical sub-committee report.

50. GWI minutes, 27 December 1887: house sub-committee report.

51. GWI minutes, 31 January 1888: medical committee meeting.

52. GWI minutes, 21 February 1888: medical committee meeting.

3

# Welfare Agencies and Migrant Settlers in Scotland, c.1919–22

## Jacqueline Jenkinson

This chapter considers the relationship between two groups of economic migrants and a range of welfare agencies in the years immediately following the First World War. Black British colonial subjects from Africa and the Caribbean came to Britain before and in increasing numbers during the war and worked principally in the merchant navy and also in wartime industry. Lithuanians settled in the west of Scotland (chiefly Ayrshire and Lanarkshire) in the late nineteenth and early twentieth centuries and worked mainly in mining and other staple industries.

The parallel histories of these two migrant populations residing in Scotland in the post-war years reveal their fragile position both in the workforce and within Scottish society during a national economic downturn. Overt hostility towards their presence was apparent in the central government policy of 'repatriation' implemented against both groups. However, the reactions of local government, welfare agencies and trade unions to the plight of the unemployed, destitute and dependent among the two groups were more complex. The purpose of this chapter is to examine the experiences of these groups of settlers in their own words and in the attitudes of the agencies which dealt with their presence in a society facing up to harsh post-war economic realities.

### Settlement History of the Two Migrant Groups

The majority of African and African-Caribbean people who came to Scotland lived and worked in Glasgow. The black population of the thriving port was of long settlement and by the early twentieth century included sailors, families, students, professionals and skilled workers. Although there are no specific figures available for black people from British colonies resident in the city (since this information was not recorded in the census), based on figures for unemployed black sailors after the war and the presence of families as well as a middle-class element, the black population of Glasgow was several hundred strong. This community supported its own political organisation (the African Races Association of Glasgow) and a social club.[1]

Links between Glasgow and the black Atlantic world originated through trade. The city's merchant guilds developed a regular direct connection with the Caribbean in the late seventeenth century, in addition to a flourishing trade with the colonial plantations in mainland North America.[2] Glasgow was involved in the slave trade, but to a much smaller degree than the major slaving ports of Bristol, London and Liverpool. Trade with Africa remained negligible until Britain began to extend its empire in the latter half of the nineteenth century. Glasgow's crucial tobacco trade was severely affected with the outbreak of the American civil war in the 1860s. Hence the conditions were ripe to look to Africa for fresh markets: Glasgow's trade links were initially with West Africa in the early 1870s.[3] The expansion of trade with Africa due to the increased use of steamships also created a demand for local sailors, particularly those who plied the overseas trading routes. Most African and African-Caribbean sailors were employed below decks as firemen and trimmers.[4]

The number of black colonial seamen sailing from Glasgow and other ports increased markedly during the war as British merchant sailors joined the Royal Navy and enemy nationals were excluded from the merchant fleet. However, the reduction in the merchant shipping fleet to suit peacetime requirements and the flooded job market following the demobilisation of many thousands of white (and some black) British sailors from the Royal Navy and the other armed forces meant that black colonial sailors faced post-war unemployment.

Growing competition for employment was compounded by the attitudes of the sailors' unions which sought to enforce a 'colour' bar on black sailors. In Glasgow, the main sailors' union, the National Sailors' and Firemen's Union (NSFU), was joined in this campaign by the Seafarers' Union under the leadership of prominent local trade union leader and future Labour MP, Emanuel Shinwell. In fact, Shinwell's apparently more politically radical union refused black membership, while the NSFU tolerated black members but sought to replace them with white labour (including non-British) wherever possible.

The competition for jobs led to a riot in Glasgow harbour in January 1919, when a large crowd of white sailors chased and attacked a group of black West African sailors out of the mercantile marine office in James Watt Street. The riot began as sailors congregated while waiting for their chance to be 'signed on' to a ship. Competing groups of black and white sailors jostled and shouted insults at each other. This escalated into a pitched battle which spilled out of the shipping yard onto the street.[5] More than 30 black sailors fled the sailors' yard pursued by a large crowd of white sailors. White locals joined the crowd, which grew to several hundred. The rioters chased the black sailors towards the nearby Glasgow sailors' home on the corner of James Watt Street and Broomielaw Street,[6] and smashed the windows of the sailors' home before invading it. Over 50 police officers intervened and cleared the two groups into the street.

The black sailors then fled to their own boarding house at 118 Broomielaw Street. White rioters sought to force the sailors back out into the street by smashing the windows with missiles, surrounding the building and then forcing entry. In response, some of the black colonial sailors fired shots down at the crowd. Cornered in their boarding house the black sailors offered no resistance when the police force entered the premises. However, to restore order, the police removed 30 black sailors from the boarding house and into 'protective custody'. All were subsequently charged with riot and weapons offences. None of the large crowd of white rioters was arrested.

Three people were seriously injured during the riot. Two were white sailors: Duncan Cowan, who was shot; and Thomas Carlin, who had been stabbed. West African sailor Tom Johnson was also stabbed. Local press reports displayed little sympathy for Johnson, who was described, in racist terms, as 'a darkie from Sierra Leone, who speaks little English. [He] complained of having been stabbed, but his wound was not serious.'[7] In contrast to the immediate arrest of the wounded Johnson and the mass detention of a group of black sailors, only one white person was later arrested for an alleged assault on a police officer during the riot.

All the arrested black people were British subjects who had served in the merchant navy before and during the war. During the trial, their solicitor, David Cook, underlined their service record in the merchant navy:

> During the whole period of the war and for some years before the war they were manning British ships and were, of course, entitled to the protection of the British Government. Some of them had formerly sailed from Glasgow, but on this occasion a number of men had come from Cardiff to man ships in Glasgow Harbour.[8]

The Glasgow press discussed the employment competition that lay behind the riot in terms of black sailors taking jobs away from local whites. One account noted that between 400 and 500 white sailors were then unemployed in Glasgow.[9] Another stated that the riot had broken out because white sailors believed that black sailors had come up from Cardiff 'to take their jobs'.[10] The *Glasgow Herald* stated: 'It is understood that the disturbance originated because of an alleged preference being given to British seamen over coloured seamen in signing on the crew of a ship at Glasgow harbour.'[11] The use of the term 'British' here to distinguish white from black sailors illustrates the practical difficulties faced by black colonial subjects in the metropole in establishing their British identity, particularly among hostile sections of the white population.

A wave of riots directed against black residents broke out around Britain's ports over the next few months. These peaked in June 1919 when widespread riots in Liverpool, Cardiff, Newport and Barry led to the deaths of five people. Government intervention on the issue resulted in the launch of a paid repatriation scheme for black colonial sailors to return to West Africa and the Caribbean. All British subjects had the right to settle in Britain and could not be involuntarily removed. Repatriation for individual unemployed black colonial workers had initially been made available via the Marine Department of the Board of Trade in February 1919. The offer was principally directed at sailors who had come to Britain during the war years. The more comprehensive government repatriation scheme open to (and urged upon) all black colonial sailors was launched after the outbreak of widespread riots in south Wales and Liverpool in June 1919. To encourage departure and promote the idea of repatriation among black colonial sailors the government put up cash incentives with the inducement of voyage and settlement allowances totalling £6.

In Glasgow and the other ports few black colonial workers took advantage of the offer, preferring to stay on in Britain, where many had put down permanent roots and started families. However, those who refused the scheme were left without much hope of employment in the continued poor economic climate of 1920–2. Moreover, in the wake of the port rioting (with violence often breaking out in the mercantile marine hiring yards as had been the case in Glasgow), employers were now even more wary of offering jobs to black colonial sailors.

Black colonial workers represented a 'reserve army of labour' before and during the First World War. Lithuanians occupied a similar status in the Scottish workforce. About 1.25 million peasants and agricultural labourers left the area described in British contemporary sources as 'Russian Poland' between 1870 and 1914, following the emancipation of the serfs in 1861 and during a time of growing population. From the 1880s onwards Lithuanians from rural communities came to Scotland and were employed in Ayrshire and particularly Lanarkshire in heavy industry: mining, iron and steel. The number of 'Russian Poles' residing in Scotland rose steeply from 478 to 4,929 between 1891 and 1901. Most of the new arrivals worked in the mines. In 1901, 1,135 of the near 5,000 Lithuanians in Scotland worked in coal mining, by 1911 there were 2,611 so employed.[12] Trade unions opposed the hiring of cheaper, unskilled foreign labour. James Keir Hardie, secretary to the Ayrshire Miners' Union and to the Scottish Parliamentary Labour Party, gave evidence before the government's Select Committee on Emigration and Immigration (Foreigners) in July 1889. He reported that around twenty 'Poles' were employed at the Glengarnock Iron works and the neighbouring steel works as day labourers. He believed that the Russian consul in Glasgow had something to do with sending them to these two non-unionised works. He recalled that

labourers' wages had been 17 shillings per week in 1882, 'but since the introduction of foreigners the wages have been brought down to 12s. a week for the same
class of work . . . and the men accept those low wages because I believe the impression prevails amongst them that if they do not accept the wages offered them, other
foreigners would be brought in to take their place'.[13] He described the 'Poles' as:
'very filthy, six or seven males occupying a one-roomed house, and having a woman
to cook for them, perhaps, and look after them; but their presence is complained of
very much by the neighbours'.[14] He went on to give evidence that 'there is a very
strong ill-feeling existing between them and the Scotch workmen; the latter do not
care to mix much with them'.[15] He recommended a prohibition on the employment of foreign workers unless they were refugees or it could be guaranteed that
foreigners would receive the same wages as local workers, ending with the
comment: 'strong diseases require strong remedies'.[16] Miners' union representatives also raised questions about the safety of mines where those with little or no
English were employed. As the newcomers became unionised, local animosity less-
ened and during a strike in 1905 Lithuanian miners strongly supported the
Lanarkshire Miners' Union. Lunn has argued that both native workers and the
Lithuanian migrant labour force came to adopt socialist principles around the same
time in the early years of the twentieth century.[17] In 1912 Lanarkshire's Lithuanian
miners joined the national miners' strike for a minimum wage.[18]

During the First World War the position of the migrant Lithuanian population in the Scottish workforce was challenged. Under the Anglo-Russian
(Military Service) Convention (an agreement reached between the British and
the provisional Russian government in 1917) Lithuanian men of military age
were given the choice of joining the British army or returning to the Russian
empire to join the imperial army in fighting the Axis powers. Despite the
employment of Lithuanians in key areas of Scottish war production such as
mining and the iron and steel industries, the Home Office resolved to push for
the application of Convention guidelines. Information supplied by local police
forces regarding the socialist tendencies among the Lithuanian settlements
helped sway this view. A Home Office memorandum noted:

> the great majority, if not practically all the miners of military age have
> elected for Russia: in the belief, according to the police, that they will
> somehow or other evade service there. The Chief Constable of Glasgow
> says of the 500 Lithuanians in Glasgow that they are all regarded as
> Socialists or revolutionaries.[19]

The view of Hamilton's chief constable was similar: 'Bellshill is the centre of
the largest Polish [sic] population in Lanarkshire, and is the place where the

meetings of the most advanced Socialistic and Anarchist Poles have been held over the last twenty years.'[20] Eventually, 1,100 Lithuanians left Scotland under the Convention and a further 700 joined the British army.

The successful Russian revolution, the proclamation of Lithuanian independence in December 1917 and the signing of the Brest-Litovsk peace treaty with Germany in March 1918 left many Lithuanian soldiers in the Russian army in limbo. It also meant that their families in Scotland were without a crucial breadwinner in the longer term, since those who could not prove they had fought alongside the allies rather than switch to the revolutionary Soviet forces were not allowed to return.[21] Thousands of Lithuanian women and children (many Scottish-born) were left with little means of financial support. The prolonged absence of this group of industrial workers meant their families were forced to vacate company houses. This placed a further burden on local authorities which then had to find additional local housing for Lithuanian dependants. Some Lithuanian women gained jobs locally in brick making and as surface workers in the mines in order to bring in a small income.[22] Others were forced into theft to keep the family fed and warm. According to Joe Smith (Cesaikas):

> some o' the wimmin suffered awfy badly an' were reduced tae daein' onythin' tae feed their weans an' heat the hoose. Lumps o' coal oot the ironworks wagons an' tatties and turnips oot the fields were lifted – mebbe it wisnae richt but maist folk turned a blin' e'e.[23]

## Support from Welfare Agencies, Self-Help and Repatriation

Black colonial sailors made unemployed after the war initially received an 'out of work donation' via the Ministry of Labour. However, this entitlement ran out after 16 weeks of payments. Some of the long-term unemployed sailors were allowed to stay on at their lodging houses free of charge, but such arrangements were not indefinite. By February 1920 a group of destitute black colonial sailors was admitted to Glasgow's Barnhill poorhouse.[24] As desperate as this may seem, according to Levitt resort to the poorhouse by 'men on the fringe of the labour market' was nothing new. The number of the 'pauper' unemployed increased steadily from the beginning of the century and by 1909 over 100 unemployed per day applied as 'disabled' for poor relief in Glasgow.[25]

Sailors and their families were also given relief by the Glasgow branch of the Charity Organisation Society (COS). However, the COS was reluctant to assume long-term support for this group. In February 1920, the COS branch secretary wrote to the Scottish Board of Health, the national agency which dealt with matters of welfare, to request central government assistance for dozens of destitute black sailors in Glasgow:

> There are over 100 unemployed coloured men in Glasgow, and two-thirds of them are destitute. As you are aware the Government offered to repatriate them but most of them refused the offer on the ground that they have nothing to go back to and that having served us during the war we should not send them away penniless when peace came . . . Even in the case of those who are willing to be repatriated considerable delay has occurred in arranging shipping. The Board of Trade officials in Glasgow have done everything in their power to get them away or get employment but during the past six months not more than half a dozen coloured men got employment from Glasgow, while ships that came in with black crews left many of them behind. The result is that the numbers are gradually increasing. Apart from humanitarian considerations, the presence of so many discontented and semi-starved men is a positive danger.[26]

Regarding the welfare of British colonials as outside their remit, the Scottish Board of Health passed the letter to the Colonial Office for consideration. The Colonial Office response was that only parish relief could be offered to destitute black colonial sailors who had refused the offer of repatriation. The government policy of mass repatriation to solve unemployment and social problems was also used against the Lithuanian settlements in Scotland the following year.

Other non-governmental agencies offered some temporary assistance to unemployed black colonial workers. The Scottish advisory committee of the National Relief Fund (which aided war veterans) temporarily relieved some of the long-term unemployed black British subjects in Glasgow. Similar short-term assistance was given by the King's Fund for Ex-Servicemen. The fate of this group failed to improve as the post-war recession worsened. For example, in March 1920 the *Glasgow Herald* reported that 600 former soldiers daily were 'walking the streets' of the city looking for work.[27]

The unemployment experienced by black British sailors was extreme but by no means untypical of the difficulties faced by industrial workers in Scotland following the armistice. Unemployment benefit entitlement was temporarily extended after the war in part due to organised protests from unemployed veterans. This interim measure described by Levitt as the 'original "dole"', lasted until March 1921.[28] Severe unemployment continued throughout 1921, with 250,000 Scottish workers (20 per cent of the workforce) unemployed. In August 1921 parish councils in Scotland for the first time began to make payments of 21s (£1.05) to the able-bodied unemployed in cases of 'absolute destitution'. These payments were formalised to cover the able-bodied unemployed who had no benefit or whose benefits were insufficient under the Poor Law Emergency Provisions (Scotland) Act of November 1921. This short-term arrangement ran for six months until May 1922.[29] Black colonial sailors in Glasgow were eligible for these benefits.

Rather than rely on the intervention of local charities and welfare agencies or trust to the actions of central government, members of Glasgow's black population worked together to publicise growing destitution among their number caused by long-term unemployment. After an appeal to Glasgow's lord provost for assistance evoked no response, a 'delegation' representing 132 black sailors sent a letter and signed petition to the ultra-patriotic journal *John Bull* in March 1919 complaining about the imposition of a 'colour' bar on British ships by trade unions in Glasgow. The petitioners blamed their unemployment on the actions of the sailors' unions, who were 'working to have coloured men abolished not only from British ships but expelled altogether out of Britain'.[30] The group's protest focused on the unfairness of denying colonial Britons a chance to work while white Europeans found no difficulty in gaining jobs. The tone of the petition also illustrated the politicising effect of war on black British colonial subjects: 'The great European war have [sic] brought the aspirations of every race to the forefront. We are not living in the stone and iron age, neither are we living in the days when Negroes was [sic] fooled with Bits of Glass and Beads.'[31]

*John Bull* incorporated the protest letter into an article which portrayed the dismal existence faced by unemployed black colonial sailors in Glasgow and at the same time highlighted the employment of aliens on British ships:

> We make no apology for returning to the subject of coloured seamen, British-born subjects, in Glasgow. The apology is due from the National Sailors' and Firemen's Union which took the disgraceful step of refusing them – although members – to serve on British ships. The only shadow of an excuse is the shallow pretence that the places the coloured men would take are to be reserved for discharged soldiers. That is sheer bunkum. One poor fellow has died as the result of privations, and of 'sleeping out' for he had no money and no bed. Yet he was a Briton who had defied the Hun and his devilries for the sake of Britain. There are 132 of these ill-treated fellows in Glasgow most of these without a square meal any and every day ... They are modest enough to say – 'first place for white Britishers; after that coloured Britishers'. Yet they are ordered to 'clear out' from ships at Glasgow, while they see Norwegians, Swedes and Spaniards taken on.[32]

A later report in April 1919 in the black-published and written London-based newspaper the *African Telegraph* took its cue from the *John Bull* article: 'In

Glasgow there are more than 130 British seamen walking on their uppers, down and out. They happen to be coloured men, but they are all true British-born subjects, who have served on British ships during the war.'[33]

The sailors' petition was passed to the Colonial Office for its consideration. The government's response had not changed in the few weeks since it dealt with the letter from the Glasgow branch of the COS requesting assistance for this same group of workers: the Colonial Office directed the petitioners to the Board of Trade repatriation scheme as the only central government solution to their unemployment problem. An internal memorandum revealed that some in the Colonial Office felt 'helpless' in the face of the 'Union attitude' to tackle the destitution of black colonial sailors in Britain's ports since it could not enact the legislation that would be required to ensure that a proportion of every ship's crew consisted of 'British subjects'.[34] The official reply said nothing about the seamen's union intransigence; instead it blamed black unemployment on the 'unusually large numbers of seamen' then in Britain owing to demobilisation from the navy and the return of sailors from imprisonment in Germany.[35]

The weak official response to their petition did not satisfy the Glasgow sailors, who submitted a further appeal to the Colonial Office. This second letter was more strident in tone, noting that they were well aware of the over supply of sailors at that time. The letter returned to the petitioners' chief grievance, namely, that foreign sailors ('Spaniards, Swedes, Greeks and Chinese') were getting jobs while they as Britons were out of work. This letter also mentioned the riot at the harbour as further evidence of the extent of racism in Glasgow harbour. It concluded by reiterating the loyalty of the black population: 'we are not Bolsheviks . . . but we wants to enjoy the freedom which is the basis of Great Britain'.[36] The Colonial Office's reply referred the unemployed sailors' representatives to the department's original letter and said that they had nothing further to add.

For those who were unwilling to accept repatriation the future was bleak. Unemployment and the threat of further riots remained. In June 1919 a letter to the local press from the African Races Association of Glasgow (ARAG) spoke out against the riots and reinforced the employment grievances felt by black colonial seamen in the port:

We, the members of the African Races Association of Glasgow, view with regret the recent racial riots in different parts of Britain, and resent the unwarrantable attacks that have been made upon men of colour, without exception as one common herd of inferior beings. It seems from the newspaper reports that the seat of the trouble lies in the fact that men of colour are employed at seaport towns, while demobilised soldiers are unemployed. Is it not a fact that there are in the same towns ex-service coloured men also unemployed?

But, granting that some coloured soldiers are employed are they not in the minority – about 1,000 to 1, and are they not British subjects the same as the white men, and consequently deserve the same consideration?

Did not some of these men fight on the same battlefields with white men to defeat the enemy and make secure the British Empire? Why can't they work now in the same factories with white men? Did they not run the risks of losing their lives by the submarine warfare in bringing food for white women and children in common with white men?[37]

The letter was signed by Leo W. Daniels, secretary of the ARAG. Daniels was from Ontario, Canada and had lived in Glasgow since 1886 working as a journalist and small trader. ARAG membership was made up of students, skilled workers and professionals and included members from Ghana, Jamaica and the United States. The association had been active during the war and functioned for at least a further decade. In 1928 it affiliated with the London-based West African Students' Union (WASU; established in 1925).[38]

The activities of ARAG echoed the organised efforts of the black sailors who petitioned the government over unemployment in March 1919 and suggests a sense of community among the black colonial population in Glasgow, including their families. According to the account of white local resident William Adams, who was a boy of 12 in 1919 and recalled witnessing the Glasgow harbour riot, black colonial sailors put down roots in the city. According to Adams many of the black sailors were 'properly married' to local women. He remembered a lot of 'coloured' children in the area.[39] In June 1919 the white wife of a black sailor was prompted to write to the Glasgow *Evening Times* after racist remarks made in the 'Hal o' the Wynd' opinion column which ended with a recommendation for the repatriation of black colonial people:

One of our readers who has been ten years in West Africa directs our attention to the coloured question in Glasgow. The other day he noticed a white girl in the company of three Negroes and he suggests that in the interests of law and order our city authorities should urge the Colonial Office to repatriate our embarrassing visitors immediately.[40]

Signing herself 'live and let live', the woman made clear that she was not the only local woman who had married a black sailor and had found the experience suited her:

I think as the white wife of a British coloured man I have a right to speak. 'Hal o' the Wynd' thinks it repulsive to see a white woman in the company

of a coloured man. It is a shame to say that. They are as God made them;
they cannot help the colour of their skin. We, the white wives know better
than anyone what they are. We have been married for years and find the
British coloured man – I don't say all, but I say most – make us very good
husbands.[41]

Around the same time as black colonial workers sought welfare assistance and
worked together to try to improve their position, Lithuanian families left without
key breadwinners due to their enforced military service in Russia turned to
various agencies for support. The Lanarkshire branch of the Miners' Federation
was content to allow the return of Lithuanian miners who had fought overseas
during the war. The miners' union position was in contrast to that of the two
sailors' unions in Glasgow which opposed the employment of black colonial
workers.

The local miners' union position became a factor during central governmental discussions at the Aliens and Nationality Committee on 31 October
1919 on whether some of the Lithuanian war veterans should be allowed to
return to Scotland. W. Haldane Porter of the Home Office, who chaired the
meeting, declared that, 'the present moment was not a very propitious one for
any relaxation of the rule against the re-admission of "conventionists" who had
not fought in the allied forces'. However, he 'referred to the application of
250 Lithuanian miners to be allowed to return to their families in Lanarkshire'.
He reported that the local union had raised no objection to the return of
82 Lithuanians who had served in the Slavo-British Legion and would probably
raise none in the case of these men, although they had not served. The
committee 'resolved to recommend that if the local miners' federation raised
no objection the return of the 250 Lithuanians should be considered'.[42] The
readmission of a small proportion of Lithuanian adult males who had served
overseas was a long and drawn-out process.

In the meantime, Lithuanian families were given financial assistance by their
local parish councils. On application to the parish an adult received a destitute
alien's grant of 12s 6d (63p) a week. The grant was paid locally but was
reclaimable from the Treasury. In addition, parish councils under Poor Law
regulations provided an allowance for rent plus help with clothing. For parish
councils in areas of concentrated Lithuanian settlement administering the grant
and making additional payments represented a heavy financial burden. Towns
in Lanarkshire were most affected.[43] Bothwell parish, which included the town
of Bellshill, bore the brunt of the financial cost. For example, of the £33,000
expended on destitute aliens' relief for the whole of Scotland in the year ending
May 1919, £12,530 was spent in Bothwell parish alone.[44] While sympathetic to

the plight of local Lithuanian families, members of the parish council felt that they were being unfairly asked to support people whose destitution was beyond local control:

> The Parish Council did not seek to shirk responsibility for the mainte-
> nance of those unfortunate people, whose poverty was brought about by
> the nature of circumstances, but as the Government had taken away the
> husbands and breadwinners of those Lithuanian women and children, and
> in some cases would not allow the husbands to return to this country, they
> contended that so long as the women and children were chargeable, the
> cost of their full maintenance should be a charge upon the Imperial Taxes,
> and that no part whatever of the expense should fall upon the local rates.[45]

The destitute aliens' grant, like the Poor Law Emergency Provisions (Scotland) Act of November 1921, which allowed for payments to be made to the able-bodied unemployed poor, was not a permanent payment. Throughout the period 1918–22 the Treasury attempted to free itself of the costs of maintaining poor Lithuanian families. Payments made under the grant were placed under review, capped, renewed for three months at a time and often spoken of as coming to an end.[46] For example, in both September and December 1919 the Treasury sought to end the grant. Pressure from the Scottish Office, the Scottish Board of Health and the local parishes helped to keep the payments coming.[47] In addition, members of the inter-departmental Aliens and Nationality Committee, including Sir John Pedder of the Home Office, felt that there was a 'moral obligation' from the state to maintain the Lithuanian dependants:

> until it is possible to allow the return of Russians who left under the Anglo-
> Russian convention, or conditions in Russia have improved sufficiently to
> permit of the repatriation of their dependants without inhumanity[,] it is
> desirable that Treasury assistance towards the cost of maintaining such
> dependants should be continued for a period of six months from 31
> December [1919] in the first instance.[48]

The destitute aliens' grant was extended for another year in December 1920 following a further meeting of the Aliens and Nationality Committee at which Dr Christopher Addison, minister of health, pleaded the case of the destitute dependants of the former Russian empire:

> he feels assured that unless assistance continues to be afforded by the
> Exchequer the possibility of these women and children being able to

maintain themselves by their own industry is, owing to the lack of employment and the state of trade generally, considerably less today than it has
been since . . . March this year.[49]

The Scottish Board of Health took a humanitarian view over the needs of the
Lithuanians' families in Lanarkshire and also supported the local parish councils
in their campaign to recover all payments made in this connection from the
Treasury. Time and again the Scottish Board of Health acted as the conduit for
the complaints of local authorities regarding the financial burden of supporting
the Lithuanian families. The secretary for Scotland, Liberal MP Robert Munro
also fought the cause of the parishes and their Lithuanian residents against the
Treasury. In August 1919 he expressed concern about the 'very heavy burden'
that would fall on the local parishes if the destitute aliens' grant was ended as the
Treasury intended. He also declared that there was a great deal of local sympathy
for the plight of the Lithuanian families: 'It would in his opinion, be most unfortunate if eviction proceedings should be carried out, with the probable outcome
of serious disturbances in the mining districts where these families for the most
part reside.'[50] As in the case of the COS and its plea to the Scottish Board of
Health for assistance for 'discontented and semi-starved' black colonial sailors in
early 1920, the 'danger' to public order played a part in official reactions to the
destitution of Lithuanian families.

The Scottish Board of Health also shared the parishes' concerns over what it
regarded as miserly rates of financial support given to the Lithuanian dependants.
Parish councils regularly complained at the inadequate level of the destitute aliens'
grant. For example, in January 1921 Bothwell parish council decided to 'make a
strong representation to the Scottish Board of Health against the grossly inadequate allowances which it is still proposed to pay to the dependants of those
Lithuanians'.[51] The initial destitute alien's grant of 12s 6d (63p) per week for an
adult and 2s 6d (13p) per child was well below the average miner's wage of 8s
(40p) per day. By late 1920 payments had increased to 15s 6d (78p) per week for
adults and 5s (25p) for children. In July 1921 payments to adults were cut back to
the original level of 12s 6d for adults and reduced to 3s (15p) per child.

The Treasury sought to impose cost-cutting measures in the post-war
slump.[52] In December 1920 it sent a directive to all departments including the
Scottish Board of Health to announce restrictions on planned expenditure in
many areas of government for the financial year 1921–2.[53] The Treasury's
commitment to financial retrenchment ultimately had a devastating impact on
the Lithuanian population in Scotland. It sought to permanently rid itself of
the burden of payments to the Lithuanian dependants and became a driving
force behind a repatriation scheme for 'Russian' dependants from Britain. The

absence of shipping facilities in 1918 and 1919 to the former Russian empire
due to the economic and political situation delayed the move until the beginning of 1920.[54] Domestic political reasons also lay behind the desire to repatriate Lithuanians, who as has been seen were regarded as Bolshevik agitators by
local police forces and the Home Office.[55]

### The Fate of the Two Migrant Groups

For black colonial sailors the offer of repatriation (though no longer with
allowances from December 1919) remained available until the 1920s. The alternative was a life of continued economic hardship and only the remotest chance
of getting a job in an industry in long-term decline. The lives and employment
opportunities for the vast majority of black (and other racialised minority
ethnic) groups in Glasgow and elsewhere in Scotland remained bleak. Trade
union attempts at imposing a 'colour' bar in the labour market also spread into
the mining industry. In March 1920 white local miners protested against the
employment of four Indians ('Lascars') at Kingshill colliery, Lanarkshire,
alleging that they were 'cheap labour'. The district coal association later issued a
statement defending the rights of capitalists to employ whom they wished and
incidentally mentioning that the Indian workers were war veterans who were
hired via a labour exchange and were paid the same rate as local miners.[56] In
March 1921, a demonstration against the employment of 'Asiatic' sailors was
held at the mercantile marine office at Glasgow harbour. Police were called as
the protest unravelled into violence. The white sailors opposed the hiring of
Chinese sailors to replace a traditionally white crew on a voyage to Colombo,
Ceylon (Sri Lanka), at a third of the usual rate of pay for this journey.[57]

  Further government intervention into the lives of black colonial Britons came
in 1925 with the passage of the Special Restriction (Coloured Alien Seamen)
Order, which removed subject status for black sailors unable to prove their British
identity (previously their seamen's identity card was taken as proof of status), thus
making it even more difficult to obtain a job in the ports. The order imposed alien
status and police controls on many black British subjects. Although it was principally directed at controlling the movement and restricting the employment of
'Arab' sailors, many black African and African-Caribbean residents were reclassi-
fied as 'alien', particularly in Cardiff under the strict registration procedures of the
1925 order. Initially restricted to South Shields, Hull and Cardiff, the 1925 order
was extended to all ports in 1926. The Glasgow police used powers to register
South Asian peddlars and sailors as aliens under the new regulations.[58]

  Following the declaration of Lithuanian independence in December 1917
hopes were raised that this would mean the return of Lithuanian soldiers from

the Russian army to Scotland. Joe Smith (Cesaikas) from Stevenston in Ayrshire recalled:

> Every wan o' the Lithuanians in the raws was over the moon that Lithuania had managed tae get free frae Russia even although the Germans were still there. It was a' the talk when the auld yins gathered thegither an Ah min' ma mother sayin' Oh! It might no' be long till yer faither's hame! Little did we ken then it would be mair nor six years [that is, 1923] afore we saw him.[59]

In autumn 1919 the 82 Lithuanians who had served in the Slavo-British Legion were returned to Scotland. They were found by British military authorities to speak 'no Russian but only Lithuanian and broad Scotch'.[60] This small positive step was soon far outweighed by the next government initiative.

In January 1920 the plan to repatriate Lithuanian dependants was officially announced. The first party left in mid-February, but the largest group left Glasgow on 11 March – on a specially arranged service by Caledonian Railway bound for a ship at Southampton.[61] Their departure attracted some press attention. The *Glasgow Herald* report focused on the quaint aspects of the party being expelled from Scotland: 'bound for Lithuania – interesting group leaves Glasgow'. The train had about 240 women and children on board, 'some 60 families from the coalfields of Lanarkshire'. This large group included 'flaxen-haired, rosy-cheeked children'. The newspaper went on to report the departure in the most jovial tones:

> The experience was obviously enjoyed, although some of the women were regretful at leaving this country, of which they spoke with gratitude for what had been done for them in the absence of their husbands ... Conversation was conducted in their native tongue though most of the children spoke good English ... The party left the station in a spirit of cheerfulness, waving their hands at those gathered on the platform.[62]

In contrast, Joe Smith (Cesaikas) recalled:

> There were twa or three families' frae Glengarnock sent back ... but there was nae joy wi' them, only floods o' tears. It was an awfy sad day when they left, they had nae idea whit was ower there for them or whether they wad find their menfolk or no' an' they were leavin' friens they had leeved wi' for years behin'.[63]

Bothwell parish council minutes recorded that by May 1920 around 100 women and 263 children from different parishes around Scotland had been repatriated.

By September 1920, 63 women and 174 children had left Bothwell parish alone.[64] These figures are supported by Rodgers, who states that over 400 women and children were eventually repatriated to Lithuania.[65]

However, many more remained. The repatriation programme for Lithuanian dependants did not end the financial burden on the Treasury and local parish councils. For example, in Bothwell parish there remained almost 350 Lithuanian families who were 'likely to become a permanent burden upon rates'.[66] In January 1921 the government's Alien and Nationality Committee heard from Treasury spokesperson, Mr Hurst, that the Exchequer 'attached great importance to the cessation or at least reduction of the charge on public funds in the maintenance of those dependants'.[67] However, the committee decided that it would be 'impracticable at the present time to deal with the problem as a whole by any scheme of compulsory repatriation of dependants'.[68] It decided to allow the Scottish authorities to submit the names of Lithuanian males who had gone to Russia for military service to the Home Office for consideration of their readmittance to Britain. However only 'good cases' where there was a 'satisfactory prospect of their being able to maintain their families here' were to be presented to the Home Office.[69]

Despite this decision there is no evidence to suggest that many families were reunited in Scotland by this initiative. Only a minority of the 1,100 who left Britain later returned. White put the figure at 'a hundred or so'. Of the rest 'some died in the civil war, probably a larger number died of illness or starvation, some settled in the Soviet Union, while others made their way back to Lithuania'.[70] Grace Miller (Klostaitis) recalled what may have been a typical family experience of this period:

> I had four sisters, all much older than me for they had been born in Lithuania, and in 1917 they were all already married to Lithuanian boys. All four of the lads went off to fight in Russia for they were our allies then. Three of them we never saw or heard a word from ever again. The other lad survived the war and managed to make his way to Lithuania which by then was a free republic. He sent for his wife, my sister, and the two of them never came back to Scotland.[71]

The deepening economic depression in 1921 meant that Lithuanian women in Scotland faced reduced chances of gaining work and staying off benefits. The total sum paid out in destitute aliens' grants increased, and in an atmosphere of growing financial prudence the Treasury once more announced that the grants were to cease, this time in April 1921. Local parishes again spoke out and their protests were conveyed by the Scottish Board of Health and by Robert

Munro.[72] Once more the Treasury grudgingly agreed to maintain the payments, 'in deference to the representations of the Secretary for Scotland'.[73] The grant was renewed until June 1922.[74] However, the number of applicants for welfare support was such that the recommended level of weekly payments was cut back by the Treasury in July 1921 by 3s per adult and 2s per child. Bothwell parish council resisted this cost cutting measure until February 1922 when it was forced to make the reduction: 'In view of the number of Lithuanian women who were now idle, it would not be possible to continue the present allowance.'[75]

## Conclusion

The First World War altered the lives of migrant black colonial and Lithuanian workers and families living in Scotland dramatically and with far reaching consequences. Black colonial sailors who had risked their lives in the armed forces and particularly in the merchant navy during the war found jobs hard to come by in the post-war period. Moreover, black residents of Britain's ports including Glasgow faced attack by disaffected white residents. Sailors' unions in Glasgow and elsewhere also sought to 'bar' black workers from employment on board ships to preserve work for white sailors. The operation of the Anglo-Soviet Military Convention of 1917 removed 1,100 Lithuanian adult male workers from their loved ones and left thousands of Lithuanian families in Scotland dependent on outside agencies for support.

These two groups of migrants faced destitution for differing reasons in the post-war period. Each sought to help themselves out of their situation. In the case of black colonial sailors this included petitioning the government. Lithuanian women obtained employment where they could, others resorted to theft to feed their families and heat their homes. Those in need were assisted by local authorities and charities. Members of these agencies often expressed anger at government policies that had prompted the situation. However, voluntary agencies and local parish councils could not cope with the financial burden of supporting destitute migrant workers and their dependants. During 1919 and 1920 repatriation was the 'cure-all' proposed by central government to the difficulties faced by these migrant communities in Scotland. However, this was never a complete solution as the large numbers of people who refused repatriation had still to be maintained. By 1921 long-term unemployment and growing destitution were apparent in large sections of the British working class, so that black colonial workers and Lithuanian families were no longer 'troublesome' special cases but part of the wider group of long-term recipients of unemployment benefits and poor relief.

## Notes

1.  A private 'coloured men's club' named the 'Order of the Star of Bethlehem's Shepherds' was set up in the Gorbals in late 1918.
2.  Smout, T.C., *A History of the Scottish People* (London, 1969), 169.
3.  Thompson, W., 'Glasgow and Africa: Connexions and Attitudes, 1870–1900', PhD thesis, University of Strathclyde, 1970, 250.
4.  Trimmers loaded and balanced coal during the voyage; firemen loaded the coal into the furnaces to fuel the steam engines on board ship.
5.  *Daily Record and Mail* (Glasgow), 24 January 1919.
6.  The central Glasgow harbour area is known locally as the 'Broomielaw', after the long street which runs adjacent to the river Clyde.
7.  *Bulletin* (Glasgow), 24 January 1919. See also *Glasgow Herald*, 24 January 1919. In addition to the *Bulletin* and the *Glasgow Herald*, two other daily Scottish newspapers were consulted for this article, the *Scotsman* (Edinburgh) and the *Daily Record and Mail*. The first three held Unionist (Scottish Conservative) sympathies; the *Daily Record* was Liberal. Three Glasgow evening newspapers were also consulted: the *Evening Citizen*, *Evening News* and *Evening Times*.
8.  *Evening Times* (Glasgow), 29 January 1919.
9.  *Bulletin*, 24 January 1919.
10.  *Evening Citizen* (Glasgow), 29 January 1919.
11.  *Glasgow Herald*, 24 January 1919. The *Herald*'s sister paper, the *Evening Times*, expressed the same view, using exactly the same words, on 24 January 1919.
12.  Lunn, K., 'Reactions to Lithuanian and Polish Immigrants in the Lanarkshire Coalfield, 1870–1914', in Lunn, K., ed., *Hosts, Immigrants and Minorities: Historical Responses to Newcomers in British Society, 1870–1914* (Folkestone, 1980), 308–42, at 310, 314.
13.  Report from the Select Committee on Emigration and Immigration (Foreigners), *British Parliamentary Papers – Emigration*, vol. 8 – session 1888–9, minutes of evidence by James Keir Hardie, 22 July 1889 (Shannon, 1969), 65.
14.  Select Committee Evidence, 1889, Keir Hardie, 64.
15.  Select Committee Evidence, 1889, Keir Hardie, 64.
16.  Select Committee Evidence, 1889, Keir Hardie, 64.
17.  Lunn, 'Reactions to Lithuanian and Polish Immigrants', 327
18.  Lunn, 'Reactions to Lithuanian and Polish Immigrants', 327.
19.  The National Archives, London, (TNA), Home Office (HO) 45/10821/318095/421, Home Office memorandum on applications to return to Russia under the military service convention, 16 August 1917.
20.  TNA HO 45/10821/318095/421, letter from Captain Despard, chief constable of Lanarkshire to J.F. Henderson, Home Office, 15 August 1917.
21.  White, J.D., 'Scottish Lithuanians and the Russian Revolution', *Journal of Baltic Studies* 6 (1975), 1–8, at 7.
22.  Rodgers, M., 'The Lanarkshire Lithuanians', in Kay, B., ed., *The Complete Odyssey: Voices from Scotland's Recent Past* (Edinburgh, 1990), 22–9, at 23.
23.  Millar, J., (Jonas Stepsis), *The Lithuanians in Scotland* (Argyll, 1998), 105.
24.  *Glasgow Herald*, 26 February 1920.
25.  Levitt, I., *Poverty and Welfare in Scotland, 1890–1948* (Edinburgh 1988), 83.
26.  TNA, Colonial Office (CO) 323/843, Colonial Office memorandum on destitute seamen in Glasgow, 14 February 1920.
27.  *Glasgow Herald*, 5 March 1920.
28.  Levitt, *Poverty and Welfare in Scotland*, 107.
29.  Levitt, *Poverty and Welfare in Scotland*, 112, 115.
30.  TNA CO 323/812, letter from distressed black sailors in Glasgow to the offices of *John Bull*, forwarded to the CO, 4 March 1919.

31. Letter from distressed black sailors in Glasgow, 4 March 1919.
32. *John Bull*, 29 March 1919, 7.
33. *African Telegraph*, vol. 1/11, April 1919, 184.
34. TNA CO 323/818, CO internal memorandum, 2 May 1919.
35. TNA CO 323/818, draft CO reply to 'delegates of coloured seamen in Glasgow', 2 May 1919.
36. TNA CO 323/813, letter from 'delegates of coloured seamen in Glasgow' to CO, 7 May 1919.
37. *Daily Record and Mail*, 25 June 1919.
38. The affiliation was reported in the London group's newspaper, also called *Wasu*. See Geiss, I., *The Pan-African Movement* (London, 1974), 299.
39. Transcript of author's telephone interview with William Adams, 15 August 1984.
40. *Evening Times*, 18 June 1919.
41. *Evening Times*, 21 June 1919.
42. TNA HO 45/11068/374355, minutes of meeting of Aliens and Nationality Committee, 31 October 1919.
43. Glasgow City Archives (GCA), Mitchell Library, Glasgow, CO1/23/18 (May 1918–July 1920) minutes of Bothwell parish council, Bellshill, Lanarkshire, 11 September 1919.
44. GCA CO1/23/18 (May 1918–July 1920), minutes of Bothwell parish council, 31 July 1919.
45. GCA CO1/23/19 (July 1920–May 1922), minutes of Bothwell parish council, 11 November 1920.
46. In January 1920 the Bothwell town clerk stated that the parish council 'resented this system of continuing the grant from month to month, which caused no end of trouble to officials and others'. GCA CO1/23/18, minutes of Bothwell parish council, 5 January 1920.
47. TNA HO 45/11068/374355, James M. Dodds, Scottish Office to secretary to the Treasury, 16 August 1919 and John Lamb, Scottish Office to Treasury, 8 September 1919; Treasury memorandum 26 September 1919.
48. TNA HO 45/11068/374355, Sir John Pedder, Assistant Secretary, Home Office, minute of Aliens and Nationality Committee, 28 November 1919.
49. TNA HO 45/11068/37435, Dr Christopher Addison, Minister of Health, memorandum to Aliens and Nationality Committee, 15 December 1920.
50. TNA HO 45/11068/374355, letter from James M. Dodds, Scottish Office to secretary to the Treasury, 16 August 1919.
51. GCA CO1/23/19, minutes of Bothwell parish council, 13 January 1921.
52. The Treasury exerted increased financial restraint over government departments from 1919 when its authority was strengthened in an attempt to create a powerful central government department to control expenditure and cut out waste. For more on this see Peden, G.C., 'The Treasury as the Central Department of Government, 1919–1939', *Public Administration* 61 (1983), 371–85, at 381.
53. Jenkinson, J., *Scotland's Health, 1919–1948* (Bern, 2002), 80–1.
54. Rodgers, M., 'The Anglo-Russian Military Convention and the Lithuanian Immigrant Community in Lanarkshire, Scotland, 1914–20', *Immigrants and Minorities* 1 (1982), 60–88, at 75.
55. Rodgers, 'Anglo-Russian Military Convention', 76.
56. *Glasgow Herald*, 5 March 1920. See also Dunlop, A. and Miles, R., 'Recovering the History of Asian Migration to Scotland', *Immigrants and Minorities* 9 (1990), 145–67, at 158–9.
57. *Glasgow Herald*, 3 March 1921.
58. Dunlop and Miles, 'Recovering the History of Asian Migration to Scotland', 156.
59. Millar, *Lithuanians in Scotland*, 99.
60. Cited in Rodgers, 'Anglo-Russian Military Convention', 75.
61. National Archives of Scotland (NAS), West Register House, Edinburgh, HH75/02, minutes of the Scottish Board of Health, 13 May 1920.
62. *Glasgow Herald*, 12 March 1920.
63. Millar, *Lithuanians in Scotland*, 112.

64. GCA CO1/23/19, minutes of Bothwell parish council, 9 September 1920.
65. Rodgers, 'Lanarkshire Lithuanians', 24.
66. GCA CO1/23/18, minutes of Bothwell parish council, 13 May 1920.
67. TNA HO 45/11068/374355, Mr Hurst, Treasury, minutes of Aliens and Nationality Committee, 11 January 1921.
68. TNA HO 45/11068/374355, minutes of Aliens and Nationality Committee, 11 January 1921.
69. TNA HO 45/11068/374355, minutes of Aliens and Nationality Committee, 11 January 1921 and (in same file) letter from Home office to Scottish Office, 1 February 1921.
70. White, 'Scottish Lithuanians and the Russian Revolution', 7.
71. Millar, *Lithuanians in Scotland*, 103.
72. TNA HO 45/11068/374355, letter from Bothwell parish council to Scottish secretary, Robert Munro, 7 January 1921.
73. GCA CO1/23/19, minutes of Bothwell parish council, 13 January 1921.
74. GCA CO1/23/19, letter from SBH to Bothwell parish council 12 May 1921 cited in minutes of Bothwell parish council.
75. The Scottish Board of Health sent a letter to all parish councils dated 8 July 1921 to report the Treasury decision 'in view of the continued fall in the cost of living and the present financial situation' to cut the destitute aliens grant to 12s 6d for each woman and 3s per child. On 9 February 1922 Bothwell parish council decided to implement the new reduced rates. GCA CO1/23/19, minutes of Bothwell parish council.

# 4

# The Jews of Glasgow
## Aspects of Health and Welfare

**Kenneth Collins**

## Introduction

In his foreword to my book *Be Well! Jewish Immigrant Health and Welfare in Glasgow 1860–1914*, Chief Rabbi Sir Jonathan Sacks commented on the plight of the Jewish immigrants fleeing poverty and persecution in Eastern Europe only to experience poor health, hygiene and housing in Britain. He referred to Beatrice Webb's study of poor Jews in London which indicated that the newcomers had what modern economists call 'social capital', that is strong families, a collective ethos, an ancient but vigorous faith and a deeply rooted sense of hope. Individually vulnerable, they gave each other strength. It was this hope and strength that enabled them to break free from the cycle of deprivation within a generation or two.

The health experiences of the Jews in Glasgow have been replicated in studies of Jewish communities in North America as well as western and central Europe.[1] Lara Marks also notes the better Jewish health indices in the East End of London and the social and religious structures which she feels enabled the Jewish community to benefit.[2] Common factors related to communal structures and organisation emerge as does constant evidence of better Jewish health indices than those in the surrounding population. The new arrivals saw their goals as personal economic stability combined with uptake of the local educational facilities which would enable their children to advance. Glasgow's Jewish community was a further example of the path followed by other communities in Britain and Germany where health and welfare provision was more extensive and of a higher quality than what was on offer in the wider community, providing Jews with the opportunity to use these facilities to strengthen their Jewish identity.[3]

Health has always been important – and there are echoes even today of some of the issues faced by Jews arriving in Glasgow 100 years ago. When there is talk now of asylum seekers and economic migrants, and of concerns related to their health, we need to understand that the history of such matters in Glasgow, a city with its own chronic health problems, is a long one and that there may be lessons from the past that can help us to deal with contemporary issues. There is much to consider in the social, welfare and health history of the immigrant period of

the Glasgow Jewish community to enable understanding of what is important in
the health achievements of Jewish immigrants in the city.[4]

## The Origins of the Glasgow Jewish Community

Although Jews had been living and working in Glasgow since the last years of the
eighteenth century, it was not till 1823 that a Jewish community, known as the
Glasgow Hebrew Congregation, was formally established.[5] Attracted by Glasgow's
rapid industrial growth, and by the development of a settled middle class, Jews
took advantage of the opportunities for traders and merchants to establish new
businesses. Initially, they came from other parts of Britain or from Holland or
Germany but gradually more Jews arrived from Poland, Lithuania and Russia, and
it was this Eastern European element that predominated. Glasgow attracted its
Jews from two main sources: first, from the merchants and traders from elsewhere
in Britain, but also from travellers, or trans-migrants, intending to reach the United
States of America. As time went on increasing numbers of Jews came to Glasgow
to join family and friends already settled in the city.

From around 30 Jews in 1831 there were about ten times as many about
30 years later, when the first major synagogue, in George Street, was opened. By
the time of the building of the Garnethill synagogue, north-west of the city
centre, in 1879 that number had increased to about 700. At this time the first
Jews appeared in the Gorbals, south of the river Clyde, where *chevrot*, small
prayer houses, appeared. There were some 2,000 Jews in Glasgow at the time of
the 1891 census, almost equally split between the 'old' community in the city
centre and the 'new' community in the Gorbals. Millions of Jews were on the
move during the last two decades of the nineteenth century and the first of the
twentieth. About 120,000 Jews arrived in Britain between 1880 and 1914, drawn
by the prospects of future prosperity away from the pervasive, and sometimes
violent, anti-Semitism prevalent in Eastern Europe. Glasgow Jewry grew rapidly
from the 1890s, reaching about 6,000 by the turn of the century and about
10,000 by the outbreak of the First World War.

## The Formation of Welfare Bodies

The Jews of Glasgow brought their own well-developed traditional communal
structures from Russia and Poland with them to Glasgow, in the form of a
society adapted to self-help and a propensity to develop organisations for every
possible area of perceived welfare, educational, religious or social need. If the
existing community had thoughts that there was any alternative to aiding their
weary and impoverished brethren, the public clamour over such issues as

sweated labour and alien immigration ensured that the settled communities had to take action. The size of the older and more integrated community meant that this elite was too small to dominate the relatively large influx which later overwhelmed it.[6]

The first Jewish welfare services in Glasgow began with the Glasgow Hebrew Philanthropic Society, which functioned initially within the synagogue before becoming an independent body in 1875.[7] The society was the precursor of the Glasgow Jewish Board of Guardians, which later became the Glasgow Jewish Welfare Board and is now Jewish Care Scotland. It was in existence in 1858 when the first Glasgow Jew to qualify as a doctor, Asher Asher, was its medical officer.[8] At the time of a congregational split in the 1840s the smaller group had its own welfare body and we can only presume that the larger group had its own too. The first Jewish welfare body in Edinburgh was established in 1838 so it is likely that the Hebrew Philanthropic Society was also a product of that period.[9] These early welfare bodies concerned themselves with the direct relief of poverty. They doled out cash, in very small sums, to help members of the local community, to cover the costs of funerals and to help indigent travellers on their way so that they would not be a permanent charge on meagre communal resources. However, this risked attracting wayfarers hoping to obtain money to fund their onward travel.

Glasgow's Jewish fathers, in a position of authority because of their earlier arrival in the city, had to strike a balance between community discipline and immigrant innovation in the provision of welfare. That is not to say that conflict between the Jewish groups north and south of the river Clyde did not exist. In London, the Jewish Board of Guardians had an active repatriation policy returning many thousands of Jews to Eastern Europe.[10] This policy may have reduced, but it could not stop, the growing influx of Jewish migrants into London's teeming East End, and was to cause great resentment among those targeted to return home. In Glasgow the Jewish Board of Guardians hardly ever attempted to send Jewish migrants back to Eastern Europe, except to reunite families separated during the migration process.[11] While the Aliens Act of 1905 was heralded as a means of limiting Jewish immigration, it had little effect on the numbers of Jews continuing to arrive. Most Jews could meet the health and financial criteria for admission and the incoming Liberal administration in 1906 refused to enforce its provisions strictly.

The Glasgow Jewish Board of Guardians was based at Garnethill until 1912, when the community leadership could no longer ignore calls for a welfare centre in the heart of the community it was serving.[12] The Board of Guardians, an austere and patronising though well-meaning body, tried to maintain a coherent community-wide welfare strategy but it had neither the resources nor the ability to control the small Gorbals welfare bodies to make such a strategy successful.

In addition, its disbursement of charity was often fairly heavy-handed and this in itself was a stimulus to self-help.


## Social Aspects of Health

Writing in *Health Care as Social History* in 1982, Olive Checkland and Margaret Lamb noted Glasgow's notoriety in health and health care.[13] For the Jewish community, the arrival of thousands of impoverished Jews from Eastern Europe into a city famed for its health problems posed difficulties. Jews have a proud medical tradition and as the Jewish writer Chaim Bermant observed, 'Among Jews in Eastern Europe the parting greeting was not the meaningless "cheerio" or "goodbye" or even "au revoir" but *zei gezunt* (stay well) . . . The expression represents not merely a benign wish, but is tantamount almost to a positive commandment.'[14] It is in this context of competing health problems and provision that Glasgow Jewry's struggle for health needs to be understood.

One potential area of friction between the Jews and their neighbours in the Gorbals was housing. There were concerns about anti-Semitic attitudes in the rented housing market and some property-owners were said to prefer their flats remaining empty rather than let them to Jews.[15] However, housing conditions in Glasgow had been atrocious before the arrival of the Jewish newcomers. There were slums in other parts of the city not settled in by Jews. There were cholera outbreaks in the 1840s and 1850s before the opening of the water supply from Loch Katrine guaranteed good clean water.[16] Jewish homes were often overcrowded, given the large families and the presence of lodgers. In 1891 Gorbals Jewish homes had an average of 3.5 inhabitants to each single-room apartment, rising to 5.2 in the two-room flats.[17] Studies carried out by the Glasgow Corporation Sanitary Department showed that Jews were under-represented in the worst of the housing stock, and Jews were not involved in the outbreaks of smallpox and bubonic plague that occurred in the Gorbals in 1899.[18]

At work Jews were concentrated in clothing, shopkeeping and cigarette and furniture making, but it was the first that received most criticism for its practices. The *Lancet* conducted a study of sweated labour around the UK in 1888 concentrating mainly on problems in Jewish workshops, especially in the conurbations of London, Manchester and Leeds.[19] In Glasgow, Scots and Irish migrants as well as Jews were found to be involved in sweated labour, entailing long hours in unhealthy conditions. Subcontracting work further isolated and marginalised employees.[20] In Glasgow some large textile firms were involved in perpetuating the sweating system by subcontracting out to home workers, and it did not appear that Glasgow's ethnic minorities could be blamed for the creation of sweated labour in the city.

A survey of diets in Glasgow, carried out by Dorothy Lindsay in 1911 and 1912, included five Jewish families among the 60 'working class families' studied.[21] There were health problems in all the families but the Jewish families ate more fish and chicken and their men drank less alcohol. The researcher expressed her admiration for the Jewish family of ten who made a half chicken the high point of their Friday evening meal. Lindsay produced an amazing snapshot of contemporary life but her conclusions were somewhat patronising. She concluded that the poor should abandon meat, fish and eggs as being too expensive and concentrate on porridge, milk, pulses and vegetables, advising that they read the pamphlet *How to Feed a Family of Five on 12/9 a Week*.

### Jewish Welfare

Victorian welfare had its own style. Support was not given on an indiscriminate basis. Care was taken to show that the poor were truly 'deserving', enabling the communal leadership to maintain its patronage over the newer arrivals. Charity was not seen as an end in itself. There was a fear of pauperising the recipient and creating a climate of dependency. The best goal was to encourage self-help and this was aided by the free loan society, officially known as the Glasgow Hebrew Benevolent Loan Society, or the 'penny society'. This name derived from its being one of the first Jewish bodies in Glasgow to finance its activities by taking 1d each week from members' subscriptions.

The Philanthropic Society employed a medical officer to provide care and dispense medication to the Jewish poor. Doctors were engaged at an honorarium of 5 guineas a year. By the late 1870s more of the welfare cases were living in the Gorbals and the first doctor from the south side of the city, Dr Morton, was appointed medical officer in 1881.[22] He conducted surgeries in Main Street, Gorbals, charging 2s for a house call and 1s for a surgery consultation. With the rapid growth in Jewish immigrants the needs and numbers of the poor increased and the cost of providing welfare services escalated sharply. The budget of the Philanthropic Society had been £200 in 1878. By 1898, the budget of the renamed Jewish Board of Guardians had expanded to £523.

Some of these funds provided direct poverty relief. About 13 per cent was spent on steamer and train fares as the board attempted to reunite families. Besides the Board of Guardians many supplementary welfare bodies were formed. These included the Hebrew Boot, Clothing and Employment Assistance Guild and the Jewish Children's Fresh Air Fund, which provided a week's summer holiday with kosher food. Competition with these Gorbals-based charities irritated the Board of Guardians. They felt that they were trying to develop a communal strategy for the management of welfare but the newer bodies, while obviously motivated by a desire to help the neediest members of the community, were linked into *ad hoc* arrangements, and this detracted from their carefully planned efforts.[23] This strategy was often seen as aloof, and fuelled resentment.[24]

Glasgow Jewry showed its ability to assimilate traditional Jewish patterns of philanthropy to those around them in Victorian Scotland. Charitable endeavour marked out the successful, gave them a key role in voluntary work and enhanced their social status. In an age of rudimentary statutory help Glasgow's Jews could fall back on patterns of care learned in Eastern Europe while gaining support from a city keen to encourage voluntary help as a means of reducing the burden on the city's rates.

The social cohesion of the Jewish community was considerably enhanced by the proliferation of a network of Jewish friendly societies. The first Jewish friendly society, the Glasgow Hebrew Sick Society, started in the Gorbals as early as 1868.[25] These bodies enabled their members to receive assistance and medical care during illness and bereavement, and encouraged a sense of self-reliance through mutual benefit. The provisions of the friendly societies were seen as much more sensitive than those of the Jewish Board of Guardians. These societies provided valuable savings benefits but their crucial impact was the welfare section, which could provide medical, sickness and unemployment benefits for families for a weekly subscription of 3d. It supported families through the week-long mourning period, or *shiva*, an essential provision given the frequency of child deaths. Many Gorbals doctors relied on friendly society members and derived much of their income from them. The societies also appealed to the immigrants' need to escape from the drabness of Gorbals life. With their colourful uniforms and rituals as well as their social activities the friendly societies had a function beyond the purely welfare. Some lodges were based on the links fostered by immigrant groups from the same Eastern European towns and villages and they formed a traditional, and often religious, bulwark against assimilation compared with the fraternal orders which often promoted acculturation.[26]

The model of self-help could be found in a wide range of new welfare bodies such as the Glasgow Jewish Naturalisation Society, the Glasgow Hebrew Benevolent Loan Society and the Glasgow Hebrew Burial Society, all founded between 1888 and 1907. Women's lodges did not appear until the National Insurance Act of 1911, a landmark provision which revolutionised welfare. This Act did not cover the many non-naturalised aliens and it was not until 1918 that the whole Jewish community could take advantage of its terms.[27] By the 1930s there were more Jewish friendly societies in Glasgow than any other type of Jewish body, including synagogues.

## The Medical Conflict with the Missionaries

Jewish–Christian relations in Glasgow during this period had two faces. On one side the major Christian bodies, both Protestant and Catholic, were well represented in protests against the persecution of Jews in Russia, and were sympathetic to the plight of impoverished newcomers arriving in Scotland. However, one of the most contentious issues dividing Jews and Christians was Christian mission. For Jews, this symbolised hostility to their religion which questioned the legitimacy of their faith in the contemporary world.[28] For many Christians, mission was seen as an act of love, and increasingly Jewish missions were formed in numbers which belied the numerical importance of Jews in the Christian world. Some Christians looked on the Jewish discomfort at missionary activity as the price they should be expected to pay for living in a Christian country. Yet there were also Christians who opposed the missionary endeavour, believing that it brought an 'atmosphere of meanness and hypocrisy and brings discredit both to charity and religion'.[29]

In Glasgow, as in other cities with large immigrant populations, a key target of Christian mission was the Jewish poor. Paradoxically, it was the strenuous efforts of the local Jewish community to thwart evangelising of the Jews by providing better welfare facilities that produced a stronger and more cohesive community. The Scottish churches had a history of mission to the Jews even before there was a significant Jewish community in Glasgow.[30] Based in Hungary, Rumania and the Holy Land, Scottish Christian mission had elements of redemption but also was strategically placed in Central Europe where baptism was seen as the passport to entry into a wider society, which was often restricted to Jews.[31] There had been some examples of Christian mission activity to the Jews in Glasgow from the early 1880s. As the Jewish community grew, some mission activity became more strident, as this statement from the Bonar Medical Mission of 1909 indicates:

> the presence of so large a Jewish community in Glasgow was a challenge to the whole Christian community of Glasgow. The invasion of our country by a large alien population was a new phase in our national life and the Church could not stand idly by if the country was to remain a Christian country.[32]

A variety of Christian missionary agencies in the Gorbals began to provide medical and social services to the Jewish poor. Success could not easily be quantified in the number of converts. Christian sources claimed dozens of successes while Jewish communal leaders put the number of converts at 'just one or two'. Christians felt that judging their efforts by the number of converts was not a fair test to apply and often attributed their lack of results to the negative attitudes to Christianity brought to Scotland from Eastern Europe.[33]

The missionaries engendered much hostility in the Jewish community. There was no doubt that some Jews had gone over to Christianity, and that some of the most determined Christian medical missionaries were former Jews, usually Yiddish speakers like the immigrants. Inhabiting neutral ground between the two communities, they used their Jewish knowledge and their medical training while holding out financial and welfare inducements to the neediest members of the Jewish community. Spurred into action by the Christian medical missions, the Jewish community responded by setting up a number of specific health and welfare bodies.[34] Jewish spending on social welfare for the needy of the community far exceeded the sums provided by the missionary bodies.

The Glasgow Jewish Hospital and Sick Visiting Association began, in 1900, to provide the 'lines' required by the private hospitals to confirm rights to admission, which had previously been supplied by the missionaries. In 1911, a Glasgow Jewish Dispensary was set up despite the open access to the major dispensaries attached to the city hospitals. The Jewish Dispensary was designed to compete with the Christian medical mission halls and provide an alternative for the Jewish poor who had become accustomed to taking their prescriptions from the Jewish Board of Guardians doctor, who could not dispense, to the Christian dispensary. The president of the Jewish Dispensary, Joseph Fox, commented that in 'the missionary dispensaries . . . very often, after receiving medicine for the body they get a double dose of poison for the soul'.[35]

**Residential Care**

The last years of the nineteenth century saw the beginnings of Glasgow Jewish residential care. The first such institution was a refuge hostel, set up in 1897, to provide accommodation and welfare for Jewish migrants reaching the city.[36] There were frequent health scares related to these travellers, such as the fear of a cholera outbreak in 1893. The Glasgow Jewish Refuge operated until about 1911, accommodating some 400 travellers each year, usually for up to seven days, before onward travel to North America. The refuge was seen as ensuring safety for newcomers at the docks where, by employing an interpreter and a retired policeman, they prevented the migrants being tricked and robbed.

It was the committee of the Jewish Refuge who first proposed the idea of a residential home for the Jewish elderly in Glasgow.[37] It was suggested that the home should start with just two or three male residents, who could perform religious services in return for their board and keep. A tenement flat in Nicholson Street in the Gorbals was rented but the project did not survive long and it was not until 1949 that a stable residential home for the Jewish elderly in Scotland was established in Pollokshields. After the First World War the friendly societies nationally began to provide convalescent homes. In 1921 the 20 Jewish friendly societies in Glasgow and Edinburgh opened a home, aimed at patients with tuberculosis returning from sanatorium treatment in England, at Binniehall House near Slammanan.[38] The home was, however, expensive to maintain and it only survived for about four years.

These years saw much family separation and premature death from tuberculosis, so the case for a Jewish orphanage in Glasgow had become overwhelming by the first years of the twentieth century.[39] In 1913 the Jacobson family donated a building in memory of their daughter Gertrude and some funding was obtained from the local authorities in Glasgow and Govan. Initially operating in a small semi-detached Victorian villa in Millbrae Road, it looked after about ten local orphans with some Jewish refugee children from Belgium. After the war new, and larger, premises were obtained, which could accommodate up to 40 children.

## Hospital Meals

Victorian hospitals were very formal institutions and must have appeared somewhat forbidding to the Jewish immigrants. Visiting hours were strictly limited and relatives were not allowed to bring in food. This caused particular hardship to Jewish patients who were unfamiliar with Scottish food and had a religious requirement for a kosher diet. There were a number of attempts to arrange kosher meals in the Glasgow hospitals. In 1910, the Victoria Infirmary turned down a request to provide kosher food as they did not want to establish a precedent, which might entail them offering similar special provision to other groups in the future.[40] Merryflatts Hospital, run by the Glasgow Corporation, now the Southern General Hospital, then agreed to the provision of a kosher kitchen, under religious supervision, in 1914.[41] A further approach was then made to the Victoria Infirmary to permit kosher meals to be delivered from the Southern General but this was also refused, the Victoria pointing out that some Jewish patients seemed content with the regular hospital fare.[42]

## Anti-Semitic Attitudes

During the immigrant period the Jewish community had both supporters and detractors. Claims of insanitary habits were commonly made and were rebutted frequently. However, the allegation made in July 1910 that Jewish children in Glasgow were drinking methylated spirits was baseless and was clearly anti-Semitic in intent.[43] This was the period when the eugenists' attitudes to so-called weak Jewish eyes and an alleged higher prevalence of eye disease were used to influence the current debate on health and alien immigration in the lead-up to the passage of the Aliens Act in 1905.[44] Dr David Heron carried out work in 1910 on the influence of 'defective physique and unfavourable home environment on the intelligence of schoolchildren' and concluded that intelligence was hereditary and racial and that Jewish immigrant children compared unfavourably with their Scottish peers.[45]

There were real concerns about the health of British children in the first years of the twentieth century after many potential recruits failed the fitness test for entry to the army during the second Boer War of 1899–1902. The report of the Interdepartmental Committee on Physical Deterioration in 1904 clearly indicated that Jewish children, all over Britain, were actually better fed than non-Jewish children.[46] A more sympathetic view was that expressed by Dr Syme of the Ruskin Society who referred, at a meeting in Glasgow in January 1911, to there being 'something interesting and mysterious' about the Jew and that the women of Glasgow might learn a good deal from Jewish mothers.[47] He felt that there was more care in the area of cleanliness and hygiene by second-generation families, but he accepted that there was no Jewish racial immunity from certain infectious diseases and indicated that better Jewish health in Glasgow was due to the greater care taken by Jewish mothers of their children, especially in diet, and to the activities of the many Jewish associations and societies. Key factors may have been the fact that fewer Jewish women in Glasgow were working outside the home, and that even in cramped Gorbals conditions census returns indicate that there were young Scottish or Irish girls living in to help with the family.

### Health Statistics

During the first years of the twentieth century figures kept by the Glasgow United Synagogue showed that births averaged 290 per year, giving a birth rate of 41 per thousand, in a Jewish community of about 7,000. This figure is comparable to the London Jewish birth rate but considerably higher than that in the general Glasgow population. The Glasgow birth rate, 35.5 per thousand in 1876, had fallen to 25.5 by 1914. The Jewish death rate for the period was around 12 per thousand with a substantial proportion of the deaths, at least two thirds, among children under the age of 16. These figures confirm the youthful nature of the immigrant population, mainly young adults with many children and accompanied by very few elderly relatives.

During the first two years of the twentieth century, 1900 and 1901, the Jewish infant mortality rate was about 90 per thousand live births.[48] These rates were broadly similar to those of about 20 years earlier, at about 92 per thousand live births, when the Jewish community was far smaller. Thus Jewish infant mortality was one third lower than the appalling Scottish figures which indicate that 13 per cent of children (130 per thousand) died before their first birthday between 1895 and 1899, with the figures little changed over the next five years. These figures have been blamed on Glasgow's poor and overcrowded housing stock, which left a bitter legacy in terms of mortality and morbidity. Despite the difficult living conditions, Glasgow's higher Jewish birth rate and lower child mortality mirrored developments around the Jewish immigrant world.

In examining figures for Jews and non-Jews in London and Manchester and in selected cities with a substantial Jewish population, such as Budapest, Amsterdam and eight American cities, Lara Marks related the lower Jewish infant mortality rates to behavioural, rather than environmental, factors.[49] She considered that the inspections of the Jewish Board of Guardians, which could lead to real improvements for the families visited, were of more importance than overcrowding. Religious factors, such as ritual hand-washing before meals, may also have been important. Children may also have been protected by a longer period of maternal breastfeeding. In a study of children admitted to Belvedere Hospital in Glasgow it was noted, as it had been in Leeds, that the Jewish rate for rickets was substantially below that of the general population.[50] In his evidence to the Interdepartmental Committee on Physical Deterioration, Dr A.K. Chalmers, medical officer of health for Glasgow, put the better health and nutritional status of the children of Jewish immigrants down to the fact that 'the immigrant is vigorous with a definite intention of bettering himself. That is why he comes here.'[51]

**Muscular Judaism**

The sponsorship of athletic and other sporting activities by Jewish community organisations was often referred to as 'muscular Judaism', paralleling moves for 'muscular Christianity' in the wider community. While programmes of exercise for puny slum dwellers were often derided as an irrelevance, a key Jewish objective was promoting fitness and health, while keeping young Jews within the community framework. Indeed, the early Zionist movement believed that they needed to improve the physical lot of the Jewish masses and youngsters were encouraged to involve themselves in physical activity. A Glasgow Zionist Cycling and Athletic Club was established in March 1899, with its own distinctive Zionist badge and uniform.[52]

The Glasgow Jewish Lads' Brigade, founded in May 1903, modelled itself on the Boys' Brigade and had the dual responsibility of providing discipline, citizenship and loyalty while aiding the acculturation of the immigrant young. The Lads' Brigade quickly became popular with Jewish boys in the Gorbals, though this was often with an adult leadership drawn from Garnethill. While its aim of developing loyal Britons was openly stated, the benefit of producing fitter, and thus healthier, young men was also obvious. A non-Jewish officer, Lieutenant-Colonel I.H. Galbraith, visiting the Glasgow Jewish Lads' Brigade in July 1919, hoped 'that parents will realise what a splendid opportunity their sons are having of getting not only their bodies but their minds moulded and disciplined through the training received'.[53]

If exercise was one health solution for the weak and poorly nourished, the idea of providing an annual holiday for slum children in the countryside also had its proponents. Some rejected the concept as a distraction from the real need to provide permanent improvements in housing and nutrition.[54] Nevertheless, the scheme was widely popular. In August 1908, for example, 57 poor Jewish children were taken for a two-week holiday in the country at West Kilbride by the newly-formed Glasgow Jewish Children Fresh Air Fund and accommodated in a home rented from a missionary organisation where 'every facility was offered for the observance of the Jewish dietary laws'.[55] Supported from 1919 by the Boot and Clothing Fund of the Glasgow Jewish Board of Guardians, and the Glasgow Corporation, the 'fresh air' holidays remained popular and continued in the same format until the Second World War. Glasgow's child health generally only began to improve with such measures as the school medical services and free school meals and milk, which confronted the main problem, that of poverty, head on.[56] The Glasgow Jewish community shared concerns about the need for health improvement, and its solutions often paralleled developments in the general community.

**Mental Health**

Some studies of migrant population groups have shown an increased incidence of mental health problems among immigrant groups. These are often attributed to problems of language, integration and family separation; and the difficulties which might be faced by newcomers in any society that is radically different from that of their country of origin should not be underestimated. However, the Jewish immigrants did have some factors in their favour. Given the conditions in Eastern Europe, whether economic or political, there was little to attract Jews back there from Scotland, and Jewish immigrants were more likely to move on to other countries, such as the United States, than return home.

The case notes of the Glasgow mental hospitals, then known as lunatic asylums, give a fascinating insight into the care provided for Jewish patients with psychiatric problems a century ago.[57] There is a mine of information related to concomitant illness, especially tuberculosis, to problems related to diet, and to relatives unable to cope with the misery of untreatable disorders. But there was another, more sinister, side too. The descriptions of patients by hospital doctors border on prejudice. Some refer to concepts such as 'physical degeneracy', others to 'shifty eyes and an evil appearance', while other notes describe a patient who is 'as ill behaved as only a Jew can be'.[58]

## Tuberculosis

Tuberculosis was a major killer in Victorian Glasgow: no less than 13 per cent of all deaths in Scotland in the 1890s were TB-related.[59] It might have been thought that the first generation of Jewish immigrants, employed in overcrowded damp sweated tailoring workshops living in small Gorbals tenements, would have had a relatively high incidence of tuberculosis, and it was especially common among patients with mental illness. While TB was often said to run a long and insidious course in the poor Jewish immigrant population, studies in areas of Jewish settlement in the major European and American cities consistently showed a pattern of a lower incidence of TB among the Jewish population compared with other neighbouring groups.[60] This was the case in Glasgow too.[61] This was often attributed to Jewish emphasis on diet and sobriety, good maternal care and long exposure to urban life as well as the extensive Jewish social and welfare network with its own welfare officers and health visitors.[62]

However, there was enough tuberculosis within the Jewish community in Glasgow for the illness to consume a considerable proportion of Jewish welfare funding.[63] A century ago tuberculosis meant the early deaths of breadwinners and helped to fill the orphanages. In 1916, the Glasgow Jewish Board of Guardians decided to set up a jubilee fund to facilitate the emigration of Jewish families in Glasgow to parts of the British empire, such as New Zealand and Australia, where the better climate might facilitate a cure.[64]

However, this form of social engineering was controversial even at the time, given the strain on emigrating families and difficulties of integration in the host countries. By removing from Glasgow dependent families with a chronically ill breadwinner the Glasgow Jewish welfare services must have felt that they could only benefit by the project. The target for the jubilee fund was £3,000 but it took some time to collect even half that sum. Money was used during wartime to pay for about 20 Jewish patients from Glasgow in sanatoria in the south of England and after the war the policy of supporting emigration began.[65]

## Trachoma

Trachoma, a chronic infective eye disease eventually producing corneal scarring and blindness, was well known in the Russian Baltic provinces, the main source of Jewish immigrants to Britain and North America. There were some who saw trachoma, before its infective agent, *chlamydia trachomatis*, was isolated in 1907, as a genetic disorder particularly affecting Jews. Jewish emigrants from Eastern Europe feared the disease, because its detection at any point along the migration route could spell the end of the journey. A family might have spent all their savings on tickets for North America only to fail a medical test at Ellis Island or at one of the ports on the trans-migrant route. It might not be feasible for all the members of a family group to return home and sometimes one person might be left behind, anywhere en route, until treatment could be obtained and the journey completed.

There was another, more sinister, aspect to the attempt to label trachoma as a Jewish disease. Of all the diseases that port doctors looked out for trachoma was the most feared because of its peculiar visibility.[66] It was in 1898 that trachoma was recognised as a dangerous infectious disease in America. In that year deportations from Ellis Island related to trachoma numbered about 250, many of them travellers who had passed through the UK on the way to North America. A court case in Scotland had established that travellers deported from the USA on health grounds had to be returned by the shipping company to their last European port of call.[67] This increased the likelihood of infected migrants arriving in Britain and indeed a number of Jewish migrants with trachoma were returned from New York to Glasgow during 1906.[68] Policing the illness was not easy. Many travellers had been around much of Europe prior to sailing to North America, and establishing the precise final European port was not always simple. There were professional agents, out to dupe the shipping companies, who helped would-be emigrants evade the companies' controls. In return, the companies employed their own trachoma inspectors, who erred on the cautious side, refusing access to anyone who had any kind of eye problem, whether trachoma or not. Early in 1905 Dr George Wilson, medical officer of health for Glasgow, produced a memorandum on the incidence of trachoma in the city. He identified the principal source of trachoma as being the trans-migrants passing through the city, noting that there were often about 400 temporarily accommodated in hostels in Glasgow. It was suggested that much of the trachoma in Glasgow derived from this group of travellers, who were, in the main, Jewish. Consequently, Dr Wilson called for support for the Aliens Bill, then before Parliament, suggesting that legislation could 'cut off the supply (of trachoma) at its source'.[69]

However, the facts did not support these conclusions, and the significance of trachoma as a Jewish disease did not match the expectations of the opponents of Jewish immigration. There was no evidence of the spread of the disease within Glasgow. There was no concentration of trachoma in the parts of Glasgow, like the Gorbals, where the immigrants were concentrated. Indeed, the prevalence of trachoma in Glasgow was not very high. There seemed much to indicate that even in the climate of 1905 anti-alien or anti-Jewish sentiment was not 'politically correct', so the best form of anti-alien protest was to suggest that measures to prevent Jewish entry were purely motivated by health concerns. Yet the number of trachoma cases recorded in Glasgow for foreign Jews refused entry to Britain in the years after the Aliens Act became law remained small. In the peak years between 1904 and 1910 the average number of cases of trachoma treated in the Glasgow Eye Infirmary annually did not reach 100.[70] Of nearly 1,000 cases notified to the Glasgow medical officer of health between 1914 and 1937 less than 15 per cent were born outside the UK.[71]

## Conclusion

The story of Jewish integration in Glasgow, and the community struggle for health, is a story that was repeated in other communities in Western Europe and North America. Jewish immigrants naturally looked to their more established co-religionists for assistance, and usually help was forthcoming. Public clamour over such issues as sweated labour and alien immigration ensured that the settled communities had to aid their weary and impoverished brethren.

While there was some tension in the relationships between those who had arrived in Glasgow before the main wave of immigration in the 1890s and the later arrivals, Jews were proud of their ability to care 'for their own', to keep Jews out of the poorhouse, and to accelerate Jewish integration to make the newcomers seem less 'foreign'. The welfare state was at a rudimentary stage of development during this period of immigration, but there was enough statutory provision to ease some of the financial burdens.

The Jewish struggle for health included provision of medical, welfare and social services for the poor and sick. Jews had to ensure that their co-religionists were able to benefit from statutory welfare and health provision and that they were not discriminated against in the hospitals and other institutions. As in other communities, Jewish provision in Glasgow did not just match what was on offer in the wider society, but was more extensive in quality and quantity than available elsewhere, and provided Jews with an opportunity to strengthen their Jewish identity. In an increasingly secular society Jews turned to Jewish health and welfare groups as a means of helping to retain their Jewishness in a socially accepted form. Thus the Glasgow Jewish struggle for health involved making use of statutory provision while strengthening Jewish welfare bodies, making them sensitive to the religious and ethnic needs of the Jewish community. Glasgow Jewry was enabled to create a society that ensured its survival as a vital part of local civic and national Jewish life.

## Notes

1. See, for example, accounts of immigrant health conditions in North America in Yew, E., 'Medical Inspection of Jewish Immigrants at Ellis Island, 1891–1924', *Bulletin of the New York Academy of Medicine* 56 (1980), 488–510; Sachs, T.B., 'Tuberculosis in the Jewish District of Chicago', *Journal of the American Medical Association* 43 (1904), 390–5; Dwork, D., 'Health Conditions of Immigrant Jews on the Lower East Side of New York, 1880–1914', *Medical History* 25 (1981), 1–40; and in London in Black, G., 'Health and Medical Care of the Jewish Poor in the East End of London: 1880–1939', PhD thesis, University of Leicester, 1987.

2. Marks, L., 'Ethnicity, Religion and Health Care', *Social History of Medicine* 4 (1991), 123–8.

3. Liedtke, R., *Jewish Welfare in Hamburg and Manchester, c.1850–1914*, (Oxford, 1998), 232–4.

4. For a detailed account of some of the issues in Jewish immigrant health and welfare see Collins, K., *Be Well! Jewish Immigrant Health and Welfare in Glasgow, 1860–1914* (East Linton, 2001).

5. For the history of the Jewish community in Glasgow, see Collins, K., *Second City Jewry: The Jews of Glasgow in the Age of Expansion, 1790–1919* (Glasgow, 1990); Braber, B., *Jews in Glasgow, 1879–1939: Immigration and Integration* (London, 2007).

6. Collins, *Second City Jewry*, 15.

7. Collins, *Be Well,*, 51–62.

8. For details of Asher Asher and the first Jews in medicine in Glasgow, see Collins, K., *Go and Learn: The International Story of the Jews and Medicine in Scotland, 1739–1945* (Aberdeen, 1988); Collins, *Be Well!*, 131–50.

9. Roth, C., *The Rise of Provincial Jewry: The Early History of the Jewish Communities in the English Countryside, 1740–1840* (London, 1950), 59.

10. Alderman, G., *Modern British Jewry* (Oxford, 1992), 134–5.

11. Collins, *Second City Jewry*, 71.

12. Braber, B., 'Integration of Jewish Immigrants in Glasgow, 1880–1939', PhD thesis, University of Glasgow, 1992, 212; *Jewish Chronicle*, 3 February 1911.

13. Checkland, O. and Lamb, M., eds, *Health Care as Social History: The Glasgow Case* (Aberdeen, 1982), 6.

14. Bermant, C., *The Jews* (London, 1978), 137–8.

15. Collins, *Second City Jewry*, 164; *Jewish Chronicle*, 22 July 1910.

16. Worsdell, F., *The Tenement, A Way of Life: A Social, Historical and Architectural Study of Housing in Glasgow* (Edinburgh, 1979), 7.

17. Summary of 1891 census returns for Jewish homes in the Gorbals in Collins, *Second City Jewry*, 222–4.

18. *Royal Commission on Alien Immigration: Minutes of Evidence*, Parliamentary Papers, Cd. 1742 (1903), evidence of Julius Pinto, questions 20991–8.

19. Report of the *Lancet* Special Sanitary Commission on the Sweating System in Glasgow, *Lancet*, 30 June 1888, 1313–14.

20. *Sessional Papers of the House of Lords*, 1889, vol. 8: evidence of Julius Pinto (question 26206), George Sedwick (question 26455) and Dr James Russell, (question 26363).

21. Lindsay, D.E., *Report upon a Study of the Diet of the Labouring Classes in Glasgow: Carried out during 1911–1913 under the Auspices of the Corporation of the City* (Glasgow, 1913), 23–4.

22. See minute books and annual records of the Glasgow Hebrew Philanthropic Society and the Glasgow Jewish Board of Guardians: Scottish Jewish Archives Centre, Garnethill Synagogue, Glasgow.

23. Collins, *Be Well!*, 56.

24. *Jewish Chronicle*, 28 August 1914, 11 September 1914.

25. Collins, *Be Well!*, 62–9.

26.  Weisser, M.R., *A Brotherhood of Memory: Jewish Landsmanshaftn in the New World* (New York, 1985), 75.
27.  Black, E.C., *The Social Politics of Anglo-Jewry* (Oxford, 1998), 195; Black, 'Health and Medical Care', 93.
28.  Endelman, T.M., *Jewish Apostasy in the Modern World* (New York, 1987), 1.
29.  Booth, C., *Life and Labour of the People in London*, 9 vols (London, 1892), vol. 7, 277–8.
30.  Chambers, D., 'Prelude to the Last Things: The Church of Scotland's Mission to the Jews', *Records of the Scottish Church History Society* 19 (1975), 57.
31.  Clark, C., *The Politics of Conversion: Missionary Protestantism and the Jews in Prussia 1728–1941* (Oxford, 1995), 109.
32.  *Glasgow Herald*, 13 January 1909.
33.  *Glasgow Herald*, 23 November 1906.
34.  Collins, *Be Well!*, 165–71.
35.  *Jewish Chronicle*, 1 March 1912.
36.  Collins, *Be Well!*, 69–70.
37.  *Jewish Chronicle*, 15 January 1909, 2 September 1910, 11 July 1913, 18 July 1913.
38.  *Jewish Chronicle*, 1 April 1921.
39.  Collins, *Be Well!*, 70–2; Collins, *Second City Jewry*, 218; Reflections of Jack Cowan, 24 September 1995: Scottish Jewish Archives Centre.
40.  *Jewish Chronicle*, 16 January 1914.
41.  'Bernard Glasser at 85', *Jewish Echo*, 20 September 1957.
42.  (Glasgow) Infirmaries Consultative Committee, in Glasgow Royal Infirmary minutes, 17 November 1915: Greater Glasgow Health Board Archives, Mitchell Library, Glasgow.
43.  *Jewish Chronicle*, 22 July 1910.
44.  Pearson, K. and Moul, M., 'The Problem of Alien Immigration into Great Britain, Illustrated by an Examination of Russian and Polish Jewish Children', *Annals of Eugenics* 1 (1925–6), 5–127 at 44–6; *Annals of Eugenics* 3 (1928), 201–68 at 254.
45.  Heron, David, 'The Influence of Defective Physique and Unfavourable Home Environment on the Intelligence of Schoolchildren', *Eugenics Laboratory Memoirs* 8 (1910), 58–9.
46.  *Interdepartmental Committee on Physical Deterioration: Minutes of Evidence*, Parliamentary Papers, Cd. 2210 (1904), e.g. question 2772.
47.  *Jewish Chronicle*, 20 January 1911.
48.  Jewish infant mortality data compiled from the records of the United Synagogue of Glasgow 1898–1906; birth, marriage and death registers of the Glasgow Hebrew Congregation; records of the Jewish Cemeteries of Scotland: all at the Scottish Jewish Archives Centre. With small numbers and some under-reporting, figures for the 1880s are less reliable.
49.  Marks, L., *Model Mothers: Jewish Mothers and Maternity Provision in East London, 1870–1939* (Oxford, 1994), 84.
50.  Marks, *Model Mothers*, 73–4; Macgregor, A., 'Physique of Glasgow Children Admitted to the City of Glasgow Fever Hospital, Belvedere during the Years 1907–8', *Proceedings of the Royal Philosophical Society of Glasgow* 40 (1908), 172.
51.  *Interdepartmental Committee on Physical Deterioration: Minutes of Evidence*, Parliamentary Papers, Cd. 2210 (1904), Evidence of Dr A.K. Chalmers, question 6090.
52.  Collins, *Second City Jewry*, 118.
53.  *Jewish Chronicle*, 29 March 1918.
54.  Glasser, R., *Growing up in the Gorbals* (London, 1986), 54–5.
55.  *Jewish Chronicle*, 7 August 1908.
56.  Hamilton, D., *The Healers: A History of Medicine in Scotland* (Edinburgh, 1981), 236.
57.  Similar findings corroborating the impression of prejudice displayed in mental health patient case notes were published in Smith, L.D., 'Insanity and Ethnicity: Jews in the Mid-Victorian Lunatic Asylum', *Jewish Culture and History* 1 (1998), 27–40.

58. Case notes from Govan District Asylum are in ledgers HB 24/5/1–36 while Govan Parochial Asylum Records are in ledgers HB 17/2/136–8. Extracts quoted are from HB/FG/8/4/1916; HB/RV/31/12/1908; HB/HA/22/8/1910. All in Greater Glasgow Health Board Archive.
59. Hamilton, *Healers*, 236.
60. Feldman, W.M., 'Tuberculosis and the Jew', *Tuberculosis Year Book* 1 (1913–14), 48–54; Hardy, A., *The Epidemic Streets: Infectious Disease and the Rise of Preventive Medicine 1856-1900* (Oxford, 1993), 289.
61. *Jewish Chronicle*, 14 September 1917.
62. Marks, *Model Mothers*, 64–5.
63. Annual Reports of the Glasgow Jewish Board of Guardians, 1912–20: Scottish Jewish Archives Centre.
64. *Jewish Chronicle*, 29 September 1916.
65. Collins, *Second City Jewry*, 196
66. Henry, Arthur, 'Among the Immigrants', *Scribner's Magazine* 29 (1901), 302, quoted in Howe, I., with Libo, K., *The Immigrant Jews of New York, 1881 to the Present Day*, (London, 1976), 44.
67. Chalmers, A.K., *The Health of Glasgow, 1818-1925: An Outline* (Glasgow, 1930), 420.
68. Wilson, T.S., 'The Incidence of Trachoma in Glasgow, 1914–1968', *Health Bulletin* 27 (1969), 15–17.
69. Wilson, G.S., 'Memorandum by the Medical Officer of Health on the Presence of Trachoma in Certain Alien Immigrants', in *Report of the Medical Officer of Health for Glasgow*, 1905, 130–1: Glasgow City Archives, Mitchell Library, Glasgow, file DTC7/11/3.
70. Glasgow Ophthalmic Institution, *Annual Report*, 1907: Greater Glasgow Health Board Archive.
71. Wilson, 'Incidence of Trachoma', 15.

# 5

# The Good, the Bad and the Ugly
## Local Registrars of Births, Deaths and Marriages in Mid-Nineteenth Century Scotland

### Anne Cameron

Until the mid-1850s, the Church of Scotland was officially responsible for carrying out vital registration. Each parish kirk session was supposed to register all the births, deaths and marriages – which, for practical purposes, usually meant baptisms, burials and proclamations of the banns of marriage – occurring within its boundaries. However, most sessions recorded such events only sporadically, if at all.[1] For their trouble in writing up the registers, the session clerks generally demanded a fee from everyone reporting a family funeral, christening or forthcoming wedding. This deterred poorer parishioners from volunteering the necessary information, and because the registers belonged to the established church, people of other denominations often refused on principle to intimate their vital events.[2]

By the 1830s, the inadequacies of this system were painfully apparent. Not only did many Scots lack proof of age and parentage to support an inheritance claim, but medical corporations and statistical societies were also concerned that the registers of baptisms, burials and banns never reflected the numbers of births, deaths and marriages taking place.[3] Couples whose banns were called did not always proceed to marry, and the birth of a baby that died before baptism, as well as the death of anyone interred without a formal funeral, frequently passed unrecorded. This made it impossible to gauge the actual birth rate, death rate or size of the population.

Following several failed attempts to push a Scottish registration bill through Parliament, the old, unsatisfactory method of recording baptisms, burials and banns was finally replaced under the *Act to Provide for the better Registration of Births, Deaths and Marriages in Scotland*, passed in August 1854.[4] The Act introduced compulsory, civil registration of births, deaths and marriages from 1 January 1855, and authorised the appointment of a registrar for each parish or municipal district, to whom people were obliged to intimate these events. No fee applied for registration, but failure to register incurred a fine.[5] A General Register Office for Scotland (GROS), headed by a registrar general, was created to oversee the new system and to supply every registrar with one principal and one duplicate set of birth, death and marriage registers each year. People

increasingly came to appreciate these registers, which not only verified their
identity for inheritance purposes, but also for life insurance policies and, in due
course, old age pensions.

Though the registers remain an invaluable source for historians and genealo-
gists today, relatively little attention has been paid to the local officers tasked
with compiling them.[6] This chapter offers a preliminary exploration of the backgrounds, status, domestic environments and working conditions of the parish
registrars, and considers how well – or in some instances, how poorly – they
carried out their duties during the first few years of civil registration.

### The Role of the Registrar

The Registration Act divided Scotland into 1,027 registration districts, most of
which comprised a single parish, and each of which had its own registrar. The
registrars' job was to elicit specific information from the people who came to
report vital events, and to copy that information clearly, accurately and
promptly into both sets of register books. When a birth was reported, for
example, the registrar had to ask for:

>The child's first name, surname and sex
>The time and date of birth
>The place of birth (street and house number)
>The name and rank, profession or occupation of the child's father
>The name and maiden name of the child's mother
>The ages and birthplaces of both parents*
>The place and date of their marriage**
>The number of other children born of the marriage, whether living or
>deceased*
>The signature of the informant beside the entry
>
>* Only required in 1855
>** Not required between 1856 and 1860

And for a death, the registrar had to request:

>The deceased's name, sex and age
>The deceased's rank, profession or occupation
>The deceased's place and date of birth and how long they had been in the
>parish*
>The names and rank, profession or occupation of the deceased's parents

The name of the deceased's spouse
The names and ages of any children, whether living or deceased*
The time and date of death
The place of death (street and house number)
The cause of death and duration of the fatal illness
The name of the deceased's medical attendant and the date on which they
last saw the deceased
The place of burial and the name of the undertaker*
The signature of the informant beside the entry

* Only required in 1855

Although primary responsibility for reporting vital events lay with the people themselves, the registrars were expected to use their initiative to discover and inquire into any births, deaths or marriages that had not been intimated to them. They were instructed to inform the county sheriff of anyone who had failed to notify such an event, and of any doctor who had not provided a certificate of cause of death for registration purposes. They were further obliged to refer any 'suspicious' deaths to the procurator fiscal for investigation.

At the close of each year, the registrars retained their principal set of register books for local reference and forwarded the duplicate set to the GROS in Edinburgh, where the staff of the statistical branch tabulated the contents to produce detailed national statistics. These were printed, presented to Parliament and used to inform government policy concerning the physical and moral health of the nation. The ostensibly humble local registrars were therefore vital components in the administrative machinery of Scottish civil registration, and everything depended on their efficacy. With this in mind, a dedicated team of GROS examiners toured the country once a year, scrutinising the registrars' work. The registrar general divided Scotland into nine large districts for this purpose and appointed one examiner for each. The latter's task was to visit all the registrars within his respective district, and have each of them read out the contents of their principal set of registers while he silently read along in the duplicate set, checking that the contents of both sets matched exactly, that there were no discrepancies or omissions, and, if such were found, taking steps to have them corrected.[7] The examiner had also to inspect any supporting schedules and certificates that had been given in by informants, and to assess the general quality and accuracy of the register books, the overall competence of the registrars, the suitability of their accommodation, and whether or not the registers were adequately stored. On completing his annual tour of inspection, he submitted a comprehensive report to the registrar general, and these reports offer a valuable insight into the registrars' world and working practices.

### Occupational Backgrounds

Until at least the 1870s, the same Church of Scotland session clerks who had
noted baptisms, burials and banns under the old system generally acted as registrars under the new.[8] Section 8 of the Registration Act entitled every man serving
as a session clerk on 1 January 1855 to become civil registrar for his parish, on
condition that when these individuals died or retired, the parochial boards and
town councils could elect new registrars of their choice. This was intended partly
to placate the Church of Scotland, which would have opposed the introduction of
civil registration if its session clerks had not been given this job; but it was also the
most practical solution, for in many rural parishes the session clerk – who often
doubled as the schoolmaster – was the only person capable of carrying out registration satisfactorily. As Alfred List, examiner for the Inverness district, affirmed:
'In the North of Scotland, the parish schoolmaster should be the Registrar. He
belongs to an ill used class of men who are really the best qualified for the duty.'[9]

   On the death or resignation of a registrar, or on the rare occasion that any
session clerk refused or was considered by the parochial board to be unfit for registration duties,[10] it could be difficult to find a replacement given the shortage of
suitable candidates outside the major cities. Several country parishes succeeded in
engaging educated men – the registrars of Crieff, Aberfeldy and Campbeltown
were lawyers, for instance[11] – while others appointed postmasters, merchants or
grocers, or simply passed the registrar's post to their next session clerk. Some
small parishes had to settle for a ploughman or weaver as registrar if no one more
appropriate could be found, but James Dawson, examiner for the Dumfries
district, criticised several larger towns for using the post as an unofficial form of
poor relief:

> In too many cases the [town] Councils are apt to forget that they are
> custodians of the public interests, and to appoint men as Registrars who
> may have been unfortunate in business, or who have come recommended
> to them by private friendship . . . I know of two instances where the
> Registrars, proverbially incompetent from the very first, were chosen for
> no other reason than that they were old <u>cronies</u> of the Electors, and so
> reduced in worldly circumstances as to be objects of charity which their
> friends the Electors, chose to dispense to them at the public expense.[12]

Dawson's fellow examiners highlighted several parishes that had acted similarly,
including Kilmeny, where the registrar, Neil McAlpin, was 'so destitute that he
receives aid from the parochial funds, and holds the Office of Registrar to eik
[sic] out a miserable pittance'.[13]

**Income**

Suitably educated men were not generally attracted to the post of registrar because it was not highly paid. Parochial boards could either choose to set an annual salary for their registrar, and raise a special local rate from which to fund it; or restrict him to the 'statutory fees' laid down by the Registration Act, which were 2s for each of the first 20 events, and 1s for every subsequent event, registered in any six-month period. If the board opted for payment by statutory fees, the registrar's remuneration was tied to the number of births, deaths and marriages occurring in the parish, which could be very few indeed. The Inchinnan registers contained only 29 entries in 1855, so that the registrar's earnings were 'exceedingly trifling'.[14] Even when a registrar was paid by salary, it was often disproportionate to his time, effort and responsibility, for, as Examiner Dawson explained, 'The Parochial Boards measure their pockets, not the necessities of the public service . . . [and] have not yet arrived at a just estimate of what is due to a Registrar who faithfully and honestly acts up to his instructions.'[15] The examiners and the registrar general occasionally wrote to parishes on behalf of particularly poorly paid registrars, recommending that their remuneration be increased.[16] Several registrars also threatened to resign if they did not receive more money. At Alness, the registrar carried out his threat and the parochial board, unable to find a replacement, had to supplement his fees by 5s to retain him.[17]

Perhaps surprisingly, the earliest examiners' reports mention a few prosperous registrars. That of Strachan, who received an annual salary of £8, was purportedly 'worth as many thousands in right of his wife'; another was 'commonly called "the Jew of Fraserburgh" on account of his reputed riches', and the registrar of Aberlour was a wealthy bank agent, who donated £100 towards a new school building and £50 towards a vestry for the parish church.[18] However, these exceptional men had acquired their fortunes before accepting the registrar's job, rather than because of it. Since the income from registration was not enough to live on, most rural registrars, and even some in the major towns, were part-time officials who had to combine this duty with their own day jobs.[19]

**Working and Living Environments**

Besides often meagre earnings, the examiners' reports exposed the unsatisfactory state of many registrars' living and working environments. Urban registrars tended to have proper offices or at least a separate room for attending to people coming to report vital events; but in rural areas, parochial boards were reluctant to provide such facilities, leaving the registrars to store their registers and make all the entries in their classrooms, behind their shop counters, or in their own houses. If an office *was* provided, it might have no waiting room. Those who came to register family events could not expect privacy, but frequently had to reveal intimate personal details in front of customers, schoolchildren, or other informants queuing for the registrar's attention. Robert Gordon, examiner for the Lanark district, feared that the national statistics would suffer in consequence, and advised the registrar general that, 'especially in cases of Illegitimacy, it appears to me to be unsuitable, and to create an obstacle to truthful information that the person recording an event should have to do so in the presence of a bevy of attentive listeners'.[20]

To compound matters, session clerks and schoolteachers who served as registrars often endured cramped, damp and draughty accommodation, as the parish ratepayers would not spend money on a decent building. This not only affected their health and morale, but also the condition of the registers, which ought to have been kept in secure, dry and fire-proof places to prevent them being stolen, tampered with or damaged. Examiner Alfred List was extremely concerned about this problem, and gave the following graphic account of the schoolmaster's house at Glenshiel:

> His dwelling is a miserable hut with a thatched roof. It consists of two rooms, a bedroom and a kitchen, neither of which is floored. The window of the bedroom, (where the Books were examined) is about $1\frac{1}{2}$ foot square; the three lowest panes must have met with an accident, as their place is supplied by a parcel of wood; of the remaining six, two are open, two filled up with boards, and the last two panes are actually of glass. There are two beds in the room, which, beyond a doubt, are occupied by the entire family. There is no ceiling; nothing but the rafters and the thatch, which can hardly be discerned by means of the scanty light let in by the window, still more darkened by the smoke issuing from the other miserable apartment. The roof being pervious to rain, the Register Box has, sometimes, to be removed; while [I was] examining, a drop of rain fell upon a page of one of the books nearly spoiling it. No wonder, then, that the Books cannot be kept clean. How the heritors of this parish can allow the school and house to remain in this state after repeated expostulation, surpasses belief. It is a perfect disgrace and scandal to a Christian community.[21]

When he visited the parish again two years later, List reported that the house remained 'pre-eminent in filth, in dampness and in wretchedness . . . There is always a rumour about repairs, but while people talk, the books are being fast destroyed by the damp'.[22] The living quarters of several other schoolmaster registrars were little better, and List remarked that the teacher's accommodation at Latheron ought to be condemned by the sheriff.[23]

**The Good . . .**

The registrar general was gratified to learn from his examiners that many local registrars took their responsibilities very seriously, and discharged them to the best of their ability. George Bell, examiner for the district of Glasgow, Edinburgh and Leith, was most impressed by the registers for Heriot and Warriston (Edinburgh), where Mr Adams was 'thoroughly acquainted with the nature of the work he has undertaken, and has evinced great aptitude for the execution of it. I cannot speak too highly of the manner in which he has discharged his duties'.[24] Mr Barclay, registrar of Dalry, won similar praise 'for the admirable manner in which he has discharged his duties in this extensive and populous District', while the registrar of Govan was 'most zealous and painstaking, and the whole work of registration in this parish exhibits a high standard of excellence'.[25]

In Tradeston (Glasgow), Examiner Bell found the business of vital registration conducted with such energy and intelligence that he believed nothing had escaped the registrar's attention.[26] The registrar for Calton (Edinburgh) was another who spared no pains to inquire into every event.[27] Outside the major towns, the Montrose registers were declared 'remarkable for the beauty of the writing, general accuracy, and uniformity in the manner of entry', and the Dunfermline registers were also distinguished for 'faultless accuracy'.[28] But it was probably the registrar of Old Machar in Aberdeen who displayed the greatest devotion to duty. Suffering from rheumatic fever, he had his sick bed moved out of his house and into a back room at the registration office, so that he might continue his work there. He and his wife both lived in this room until he had fully recovered.[29]

**. . . the Bad . . .**

Conversely, numerous registrars failed to complete the registers properly, giving the examiners the time-consuming and often exasperating task of identifying and correcting their mistakes. Poor spelling and bad handwriting, which jeopardised the validity of the entries, were common. Examiner List lamented that although most registrars were schoolmasters, 'many of them find difficulty in spelling correctly', while Examiner Bell had to advise the registrar of Prestonpans to use a dictionary of names.[30] Other registrars made no physical effort to discover vital events in their parish. At Inverness, Examiner List found Mr Davidson to be

> perfunctory in the discharge of his duties, taking no active interest in the System. Informants are received when they come, but means are not taken, by moving about among the people, to ensure registration. I feel confident, in consequence of this laxity, that many cases escape Registration.[31]

These shortcomings generally stemmed from old age and infirmity, and were hardly surprising given that most registrars were long-serving session clerks and schoolteachers, not in the first flush of youth. In Baillieston, the schoolmaster registrar was 'an old worn out man, absolutely decrepit, his hands shaking to such a degree that he can hardly hold a pen . . . his defective eyesight being alone a fruitful source of error'.[32] The examiners' reports mention many similar cases, including the registrar of Abertarff ('too old, too blind, and too doted to do any good'), and the unfortunate registrar of Cupar, who was twice confined in a lunatic asylum.[33]

The Registration Act permitted, but did not compel, each registrar to appoint a permanent, paid assistant. The examiners usually encouraged elderly or infirm registrars to nominate a capable older son to this position, and, eventually, to resign in his favour.[34] This kept the registrar's office and income in the family and also afforded the parish a competent officer; but, because the registrars were obliged to pay their assistants out of their own pockets, many lacked the means to employ one. Instead, they relied on casual help from their wives, adult daughters or school-age children to fill up the registers, as at Ratho, Newbattle and North Morar.[35] In Fort Augustus, too, Examiner List noticed that the registers 'appear as if kept in a female hand differing from the writing of the Registrar's signature; and altho' the Registrar denied my challenge, yet I am persuaded that my suspicions are not unfounded'.[36]

The registrar general, William Pitt Dundas, frowned on these irregular practices. To reduce the risk of errors and falsified entries, only the registrar and his official assistant were authorised to write in the registers, and common law disqualified both women and minors from election to these and other offices of public trust.[37] However, the *Regulations for Registrars* issued by the GROS in January 1855 did not make this disqualification plain, leading some registrars and parochial boards to assume that females *could* serve as assistant registrars, and to appoint them accordingly. Pitt Dundas consulted the law officers of the crown for Scotland, who confirmed

> that a female cannot be considered a fit person to hold the office of Assistant Registrar. We hold it to be clear that the office of Registrar could not be held by a female, and considering to how great an extent the duties of the two offices are identical, we think that the same principle must apply to both.[38]

The revised edition of the *Regulations*, printed in December 1855, distinctly stipulated that assistant registrars must be male, over the age of 16, and sanctioned by the parochial board or town council, with their appointment also notified to the sheriff and the registrar general.[39] Yet several parishes persisted in approving the registrar's wife or daughter as his assistant, or, when the registrar died, allowed her to take over temporarily for the benefit of the family until a successor could be appointed. In June 1858, for instance, Alexander Nicolson, examiner for the Lothian district, discovered that Miss Foggo, daughter of the late registrar of Pencaitland, had been acting as interim registrar for the seven months since her father's death, with the sanction of the board, but in breach of the *Regulations*. The 55 entries she had made were invalid and a sheriff's warrant was required to render them probative.[40]

Nicolson's fellow examiners sympathised with those in Miss Foggo's position, for they often kept the registers more efficiently than their husbands and fathers had done. In the second district of Dundee, the registrar's daughter had assisted him, and the examiner, Andrew Jervise, acknowledged her entries to be 'superior, in every respect, to those by the Registrar himself'.[41] The registrar general also received numerous letters, including one from his own nephew, Robert Dundas of Arniston, urging him to accept women as assistant registrars; but he believed that to do so would merely give session clerk and schoolmaster registrars an excuse to hand over all their registration duties to their female relatives.[42] Citing the law officers' opinion of 1855, Pitt Dundas and his successors resisted all such pleas, and warned any parochial boards found to have sanctioned female assistants that these women must be replaced.[43] By the 1890s, Sir Stair Agnew, who was then registrar general, doubted that this position would be tenable for much longer, public opinion having 'undergone a decided change' since the date of the law officers' pronouncement.[44] However, not until the labour shortages of the First World War, when many registrars joined the forces, did the GROS finally permit women to serve both as registrars and as assistant registrars.

While elderly registrars' mistakes made much work for the examiners, their younger counterparts, susceptible to vanity, laziness and worldly distractions, could perform equally poorly. The Forgan registers suffered because the youthful registrar was 'evidently more in love with himself, than with any part of his business'. Examiner Jervise described the registrar of Drumblade as 'a fast youth' who ought to be closely watched, and the registers of New Pitsligo were kept by 'a young, flighty student of divinity, [who] takes up his head with praying at revival meetings, and fiddling at private parties, to the neglect of his duties as a teacher, it is said, and certainly to those of the registration'.[45]

More seriously, several of the registrars were habitual drunkards. Examiner Gibson Stott suspected that 'the nonsense contained in some of the [Anderston] entries can only be accounted for on the supposition that the writer was very drunk indeed', and Examiner Bell perceived that the registrar of Spott, 'a man of intemperate habits', possessed 'a maniacal tendency . . . [and] requires to be managed discretely'.[46] Others never bothered to read the *Regulations* on commencing their post, and consequently made copious errors. Examiner Bell remarked that though the registrar of Earlston was intelligent enough, 'anything not plain sailing must be bungled . . . because of [his] ignorance of details of the Statute and regulations',[47] and Examiner Jervise reported that in Dunnottar, grave circumstances had arisen from the registrar's laxity:

> The Registrar seems utterly ignorant of the workings of the Act; and, I much fear, is very careless . . . I feel convinced in my own mind that he was very much to blame for the late serious mistakes which were corrected in terms of the 63rd Sec. of the Act, and for which the Informant suffered imprisonment.[48]

Furthermore, it was not uncommon for part-time registrars to be so preoccupied with their main job(s) that they neglected the registers. The examiners maintained that preachers, merchants and certain schoolteachers were particularly guilty of this, and that lawyers who served as registrars often delegated all the registration duties to their clerks.[49] In remote country districts, so few births, deaths or marriages occurred that the registrars might not remember the correct procedures when called upon,[50] while in the Highlands, many registrars were divinity students who went to college in Aberdeen or Glasgow during the autumn. When, as in Dingwall, they could not afford to appoint an assistant, this left the people with no one to record their family events for months at a time.[51]

Those registrars who had been selected out of charity or favouritism on the part of the parochial board, rather than consideration of their qualifications and abilities, generally proved incompetent, and that of Lochmaben was no exception. The examiner concluded that, 'Mr Rogerson should never have been appointed. He is above 70 and cannot write steadily . . . It seems to have been done from charitable motives and he asked me not to be severe, as it went far to help to support him.'[52] Problems were also inevitable in very small parishes like Bedrule, where Andrew Daniel, an uneducated hedger and game watcher, kept the registers for want of anyone more appropriate. When Examiner Bell called, he found himself

> not able to give an intelligible description of these Books. The poor fellow who wrote the entries is civilly responsible for his work, [but] morally not so. He was simply elected to the office, why? is a mystery to the uninitiated, but certainly not because of his fitness . . . He is totally and entirely and in every sense incompetent, and the honest man knows and feels this.[53]

Underpinning all of these explanations and excuses for ineptitude, however, was the fact that many registrars were not paid enough to foster any care or pride in their work, and therefore lacked the motivation to do it well. The examiners were aware of this, and, as the following case illustrates, accepted that the problem would not be solved rapidly. Examiner Dawson observed that the Johnstone registrar, John Stark, had not completed a single entry properly in his registers for 1857, sometimes filling in nothing more than the child's name and date of birth in the birth register. When the examiner remonstrated with Stark, 'he complained of it not being worth his while for so poor a remuneration'. Dawson was forced to concede that

> it is not in human nature generally, to expect a very rigid adherence to rules laid down even in an Act of Parliament when the wages of labour are so meagre . . . Until the Registrars be put on a juster [sic] footing as regards their remuneration I do not expect any marked improvement in the Registration Books.[54]

## . . . and the Ugly

As well as recordkeeping abilities, the examiners often commented upon the registrars' demeanour. Jervise described the registrar of Rothes, for example, as 'one of the most pompous of men – [he] talks so very fine that I cannot understand him at times, has a curled wig of a fair reddish colour, and jumps about so that you would not know where to find him when you require him'.[55] Such affectations (perhaps put on specially to impress the examiner?) were amusing, but basically harmless, and might therefore pass without reprimand; but ugly, unpleasant or impertinent behaviour did not. The GROS could ill afford for registrars to embarrass, distress or anger those who came to report births, deaths and marriages, as this might make people reluctant to register future events, thus leaving the national statistics incomplete. Tact and sensitivity were required when attending to bereaved relatives reporting the death of a loved one, or unmarried women intimating the birth of an illegitimate child, but the examiners found that certain registrars lacked these key qualities. One such was the registrar of the first district of Dundee, who

> treats the informants – the poorer of them – in a proud, haughty, and arrogant manner, which is ill calculated to elucidate important particulars, and which probably has rather the effect to make them conceal than to confess anything that may be wrong in their respective cases.[56]

Other registrars behaved even less appropriately, with Henry Murray, registrar for the Edinburgh district of Newington, attracting the strongest criticism.[57] Murray provoked more public complaints than any registrar in Scotland, and one such complaint came from Mrs Mabelle Balfour, who accused Murray of being 'anything but civil' when she came to register a birth. Mrs Balfour's dog had followed her into the registration office,

> upon which the Registrar ... spoke to me in such a manner [as] I have never been spoken to before and said he would have thought my common sense would have taught me better than to allow my dog to come into his office. I think where a man holds a public position of that kind he ought at least to remember that he is a servant and paid to be civil. He is far above his work ... [and] it is very unpleasant to have to go to such a man's office.[58]

When the registrar general demanded an explanation, Murray replied that he had warned Mrs Balfour dogs were not allowed inside the office, and petulantly remarked that, to avoid similar altercations in future, 'I must just allow smokers, dog-owners and others to do as they like to the discomfort of other ratepayers, and submit to the nuisances and indecencies which must necessarily follow.'[59]

### Dealing with the Bad and the Ugly

Despite his flippancy, the various complaints about his conduct, and the registrar general's obvious displeasure, Murray – and many more like him – remained in post, for the Registration Act made it extremely difficult to remove any registrars, however inefficient. The registrar general might admonish them in writing, but the Act gave him no power to dismiss them. Only the county sheriffs could do so, on the formal petition of the parochial board or town council concerned and after inquiring into the alleged grounds for dismissal. Unfortunately for the GROS, such petitions were rare, as boards and councils did not wish to appear foolish by admitting they had made a poor choice of registrar and requesting his removal.[60]

Whenever the examiners reported unfavourably of the registers in any parish, the registrar general would apprise the registrar and parochial board of the situation and, if the case were particularly bad, recommend that the registrar should resign. Sometimes, especially if he had a competent son ready to take his place, the registrar *was* willing to step down, thus solving the problem.[61] An amending Act of 1855 also improved matters somewhat by allowing the registrar general to petition the sheriff directly for the removal of a registrar, if the parochial board would not do so.[62] Even so, the ejection of incompetent registrars remained fraught with difficulties, as the registrar general acknowledged in a letter of 1863:

I have found by experience that I have been obliged to put up with Registrars who I believe to be quite inefficient from indolence, want of orderly habits, bad temper and other such causes, when it was not possible to frame and support by evidence, such a formal complaint as a Sheriff acting judicially feels himself bound to require . . . I have also found that an amount of inefficiency which is thought quite sufficient to call for dismissal by one Sheriff is not so considered by another and hence a want of unity in the working of the system.[63]

In November 1859, for example, the registrar general requested the magistrates and town council of Dundee to petition for the removal of Alexander Leask, registrar of the second district of the city, following reports that his handwriting was barely legible and that he had neglected his duties and absented himself from the registration office. The council acquiesced, but on investigating the case, the sheriff substitute judged their evidence of Leask's incompetence to be insufficient, and allowed him to stay on, provided he appointed a capable assistant and met several other conditions.[64] A year later, having received further unsatisfactory reports of Leask from the examiner, the registrar general again urged the council to appeal for his dismissal, considering it 'absolutely essential for the interests of Registration in such a large and important District as the one in question, that the business should no longer be entrusted to Mr Leask'.[65] Once more, however, the sheriff substitute ruled that the council had not supplied adequate proof of Leask's ineptitude, and refused the petition, leaving the registrar general no choice but to accept the 'very disappointing' outcome.[66]

Not all parochial boards and town councils were as co-operative as that of Dundee, and when asked to prepare a petition for the registrar's removal, several requested that the registrar be given another chance instead. So long as they undertook to monitor him closely, the registrar general usually acceded to their wishes, knowing only too well that the troublesome process of petitioning for dismissal carried no guarantee of success, but that increased supervision, combined with a dressing-down from the council or parochial board, might possibly tighten up the registrar's practice. Nevertheless, if the registers showed no improvement on the examiner's next visit, the registrar general informed the board or council that if they did not take the necessary steps for the registrar's removal, he would do so himself.[67]

## Conclusion

As the foregoing sections have shown, the local registrars of mid-nineteenth century Scotland were a heterogeneous group, not only in terms of their occupational backgrounds, education and social status, but more importantly, in terms of their capacity for and commitment to their task. Some were well educated, while others could hardly write. A few were extremely wealthy, while many more lived in poverty, and some were dedicated and diligent, whereas others were slipshod and indolent. The registrar's job was both responsible and laborious, but not all parochial boards or town councils considered this when making the appointment, far less when setting the registrar's remuneration. Fortunately, the examiners' reports indicate that as the years progressed, parishes increasingly opted to pay their registrars by fixed annual salaries rather than the statutory fees, which generally left them better off.[68] Proper registration offices also became more common as time went on, and a second amending Act of 1860 permitted parochial boards and town councils to add the cost of providing and maintaining a suitable office to the local rate levied for payment of the registrar.[69]

In most cases, the examiners were satisfied with the state of the registers, but they always endeavoured to prod careless or inefficient registrars into better habits. Their reports confirm that some were genuinely anxious to improve, and succeeded in doing so. Thus, in 1856, Examiner Jervise found the registrar of Auchtermuchty 'much improved since last year', while in 1857, Examiner Gordon observed a 'decided improvement in the Rutherglen Books since [the] date of my last Examination'.[70] Even drunken and disreputable registrars could mend their ways, as Examiner Jervise discovered in 1861: 'The Registrar [of Weem], who got married a second time about last New Year, is, I am glad to say, improved in every respect – previously I found him almost always the worse of drink, and in rags. He is now a teetotaller, and well dressed.'[71]

Conversely, others never showed any willingness to do better, and some, such as James Thomson in Kirkcudbright, grew steadily worse over the years. In 1857, Examiner Dawson reported that Thomson's books were in disorder, he having 'been long addicted to occasional intemperate indulgences' that had rendered him unfit for business for several months. The sheriff substitute convinced Dawson not to recommend the registrar's dismissal on this occasion,[72] but when Dawson returned to the parish a year later, the registers still displayed 'the effects of dissipation', and Thomson's hand trembled so much that he could not write in the examiner's presence.[73] By the following year, Thomson exhibited 'such prostration of body, and even of mind', that the sheriff ordered him to retire for a season, or face permanent dismissal.[74]

While an admonitory note from the registrar general could sometimes persuade an incompetent registrar to resign, forcibly removing him was so tricky that the parish might not obtain a competent officer until after that registrar had died. However, the appointment of a capable assistant to do most of the work could provide an acceptable solution. As noted above, the sheriff substitute of

Forfarshire twice rejected petitions from the magistrates and town council of Dundee craving the dismissal of Alexander Leask, registrar of the second district. Leask remained in post, but also remained hopelessly inadequate, Examiner Jervise noting in 1862 that

> The few entries which the Registrar has [himself] made in the B[irth] or D[eath] Registers – both in respect of the illegibility of his handwriting, and a want of accuracy, bear evidence, probably more apparent even than on previous occasions, of his utter incapacity to perform the duties of his office in person . . . A common scavenger, or any person that has learned to scribble his name, might hold the office of Registrar with as good grace as Leask does, and as tolerated by the sheriff.[75]

Yet, by ordering Leask to employ an efficient assistant, the sheriff substitute *had* effected a general improvement in the registers, as the registrar general happily informed the provost:

> After all the trouble which was entailed upon the Town Council and myself from the manner in which the Registers of the 2nd District in Dundee were at one time kept, I cannot resist the temptation of calling your attention to the very gratifying contrast which they now present, since the appointment of the present Assistant. The Books are well and clearly written, and . . . I am much gratified with the result.[76]

The GROS depended on its army of parish registrars to produce the raw materials from which the national statistics derived. Through their efforts in scrutinising the registers, weeding out errors, supplying any omissions and chivvying the registrars, the examiners ensured that these raw materials were as complete and reliable as possible, and the system would certainly never have worked properly without their assistance. But, given the financial hardship that numerous registrars suffered, the fact that they were essentially part-time officers, and the less than optimum environments within which they operated, it is rather remarkable that so many of them managed to keep their registers reasonably well; and the success of Scottish civil registration can perhaps only be truly appreciated in this context.

### Acknowledgements

The research for this chapter was undertaken with the support of the Wellcome Trust, grant 069811/Z/02/Z/AW/HH, and with the co-operation of the registrar general for Scotland.

**Notes**

1. Turnbull, W.B., *Scottish Parochial Registers: Memoranda of the State of the Parochial Registers of Scotland, whereby is Clearly Shown the Imperative Necessity for a National System of Regular Registration* (Edinburgh, 1849), xiii.
2. Seton, G., *Sketch of the History and Imperfect Condition of the Parochial Records of Births, Deaths, and Marriages in Scotland, in Illustration of the Important Advantages which would be Derived from the Introduction of a System of Compulsory Registration* (Edinburgh, 1854), 48–9.
3. See Cameron, A., 'The Establishment of Civil Registration in Scotland', *Historical Journal* 50 (2007), 377–95, at 380–1.
4. There was, however, no obligation to register an *irregular* marriage that had been established by a verbal expression of consent, or by a promise of marriage followed by sexual intercourse. See Cameron, 'Establishment of Civil Registration', 9, 11.
5. Fees were applicable in exceptional circumstances, such as when a couple requested the registrar to attend their marriage ceremony and register it there and then. Fines were incurred for failure to intimate a birth within twenty-one days, a death within eight days, or a marriage within three days of the event.
6. This is also the case for registrars in England. See Mills, D., Wheeler, R. and Woollard, M., 'Some Comparative Perspectives on Two Early-Victorian Registrars of Births and Deaths in Rural Lincolnshire in the Context of National Legislation', *Local Population Studies* 79 (2007), 8–22, at 8.
7. *Regulations for the Duties of District Examiners of Registers of Births, Deaths and Marriages* (Edinburgh, January 1857), 6. By 1861, the number of districts and examiners had been reduced to six. See National Archives of Scotland (NAS), GRO1/472, Letter Book (Out-Letters) 1861, W.P. Dundas to the secretary to the Treasury, 17 June 1861.
8. When a representative from the General Register Office for England and Wales came to evaluate the Scottish system in 1871, he found that many of the session clerks appointed as registrars in 1855 were still in office. Whitaker, E., '1871 Report on Registration in Scotland', General Register Office for Scotland Library, 16–2.03, 8.
9. NAS, GRO1/2, Examiners' Notes: Registers of 1856, Report of Alfred List, 135.
10. See, for example, NAS, GRO1/291, Letters Concerning Elections and Appointments of Registrars and Assistants for September and October 1854, extract of minutes of a meeting of the parochial board of Kilmalcolm [sic], 4 November 1854.
11. GRO1/2, Report of Alfred List, 66; NAS, GRO1/4: Examiners' Notes: Registers of 1858, Report of Andrew Jervise (not paginated).
12. NAS, GRO1/5, Examiners' Notes: Registers of 1859, Report of James Dawson, 195, 200–1.
13. GRO1/3, Examiners' Notes: Registers of 1857, Report of Andrew Jervise on behalf of Robert Dundas Fergusson (not paginated).
14. GRO1/2, Report of Robert Gordon (not paginated).
15. GRO1/5, Report of James Dawson, 197.
16. See, for example, NAS, GRO1/1: Examiners' Notes: Registers of 1855, Report of Alexander Nicolson, parish of Ratho (not paginated).
17. GRO1/2, Report of Alfred List, 34 verso.
18. NAS, GRO1/6, Examiners' Notes: Registers of 1860, Report of Andrew Jervise, 6; NAS, GRO1/7, Examiners' Notes: Registers of 1861, Report of Andrew Jervise, 33, 58.
19. See GRO1/1, Report of George Bell, 39–40.
20. GRO1/5, Report of Robert Gordon (not paginated).
21. GRO1/2, Report of Alfred List, 116 verso, 117 verso.
22. GRO1/4, Report of Alfred List (not paginated).
23. GRO1/2, Report of Alfred List, 57 verso.
24. GRO1/1, Report of George Bell, 6–7.

25. GRO1/4, Report of Henry Clarence Gordon (not paginated); GRO1/7, Report of Gibson Stott, 37.
26. GRO1/1, Report of George Bell, 13.
27. GRO1/1, Report of George Bell, 6.
28. GRO1/1, Report of Andrew Jervise, 5; GRO1/4, Report of Robert Dundas Fergusson (not paginated).
29. GRO1/6, Report of Andrew Jervise, 80–1.
30. GRO1/1, Report of Alfred List, 57; GRO1/7, Report of George Bell, 33.
31. GRO1/5, Report of Alfred List (not paginated).
32. GRO1/7, Report of Gibson Stott (not paginated).
33. GRO1/4, Report of Alfred List, 73; GRO1/5, Report of Henry Clarence Gordon (not paginated).
34. See, for example, GRO1/1, Report of Alfred List, 84, parish of Moy; GRO1/7, report of Henry Clarence Gordon, 161, parish of Kirktown.
35. GRO1/1, Report of Alexander Nicolson (not paginated); GRO1/2, Report of Alfred List, 115–16.
36. GRO1/2, Report of Alfred List, 124–5.
37. NAS, GRO1/473, Letter Book (Out-Letters), Jan.–Dec. 1862, W.P. Dundas to town clerk of Glasgow, 23 April 1862.
38. NAS, GRO1/503, Letter Book (Out-Letters), 1892, Stair Agnew to sheriff of Caithness, 6 October 1892, enclosing a copy of the opinion of the law officers of the crown for Scotland, 12 December 1855.
39. *Regulations for the Duties of Registrars of Births, Deaths and Marriages, and of Assistant-Registrars* (Edinburgh, January 1855), 6; *Regulations for the Duties of Registrars of Births, Deaths and Marriages, and of Assistant-Registrars* (Edinburgh, December 1855), 6.
40. GRO1/3, Report of Alexander Nicolson (not paginated).
41. GRO1/3, Report of Andrew Jervise (not paginated).
42. NAS, SRO8/79A, Letters to deputy clerk register [W.P. Dundas] 1856, Mr Dundas of Arniston [to W.P. Dundas], 1 October 1856; NAS, GRO1/466, Letter Book (Out-Letters), July 1855–May 1856, W.P. Dundas to Major Graham, Somerset House, 19 November 1855.
43. See, for example, NAS, GRO1/442, Miscellaneous Letters Received, 1892, James Drew, Newton Stewart, to registrar general, 12 January 1892; GRO1/503, registrar general to James Drew, Newton Stewart, 14 January 1892. Only a very few parishes ignored these warnings – see, for example, GRO1/503, Stair Agnew to sheriff of Caithness, 6 October 1892.
44. GRO1/503, Stair Agnew to sheriff of Caithness, 6 October 1892.
45. GRO1/2, Report of Andrew Jervise (not paginated); GRO1/7, Report of Andrew Jervise, 68; GRO1/5, Report of Andrew Jervise, 47.
46. GRO1/7, Report of Gibson Stott, 82 and Report of George Bell, 66.
47. GRO1/6, Report of George Bell, 62.
48. GRO1/4, Report of Andrew Jervise (not paginated). Section 63 provided for the correction of erroneous entries on the authority of the sheriff. Those who wilfully made false entries in the registers could be imprisoned for up to two years.
49. GRO1/4, Report of Andrew Jervise (not paginated). See also GRO1/1, Report of Alfred List, 82, parish of Tain; GRO1/5, Report of Andrew Jervise (not paginated); GRO1/7, Report of Gibson Stott (not paginated).
50. GRO1/6, Report of George Bell (not paginated).
51. GRO1/1, Report of Alfred List, 70.
52. GRO1/1, Report of James Dawson (not paginated).
53. GRO1/6, Report of George Bell, 88.
54. GRO1/2, Report of James Dawson, 44.
55. GRO1/7, Report of Andrew Jervise, 59.
56. GRO1/6, Report of Andrew Jervise, 84–5.

57.  NAS, GRO1/504, Letter Book (Out-Letters) 1893, Stair Agnew to registrar of Newington, 15 July 1893.
58.  NAS, GRO1/443, Miscellaneous Letters Received 1893, Mabelle A. Balfour, 11 Warrender Park Crescent, Edinburgh, to registrar general, received 15 July 1893.
59.  NAS, GRO1/226, Letters Received from Local Registrars, Registration Districts K–Y, 1893, registrar of Newington to registrar general, 17 July 1893.
60.  The examiners sometimes commented on this: see GRO1/2, Report of Henry Clarence Gordon (not paginated).
61.  See, for example, NAS, GRO1/376, Miscellaneous Letters Received, May–August 1861, chairman of parochial board of Glencoe to registrar general, 27 July 1861, enclosing copy from registrar of Glencoe to chairman of parochial board, 24 July 1861.
62.  18 & 19 Vict. (1855), c. 29, section 2.
63.  NAS, GRO1/474, Letter Book (Out-Letters) 1863, W.P. Dundas to Sir Robert Peel, Irish Office, London, 29 January 1863.
64.  NAS, GRO1/273, Letters Received from Sheriffs, Sheriff Clerks and Procurators Fiscal, 1860-1, sheriff clerk depute, Dundee, to registrar general, 17 January 1860, enclosing certified copy of interlocutor dated 11 January 1860.
65.  NAS, GRO1/471, Letter Book (Out-Letters) 1860–1, G. Seton [GROS secretary] to town clerk of Dundee, 24 November 1860.
66.  NAS, GRO1/384, Miscellaneous Letters Received, 1861, town clerk of Dundee to G. Seton, 7 February 1861, enclosing 'Copy Interlocutor in Causa the Magistrates and Town Council of Dundee v. Alexander Leask, Dundee, 6 February 1861'; GRO1/471, G. Seton to town clerk of Dundee, 8 February 1861.
67.  See, for example, NAS, GRO1/472, W.P. Dundas to chairman of parochial board of Kirkmabreck, 10 June 1861 and W.P. Dundas to chairman of parochial board of Kirkmabreck, 27 June 1861; GRO1/376, copy of minute of a special meeting of the parochial board of Kirkmabreck, 25 June 1861.
68.  In 1857, for example, Examiner Nicolson reported: 'Salaries . . . I am glad to say, are becoming general.' GRO1/2, Report of Alexander Nicolson (not paginated).
69.  23 & 24 Vict. (1860), c. 85, section 8.
70.  GRO1/2, Report of Andrew Jervise (not paginated); GRO1/3, Report of Robert Gordon (not paginated).
71.  GRO1/6, Report of Andrew Jervise, 46.
72.  GRO1/2, Report of James Dawson, 112.
73.  GRO1/3, Report of James Dawson, 34–5.
74.  GRO1/4, Report of James Dawson, 75.
75.  GRO1/7, Report of Andrew Jervise, 7–8.
76.  GRO1/473, W.P. Dundas to provost of Dundee, 19 March 1862.

# 6

# Public Information, Private Lives

## Dr James Craufurd Dunlop and the Collection of Vital Statistics in Scotland, 1904–30

### Gayle Davis and Rosemary Elliot

In 1925, the registrar general for Scotland, Dr James Craufurd Dunlop, commented at length on proposed changes to the English registration system, which included additions to the birth registration system and the introduction of stillbirth registration. He stated that he failed to see 'any great advantage' in obtaining additional personal information for the purposes of registration, and described one question in particular as 'quite uncalled for'.[1] Dunlop's remarks, and indeed the proposals he was commenting on, strike at the heart of one of the most notable features of modern government: the ever-increasing central collection of personal information for the purposes of managing and reshaping social and economic life. According to Edward Higgs, the late nineteenth and early twentieth centuries brought the foundation and expansion of the modern 'information state'. This effected changes to the census and to civil registration, as well as instituting new forms of record keeping which facilitated central taxation and the mobilisation of the population during two world wars. Higgs sees this central collection of data not merely as a tool of domination and surveillance, but as 'underpinning a whole raft of rights and benefits that has helped incorporate the masses into the structures of the modern nation state'.[2]

This vast expansion of data gathering was central to governmental strategies that addressed one of the most pressing social and political concerns of the early twentieth century, namely, the quality and quantity of the population. These concerns were expressed within debates on differential fertility, infant mortality and national efficiency; debates that crossed medical, political and ideological boundaries.[3] A key impetus was the disastrous performance of Britain in the second Boer War, following which the reports of the Royal Commission on Physical Training (Scotland) in 1903 and the Interdepartmental Committee on Physical Deterioration in 1904 revealed the substantial health problems of many working-class children.[4] Addressing these concerns legitimated public policies invading private space, taking government beyond its traditional realms and into the family through measures directed at motherhood and the health of children. Such measures, including health visitors, antenatal programmes, infant welfare centres, free school meals and school health inspections, relied upon an increasing amount of information for co-ordination and monitoring purposes.[5]

At the same time, the growing eugenics movement was concerned with population health and the quality of the race, particularly the issue of differential fertility.[6] Debates centred on whether state intervention served merely to promote the survival of 'unfit' members of society, thereby contributing to the deterioration of the population, or whether state measures improved overall health. Population statistics were crucial to these debates, as, for example, in the disputes between Arthur Newsholme, chief medical officer to the Local Government Board, George Newman, chief medical officer to the Ministry of Health, and Karl Pearson, professor of eugenics at University College, London, over the cause of infant mortality.[7] The registrar general for England and Wales from 1909 to 1920, Bernard Mallet, himself a eugenicist, believed that civil registration should be central to the expanding public health system, and argued in a lengthy memorandum that '[t]he statistical data available [were] insufficient to meet the growing demands made upon the Registrar-General for information as to the facts of natality, fertility and mortality'.[8] Mallet proposed substantial reforms to the English registration system, including making registrars part of the staff of the medical officers of health (MOsH) in urban areas. MOsH would transmit registration information directly to the registrar general, replacing superintendent registrars and thus tying registration more closely to the developing public health system. Although these reforms were not adopted during Mallet's term of office, the following decades did see increases in the amount and types of data collected by registrars, mainly for public health and medical reasons.

This emphasis on public health in fact fitted into a long tradition within the English General Register Office (GRO). Concerns with public health, mortality and disease had shaped its work from the appointment in 1839 of the first medical statistician, William Farr, onwards.[9] In Scotland, however, the concerns of actuaries, lawyers and the Church sat alongside those of medical men. The public records of Scotland had a long tradition of resting in the hands of legal men, and the first registrar general for Scotland, William Pitt Dundas, was an advocate by training.[10] Indeed, until 1920, the Scottish registrar general held this post alongside that of the deputy clerk register and was required by law to be a member of the Scottish Bar of not less than ten years standing.[11] While the Royal College of Physicians of Edinburgh (RCPE) was influential in securing a medical superintendent of statistics for the General Register Office for Scotland (GROS) at its inception in 1855, the first incumbent in this position, Dr James Stark, was so dogged by ill-health that his reports appeared up to six years late.[12] Moreover, for much of the nineteenth century, the work of the GROS was shaped primarily by statutory requirements, and, although the office was in close contact with MOsH and certifying doctors, it is hard to find any substantial contribution to public health debates at a national level.

However, in 1919, the post of registrar general for Scotland was separated from that of deputy clerk register when the administration of the GROS was brought under the auspices of the new Scottish Board of Health.[13] The following year, the stipulation that the registrar general for Scotland be a member of the Scottish Bar was relaxed to allow the appointment of Dr James Dunlop, who had been the medical superintendent of statistics at the GROS since 1904.[14] Prior to his appointment to the GROS, Dunlop was already a renowned medical man who had worked as a paediatrician at the Royal Hospital for Sick Children in Edinburgh. In addition, he was an inspector under the Inebriates Act for Scotland, and a medical advisor to the prison commissioner for Scotland.[15] Dunlop held the office of registrar general alongside that of medical superintendent of statistics from 1921 until 1930, making him the first and only medical man to be appointed as registrar general in Scotland.

Dunlop's appointment to this post, given his medical credentials and the repositioning of the GROS within the Scottish Board of Health, arguably presented an opportunity for the GROS to align its work more closely with contemporary public health and medical concerns. During Dunlop's period of office, the issues most visibly connected to public health were the 1911 fertility census, the introduction of stillbirth registration, and changes to death registration. The introduction of national registration during the First World War, while not directly a medical question, also raised related issues concerning the interface between private information and public policy that were germane to the expanding boundaries of the information state. Using these four issues as case studies, this chapter explores whether the period of Dunlop's employment could be said to mark the transition from a legal to a medical framework for the GROS.

### The Early Years: The 1911 Fertility Census

As medical superintendent of statistics, Dunlop was responsible for the statistical branch of the GROS. As its name suggests, this office produced the statistical abstracts for the annual reports of the registrar general for Scotland, as well as the monthly and quarterly abstracts.[16] By the early twentieth century, these reports had become very formulaic, and provided the figures pertaining to births, marriages, deaths and vaccinations in Scotland. Unlike in England, the report provided only a sparse interpretation of these statistics, and this did not change when Dunlop entered the office.[17] Dunlop also responded to individual statistical inquiries, was responsible for deciding classifications of cause of death where there was uncertainty, oversaw the census, and made population estimates between census years.

In the first years of his appointment, Dunlop does not appear to have had a large presence in the correspondence of the office beyond the terms of his appointment, although in 1906 he published a paper on occupational mortality which drew on the 1901 census figures. Here it is clear that he was in contact with Karl Pearson, one of the foremost statisticians of the day and a proponent of eugenic views. The problem Dunlop addressed in this paper was how to state mortality rates with any certainty in occupations where there were small numbers employed with varying age distribution. Dunlop discussed various statistical methods used across other such studies, including an approach suggested to him by Pearson, before going on to present his own method.[18] This was primarily a statistical paper, which set out the results and offered no interpretation on the implications of its findings. This concentration on the statistics was to become characteristic of Dunlop's approach to his job, and is notable in his subsequent published work. Indeed, one of his obituaries reveals his accomplishments in this sphere, noting that the Faculty of Actuaries awarded him 'the signal honour of [becoming] an Honorary Fellow – a distinction very sparingly given and never before or since to a medical man'.[19]

In contrast to his counterparts at the English GRO, there is little evidence that Dunlop subscribed to eugenic thought while employed within the GROS, or indeed in his previous work. In his capacity as medical advisor to the prison commissioner, Dunlop proposed that 'weak-minded delinquents' be detained without limit of time. While this could be interpreted as eugenically motivated, his proposal was in fact to rehabilitate such offenders so as to avoid future imprisonments. In a study of 85 habitual reoffenders, published in the *Scots Law Times* in 1902, Dunlop concluded that such people reoffended because they were unable to take care of themselves and were being failed by the existing system. He proposed that specialist institutions be set up to 'strengthen [such habitual reoffenders] to take care of themselves' or to house them until 'a responsible guardian was found to take care of them'.[20] Thus, while Dunlop was concerned to alleviate the social cost of habitual reoffending and imprisonment, his writing did not employ the language of eugenics and hereditary fitness. Rather, it was infused with the idea of using social measures to create socially and morally responsible citizens who were not a burden on society.

Dunlop's views on contemporary debates around eugenic thought, particularly differential fertility, can be seen in his criticism of proposals for the 1911 fertility census. In 1909, Dr T.H.C. Stevenson was appointed medical superintendent of statistics and Bernard Mallet was appointed registrar general at the GRO in London. One of the first things that Stevenson and Mallet did was to introduce two extra columns to the 1911 census, relating to duration of marriage and number of children from that marriage, additions that historians have often held to have had a eugenic motivation.[21] The proposal for these two columns came from the Census Committee of the Royal Statistical Society in 1908, of which Mallet was a member.[22] The proposals were endorsed in 1910 by Stevenson, who stressed that these additional columns were intended to 'definitely determin[e] the very important question of the relative degrees of fertility of the various grades of society', as well as ascertaining 'an accurate comparison of the fertility of women of differing ages . . . [and] the bearing of the wife's occupation on fertility'. In addition, it was hoped that these columns would reveal the influence of duration of marriage and age of the parents upon infant mortality and 'at what age, women under different circumstances should marry'.[23]

However, Dunlop did not share his English counterparts' enthusiasm for these additional columns. In a stinging memorandum, he criticised the fertility questions on the grounds that they were intrusive, concerns that were echoed by some MPs in the House of Commons when the subject was debated in 1910.[24] He enquired how the additional census questions would deal with the contentious issues of stillborn children, illegitimate children and children of separated parents where there was the possibility of duplication in their returns. To ask about such things was, in his view, 'inquisitorial' and would 'rightly' be resented by parents. Dunlop also questioned whether the proposed 'natality tables' would in fact provide enough reliable information to study the intended questions and whether, indeed, these questions were 'of sufficient practical importance to justify the expenditure of a considerable sum of public money'.[25] This appears to be the first exposition of Dunlop's view in relation to the broader public health concerns that were shaping English political discourse at this time.

Although Dunlop was ultimately compelled to include the contentious questions, his subsequent report was a much sparser affair than the corresponding English report. While Stevenson began with a long discussion of the possible causes of the nation's fertility decline, Dunlop did not engage with any of the intellectual questions that had prompted the survey. Presenting the results to the Royal Statistical Society in 1914, he opened with the statement:

> I think I am right in asserting that it was principally on the initiative of this Society that questions relative to the fertility of marriage were inserted into householder's schedules . . . and the fertility of marriage made a subject of censal study. Under these circumstances I feel that I am not called on to make any preliminary remarks either in defence of the interest or importance of the subject, or in defence of my asking you to give me a hearing.[26]

Of course, one may read his assertion of the importance and interest in the subject in two ways: either at face value or as a way of avoiding the need to declare his views on the subject. However, it does seem that his overriding concern was with presenting statistics rather than interpreting them or becoming involved in the politics surrounding them. While he noted that the groups that had the lowest fertility were professional, he also found that domestic occupations had low fertility. Dunlop formed the uncontentious conclusion that decreasing fertility of marriage in Scotland could 'be accepted as an established statistical fact, it having been evidenced by a continuing fall of the birth rate', a fall that his own report demonstrated 'in a clear and conclusive manner'.[27]

One possible explanation for this more pragmatic approach is geographical distance from the politics of Whitehall. Since the first decade of the twentieth century, figures such as Robert Morant and the Webbs had been campaigning for a central body to co-ordinate public health and medical services, and Mallet was keen to situate the GRO at the heart of any potential new body.[28] However, Dunlop was seconded to the War Office as director of statistics at the outbreak of the war, and subsequently divided his time between London and Edinburgh, so clearly it was not only geography that underpinned his differing approach to public health issues and the role of registration within them.[29]

### National Registration

Similar concerns around personal privacy and economic pragmatism can be seen in Dunlop's correspondence on the subject of national registration. The National Registration Act was passed in 1915 in the wake of a perceived manpower shortage, in order to provide a register of all men and women aged between 15 and 65 as a way of stocktaking the nation's manpower resources.[30] The Bill's passage through Parliament was enormously contentious, as it was widely seen as a prelude to military and industrial conscription, and to betray British traditions of individual liberty. However, those opposing the Bill were depicted as 'unpatriotic', and the passage of the National Registration Bill legitimated the gathering of personal information (name, date of birth, address, nationality, marital status, occupation and employment details) on an unprecedented scale.[31]

The GRO and GROS were the bodies charged with administering national registration in England and Scotland respectively. As Elliot has argued else-where, this new responsibility provided Bernard Mallet with the opportunity to develop his earlier recommendations for a restructured registration system south of the Border.[32] From 1916 onwards, Mallet advanced proposals for a permanent universal register to be maintained after the end of the war, once again drawing on questions of public health, particularly infant mortality, as his justification.[33]

However, there was a notable lack of support from the GROS for any expansion of the boundaries of the information state. The GROS was a small office and its staff were stretched to the limits by the increased workload caused by the war, particularly national registration. The administration of the National Register was extremely problematic, due to a lack of communication between the GROS and Whitehall. There was no representative from the GROS on the various parliamentary registration committees over the summer of 1915, and the Scots were a good way into setting up their register before English plans were finalised. The Scots, believing that the register was required for occupational data, had organised their register alphabetically by district for ease of maintenance, and set up a card index which could easily be accessed by officials from the Labour Exchange and the Ministry of Munitions for occupational information. However, as it became clear subsequently that the purpose of the National Register was to facilitate military recruitment as well as to avoid labour shortages in industries crucial to the war effort, problems emerged. The English organised their register by occupation, and 'starred' those in occupations exempt from recruiting. All the original registration forms of men between 19 and 41 were copied on to pink forms for the military authorities, who then used the data for recruiting. Men who were not in exempt occupations were visited up to three times, and their reasons for not joining were recorded on a parallel index.[34]

Given that the Scots had already organised their registration forms alphabetically, Dunlop complained bitterly about this 'additional' task of providing pink forms (that is, duplicates of the originals) in occupational groups. The GROS had already released many of the volunteers who had done the original sorting work. Further, Dunlop expressed grave misgivings about the purpose of the pink forms, the extra occupational coding operations which they necessitated, and the fact that this coding was to be performed by untrained volunteers. The coding process, he argued, put a responsibility on the volunteers that was 'to say the least of it . . . questionable'.[35] He argued that 'the purpose of dividing a section of the community into recruitable and non-recruitable' was a process that required 'absolute and individual accuracy', and one that simply could not be entrusted to mere volunteers.[36] After all, this division would decide who was to be sent to war, a matter of life and death well beyond the traditional boundaries of the work of the GROS. Concerns about the privacy of the individual were also raised. Supposedly single domestic servants were asked to declare their marital status, for example, whilst the GROS received a steady stream of letters asking for the whereabouts of absent husbands, information that they could not disclose.[37]

In discussions around extending national registration to create a universal peacetime register, the Scots were more focused on pragmatic matters such as organisation and cost than expanding the remit of their registration office. The experience of rationing drove home the financial and practical implications of expanding the information state. During the latter years of the First World War, local registrars were drawn into the administration of rationing as they were required to issue application forms to new parents, collect unused coupons when a death was registered, and submit default forms to the Ministry of Food when relatives refused to hand back coupons.[38] Local registrars complained loudly about the amount of extra work they were required to do without adequate remuneration, and pointed out that the service had become increasingly stretched during the war.[39] The GROS remained ideologically opposed to adopting Mallet's recommendations for a universal peacetime register, with an apparent consensus in Edinburgh that state apparatus should not collect unnecessary data or use that information in a way that might do harm. In the face of a broader lack of political will and little public support for his proposals, Mallet failed in his attempts to have national registration extended into peacetime.

### Registration of Stillbirths

Similar economic and moral concerns about increased state collection of personal data were raised in relation to the issue of stillbirth registration. While compulsory civil registration of births and deaths was introduced to Scotland in 1855, requiring any child born alive – no matter how brief its survival – to have both its birth and death registered, the stillborn child was not incorporated into the registration system until 1939 through the Registration of Still-Births (Scotland) Act 1938.[40] A similar time lag can be charted in England and Wales, where civil registration was introduced in 1836 but stillbirth registration remained absent until the Births and Deaths Registration Act 1926.[41] This long omission appears to have occurred because the registration system was designed to record the birth of legal rather than biological persons, as civil registration was intended to improve the recording of lines of descent and the security of title to property. As John Glaister, the early-twentieth-century doyen of Scottish medical jurisprudence, noted, 'the still-born child . . . never was "a reasonable creature in being, and under the King's peace," [and thus] the State can have no concern over an infant which never had a legal existence'.[42] The stillborn child was therefore treated by the GROS as if it had never existed, and registered as neither a birth nor a death.

The non-registration of stillbirths and their absence from the vital statistics of Scotland gave rise to a range of fears during the late nineteenth and early twentieth centuries. Statistically, there was concern that accurate rates of fertility, infant and maternal mortality and morbidity were impossible to ascertain without the inclusion of stillbirth data, seriously hampering public health administration and medical research. Legally and morally, there was concern that some stillbirths were in fact cases of infanticide, the 'stillbirth' label merely a convenient classification to avoid suspicion. There was no legal obligation on doctors to certify a child stillborn in either Scotland or England and, as the Scottish Board of Health noted, it was not the general practice among doctors to do so.[43] This concern was increased by the ease with which the stillborn child could be disposed of; buried without the production of any form of medical certificate or declaration.[44] Thus, according to the *British Medical Journal* in 1909, it was, in the present state of the law, 'perfectly easy not only to kill intentionally and with the basest motives a perfectly healthy child during or immediately after birth, without running the risk of a charge of murder, but [also] to secure its interment without a medical certificate and without inquiry'.[45]

Such concerns came to the fore during Dunlop's tenure as registrar general. Within his correspondence on the issue of stillbirth, the need to protect the individual from potentially intrusive state surveillance again emerged as a prominent theme. While the 1926 legislation that introduced stillbirth registration south of the Border was not considered suitable for application to Scotland as a whole,[46] the Scottish Board of Health recognised that certain aspects of it, and notably stillbirth registration, would be of value to Scotland. The board therefore invited Dunlop to give the GROS's observations upon the 1926 Act.[47]

In his response to its various 'controversial principles', and despite the many serious problems relating to lack of stillbirth registration, Dunlop stated himself to be strongly against the extension of the registration system to the stillborn child. While he recognised the value of such information 'for statistical purposes pure and simple', he stressed that this did not necessitate civil registration. His main arguments were legal: that all events registered at this time dealt with 'civil or individual rights in some form', whereas for a stillborn child 'with no separate existence, no civil rights, and not even a name', there appeared to be little, if anything, to record permanently in a register. Thus, as he asked: 'Why encumber either a birth register, a death register, or even a special register with useless detail?'[48]

In addition, Dunlop offered more humanitarian reasons for his rejection of such registration, suggesting that it would be 'distinctly objectionable' in 'expos[ing] to public search and extract (registers [being] open to search and extract) private and intimate detail with which the public [was] not concerned'.[49] Such sentiments echoed earlier English arguments, connected to private members' bills in 1908 and 1914, that stillbirth registration 'would involve considerable public expenditure' and contain 'objectionable incidental matter'.[50] Finally, Dunlop's thrifty pragmatism shone through when he urged that regulation of the disposal of stillborn children could 'surely . . . be obtained without the expense of permanent record'.[51]

Not surprisingly perhaps, given his medical qualifications, Dunlop held the whole stillbirth subject to be 'essentially a medical or medico-legal matter and one much more akin to the functions of a medical man than to those of a lay Registrar'. He recommended that the MOsH be given the duty of keeping a record of still-births, to provide greater medical scrutiny and to 'obviate the great disadvantage of publicity'.[52] Through the Early Notification of Births Bill, introduced as an adoptive measure in 1907, and made compulsory through the Notification of Births (Extension) Act 1915, MOsH had already assumed responsibility for noti-fication to the local health authority of every birth that had reached a gestation period of 28 weeks within 36 hours of its occurrence, including the stillborn child. Dunlop's approach appears to have been pragmatic, attempting to limit any exten-sion to the duties of the already busy, and non-medically qualified, registrar; a theme that recurs with respect to medical certification of adult death.

It was not until 1 January 1939, and two Scottish registrars general later, that death registration north of the Border was extended to include any child born without sign of life after the twenty-eighth week of pregnancy. The Registration of Stillbirths (Scotland) Act was effected in 1938, amidst growing concern over persistently high levels of maternal mortality – as high as six maternal deaths per thousand births in Scotland by the mid-1930s – and infant mortality – 82 per thousand births for Scotland, as compared to 59 for England and Wales, and 31 for New Zealand.[53] There was also some degree of embarrassment that Scotland was 'almost alone among civilised nations' in not providing registration of stillbirths by this time.[54] Scottish stillbirth registration was ultimately implemented as it was in England, with certain modifications made to the normal rules of death certifica-tion. The underlying principle was that stillbirth registration was a contribution to statistics and part of the machinery to protect infant life rather than a matter of public record for public use. The public were therefore deprived of 'their usual right' of obtaining extracts from the resulting stillbirth register, no duplicate was made of that register, and its details were not made publicly accessible.[55] This would suggest that Dunlop was not atypical within registration circles, for both his English counterpart and his Scottish successors took similar steps to resist the potentially intrusive nature of state surveillance into the 'poignant tragedy of a dead child'.[56] Moreover, while medical arguments appear ultimately to have been the most weighty in the successful journey through Parliament of the Registration of Stillbirths Bill,[57] such GROS correspondence suggests some reluctance to the transition from a legal to a medical framework.

### Registration of Death

Moving to death registration more generally, civil registration of death was compulsory in Scotland from 1 January 1855 through the Registration (Scotland) Act 1854. This Act stipulated that the nearest relative present when death occurred must report it to the parish registrar within eight days, and that any medical man who had attended the deceased during his or her last illness was legally required to send the registrar a certificate of the cause of death within 14 days. In 1860 the time limit was reduced to seven days, after which, if no certificate had been received, the registrar was to apply pressure by writing to the doctor, enclosing a blank certificate for completion and prompt return. If there was no medical attendant, a relative or member of the household was obliged to certify the death and to give his or her opinion as to the cause.[58]

The theme of what we might term 'economy' is again fairly prominent within Dunlop's death registration correspondence. During his period as registrar general, various requests were made for him to elicit additional information from his registrars, most of which appear to have fallen upon deaf ears. A number of these requests related to the issue of maternal mortality. Glasgow's MOH, A.K. Chalmers, asked whether registrars could be obliged to record all cases where the death of a woman occurred within four weeks of the birth of her child, in a bid to ascertain more exactly how many deaths were related to childbirth.[59] Chalmers argued that, as it stood, many death certificates 'bore no indication' of this relationship even in the death of mothers within ten days of confinement. However, Dunlop responded that he was 'loath to make a move' in this regard as he considered that it would 'not be practicable or desirable to let registrars interfere with what is or should be a deliberate medical opinion', and in addition that it was quite possible for a woman to die within a month of child birth 'from a cause quite unconnected with it'.[60] Dunlop appears to have adopted a laissez-faire attitude in an attempt both to limit the responsibility placed on his registrars, and to demonstrate that the registration system valued the expertise of physicians. As he argued, upon further pressure from Chalmers: 'We must trust the medical profession to give us reasonable and correct certificates even although we are aware that certification is far from perfect.'[61]

Dunlop was similarly reluctant to augment his registrars' workload when, first in 1921, and then in 1928, the MOsH of Aberdeen and Glasgow respectively requested that registrars obtain information on housing accommodation as an integral part of the death registration process.[62] While the Scottish registrar general was noted to 'quite recognise' the potential significance of such information, he was said to be 'rather strongly of opinion that he could not expediently add to the death questionnaire a further non-statutory enquiry'.[63] As he noted privately shortly after his retirement from this post, 'if the door [was] opened to enlarging the questionnaire, there would be no end to it'.[64] This economical stance appears to have continued with Dunlop's successor, Andrew Froude (1876–1945), a career civil servant, who argued similarly that, while he 'fully appreciate[d] the utility and importance' of such additional labours, it 'would be going too far to impose . . . further obligation on the Registrars and on Informants without some better basis than their own goodwill', particularly since the death questionnaire was already 'full to capacity'. The Scottish registrar general continued to turn down the various suggestions made 'for the obtaining of extraneous information through the medium of the registrars', despite the contribution that such information might clearly make to medical research.[65]

Stillbirth registration was not the only aspect of the Births and Deaths Registration Act 1926 that Dunlop found objectionable. One of the English Act's main provisions was to make the certification of the fact of death by a medical practitioner or coroner compulsory, so as to allay fears of the possibility of insurance fraud, murder or premature burial in cases where a doctor had not seen the body after death. Dunlop deemed this 'a matter of medical-legal rather than registration importance', but objected to one practical difficulty that might impinge on the registration process as a result – that any such 'complication in death registration would tend to a delay . . . [in the obtaining of funeral monies and other insurance benefits] which would cause both the Department and the public very considerable inconvenience' and expense.[66] Therefore Dunlop was not simply concerned with the resources of the registration system, but also with the more private resources of those individuals attempting to register a death.

This is not to say that Dunlop was unconcerned with the accurate medical certification of death in cases where a doctor had attended the deceased. He received a number of queries from physicians who wished clarification on a particular aspect of the death certification process, or who wished to alter a given cause of death upon the results of a post-mortem examination. His standard response began by noting that he 'always welcome[d]' such correspondence.[67] This is understandable given the difficulties those converting death certificates into the nation's vital statistics experienced in some cases, a fact that Dunlop was only too aware of from his own experience as medical superintendent of statistics. At a medical meeting on death certification, much quoted in the press, Dunlop 'created great amusement' with some of the causes of death that had come to his attention in recent years, including 'result of falling into ditch', 'senile decay – duration five days', and 'probably decapitation', all of which were said to show 'how some medical men might go astray'.[68] The returns of procurators-fiscal in particular were noted to be 'very often defective', being too general or ill-defined for tabulation purposes by certifying deaths from, for example, 'natural causes' or 'sudden death'.[69] Dunlop deplored the 'anomalous position of a Registrar, who [did] not claim to have medico-legal knowledge, being called on to decide what certificates [were] satisfactory and what unsatisfactory'.[70]

As registrar general, Dunlop's medical training allowed him to police the situation more thoroughly than previous incumbents might have been in a position to. He scrutinised death certificates in some detail, and corresponded regularly with registrars when he considered a death certificate to be lacking in sufficient detail or clarity. Physicians were given strict instructions on the appropriate terminology for the certificate, including a list of terms judged to be indefinite and undesirable, and invited to correspond with Dunlop if in any doubt on the matter.[71] A certificate merely naming the diseased organ was deemed incomplete unless it gave an indication of the nature of the disease; and where tumours or cancers were concerned, both the nature and position of the growth were to be specified.

Yet, as it had been in cases of stillbirth, privacy was a prominent theme within Dunlop's death registration correspondence, and one which conflicted with accurate medical certification of death. This conflict stemmed mainly from the fact that the certificate was not a confidential document, and was generally handed to the relatives or friends of the deceased for transmission to the registrar. Doctors were asked to intimate the exact nature of the disease, but they could struggle as to whether to convey this information to a family when the cause of death would be likely to upset them or when it might conflict with the physician's sworn duty to patient confidentiality. There was said, in particular, to be a 'hesitation . . . to give the show away in such cases as venereal disease and alcoholic abuse'.[72] Attention was particularly focused on this matter by the Royal Commission on Venereal Diseases in 1913.[73] As superintendent of statistics, Dunlop openly admitted in his evidence to the commission that these particular registration figures were loaded with errors both of a 'biased' (deliberate use of a less offensive term) and 'unbiased' (uncertainty or ignorance) nature, and that the amount of deaths from these causes was 'almost certainly considerably greater than shewn by registration'.[74]

Thus, from the outset of his career within the registration office, Dunlop was aware of the problems associated with an open system of death certification. Indeed, it might be said that he conspired with doctors to disguise potentially upsetting terms which could still be 'translated' accurately by statisticians. When one physician enquired whether 'klebs-loeffler bacillus disease' would be acceptable instead of 'diphtheria', Dunlop deemed it a 'perfectly good synonym' that satisfied the requirements.[75] In fact, this view was in conflict with others in the GROS, who believed that medical certificates of cause of death should be 'in terms intelligible to laymen' so that mistakes in interpretation did not creep in.[76] Dunlop was unusual within the GROS in terms of both his detailed medical and statistical understandings of the situation. As in cases of stillbirth, he appears to have been more concerned with the protection of potentially vulnerable individuals from the intrusive state than he was with the entirely accurate compilation of vital statistics.

### Retirement and the Search for a Successor

Throughout Dunlop's career with the GROS, first as medical superintendent of statistics and then as registrar general for Scotland, it is possible to see a pattern emerge in his responses to attempts to integrate a medical and public health agenda into the collection of the nation's vital statistics. Above all, as demonstrated by our four case studies of the 1911 fertility census, national registration, stillbirth and death registration, Dunlop exhibited a consistent resistance to efforts to widen the remit of the GROS and to extend the amount of personal information they collected, whether for medical or other purposes. His correspondence reveals a deep concern to protect the integrity of the office and a keen awareness of the legal parameters of its existence.

The explanation for Dunlop's objections can be found on several levels. On a practical level, there was a concern for economy, particularly economy of manpower, and a wish to protect registration staff from what he deemed to be 'unreasonable' demands upon their time. Thus Dunlop questioned the purpose and reliability of any additional information to be gathered by the registration system, and attempted to establish boundaries around what was practicable for registrars to achieve. This related to both workload and their capabilities in engaging with subject matter that might, for example, require medical or legal training. His concern is evident in relation to both death and stillbirth registration, where Dunlop lamented the inability of registrars to engage with medico-legal matters, believing such matters were better left to trained physicians and MOsH than to the registration system. Similarly, in relation to national registration, he was concerned about coding being done by volunteers for a purpose which lay beyond the traditional remit of the GROS. It is not that Dunlop failed to appreciate the medical and public health advantages of more detailed vital statistics, but, arguably, he wished to maintain the boundaries of expert knowledge. He was keen to delineate spheres of knowledge and to protect the notional boundary that separated registration practice and the production of vital statistics from medical expertise, the expanding public health service and government policy more broadly.

On a more personal level, Dunlop also expressed great anxiety about the potentially 'intrusive' nature of the registration system as the boundaries of the information state were extended into personal lives. Such concerns partly explain his resistance to the 'fertility' columns in the 1911 census, which he perceived as 'inquisitorial'. Dunlop also rejected stillbirth registration in part because he feared that such private and poignant details should not be exposed to public attention. This concern for privacy conflicted with accurate medical certification of adult death, leading him on occasion effectively to 'conspire' with doctors to shield grieving relatives from potentially upsetting causes of death. He appears in such instances to have been more concerned with the protection of vulnerable individuals from the intrusive state than he was with the accurate compilation of the nation's vital statistics, and at all times stressed the need to balance personal privacy with medical or public health gain.

This dual rationale of preserving the boundaries of GROS responsibility whilst recognising the medical and public health need for more detailed vital statistics can also be seen in the discussions surrounding the appointment of Dunlop's successor. Dunlop retired from the post of registrar general for Scotland on 2 September 1930 upon reaching the age limit. Andrew Froude was appointed his successor as registrar general, having served previously as secretary to Dunlop (2 October 1925 to 2 September 1930). However, as Dunlop had jointly held the post of registrar general and superintendent of statistics since 1921, his replacement was not an entirely straightforward exercise. The return to a non-medically qualified registrar general generated discussion of whether or not there was a need for the GROS to make a separate appointment of a medically trained superintendent of statistics.

Both Dunlop and Froude agreed that medical supervision of the country's vital statistics was 'an absolute necessity', and that 'the production of the principal medical statistics in Scotland without medical impress would be too utterly anomalous'.[77] Although the Department of Health for Scotland (DHS) was said to be 'impressed with these propositions', both they and the GROS appear to have agreed that the full-time services of a medical man were not required. A memorandum prior to Dunlop's retirement considered the medical aspects of his statistical work under three headings: dictating the monthly, quarterly and annual reports; deciding the line of reply to statistical enquiries; and deciding how to classify individual causes of death. It was only in the last of these that there was considered to be anything that could not be performed 'quite competently' by the non-medical staff.[78] Even then, medical certificates of cause of death were said to be submitted to Dunlop for classification only because he had requested this procedure, and only in a very small proportion was it claimed that his staff were unable to make 'a definite allocation' without his assistance. It was, however, argued that a superintendent of statistics could usefully 'supplement the experience and skill of the existing staff' by presenting the vital statistical reports in such form as would 'best meet the needs of the medical profession and public health authorities'.

Thus, despite recognition of the importance of a medical man to the job, and recognition of the value placed on vital statistics by the medical community, the GROS and DHS appear to have talked down the need for a full-time medically qualified superintendent of statistics. Part of the reason for this can be found in

Treasury calls for economy. In 1927, Dunlop had been asked to state how many staff would be lost to 'natural wastage', to which he replied that the only member of staff due to retire was himself.[79] However, it is also possible to argue that, by marginalising the medical aspects of the job of the superintendent of statistics, the GROS and DHS were able to argue the case for their preferred replacement.

Both offices agreed that Dr Peter Laird McKinlay was the ideal man for the job. McKinlay was a medical man who had subsequently studied statistics to a high level under Karl Pearson and Major Greenwood. He had also worked on the Medical Research Council Statistics Committee at the London School of Hygiene and Tropical Medicine, concentrating on aspects of infant and maternal mortality, areas of expertise that fitted well within the broader political concerns of this period.[80] McKinlay had recently been appointed to the DHS,[81] and both they and the GROS believed that his appointment to the post of medical super-intendent of statistics would promote co-ordination between the medical statis-tics of both offices.[82] They agreed that McKinlay's duties should be placed under the control of the registrar general, but that he would have authority to instruct the statistical staff. The Treasury approved the appointment, but on the condi-tion that 'no additional remuneration' would be payable for this role given that McKinlay was to hold it concurrently with his appointment as medical officer of the DHS.[83] The GROS concurrently supported the promotion of 'their' McKinlay, Alexander McKinlay, who had been employed as chief clerk in their statistical branch for the last 25 years. For additional remuneration, Alexander McKinlay would take charge of the day-to-day running of the statistical branch, deferring to Peter McKinlay on questions of medical importance.[84]

In implementing this dual appointment, the GROS simultaneously gained the services of a medically-qualified statistician of considerable repute and retained the services of one with considerable GROS experience for little additional expenditure. This solution fulfilled a number of purposes: it provided medical supervision for the production of statistics where necessary, and recognised the importance of vital statistics to public health, but at the same time protected the remit and preoccupation of the GROS, allowing that office to focus upon the production rather than the politics of those statistics. At a time when the amount and types of data collected by registrars for overwhelmingly public health and medical reasons were growing significantly, as perhaps epitomised by the intro-duction of stillbirth registration, this compromise accorded well with views Dunlop expressed throughout his career at the GROS. It is not so much that Dunlop resisted the transition to a medical framework; rather, he wished to be clear about the role of the GROS within such a framework, and the extent to which individual life experiences should be scrutinised for the purposes of government.

## Acknowledgements

This research was funded by the Wellcome Trust, as part of the 'Scottish Way of Birth and Death' project [Grant 069811/Z/O2/Z/AW/HH]. We also gratefully acknowledge the co-operation of the registrar general for Scotland.

## Notes

1. National Archives of Scotland (NAS), GRO 5/887, Dunlop, J., 'Observations on Bill to Amend the Law Relating to the Certification of Deaths and the Disposal of the Dead, 15 Geo. V. Bill 132', 22 May 1925. The question he was referring to specifically related to whether or not a deceased individual had undergone an operation in the twelve months prior to his or her death.
2. Higgs, E., *The Information State in England: The Central Collection of Information on Citizens since 1500* (Basingstoke, 2004), 199–200.
3. Porter, D., *Health, Civilisation and the State: A History of Public Health from Ancient to Modern Times* (London and New York, 1999), 165–95.
4. *Report of the Royal Commission on Physical Training (Scotland)*, Parliamentary Papers, Cd. 1507–8 (1903); *Interdepartmental Committee on Physical Deterioration: Minutes of Evidence*, Parliamentary Papers, Cd. 2210 (1904).
5. Rose, N., *Governing the Soul: The Shaping of the Private Self* (London, 1999),123–34.
6. Soloway, R.A., *Demography and Degeneration: Eugenics and the Declining Birthrate in Twentieth-Century Britain* (Chapel Hill and London, 1990).
7. Lewis, J., *The Politics of Motherhood: Child and Maternal Welfare in England, 1900–1939* (London, 1980), 61–8.
8. The National Archives, London (TNA), RG 28/3, Bernard Mallet, 'Memorandum on the Registration Acts (Births, Deaths and Marriages) with Proposals for their Reform', March 1915.
9. Higgs, E., 'Disease, Febrile Poisons, and Statistics: The Census as a Medical Survey, 1841–1911', *Social History of Medicine* 4 (1991), 465–78; Szreter, S., 'The GRO and the Public Health Movement in Britain, 1837–1914', *Social History of Medicine* 4 (1991), 435–63.
10. *Stair Memorial Encyclopaedia* (Edinburgh, 1990), vol. 19, 301–7.
11. Lord Clerk Register (Scotland) Act 1879, 42 & 43 Vict., c. 44.
12. Cameron, A., 'Medicine, Meteorology and Vital Statistics: The Influence of the Royal College of Physicians of Edinburgh upon Scottish Civil Registration, c.1840–1855', *Journal of the Royal College of Physicians of Edinburgh* 37 (2007), 173–80, at 177.
13. *Stair Memorial Encyclopaedia*, vol. 19, 301–7; Scottish Board of Health Act 1919, 9 & 10 Geo. V, c. 20.
14. Registrar General (Scotland) Act 1970, 10 & 11 Geo. V, c. 69.
15. James Dunlop (1865–1944) was born in Barrhead, Renfrew, and educated in London and Edinburgh. After graduating from the University of Edinburgh in 1887, he embarked upon postgraduate studies in Strasbourg, Vienna and Paris, and was therefore a well-travelled man when he settled back in Scotland. He also worked with the distinguished physiologist Noel Paton in surveying the diet of the poorer classes at the turn of the twentieth century. See Royal College of Physicians of Edinburgh minutes, 'Obituary of James Dunlop', 2 May 1944; Craig, W.S., *History of the Royal College of Physicians of Edinburgh* (Oxford, 1976), 670.
16. NAS, GRO 4/2, James Dunlop to Treasury, 1 July 1927.
17. See *Registrar General for Scotland Annual Reports* from 1855 onwards.
18. Dunlop, J.C., 'Occupational Mortalities', *Edinburgh Medical Journal* 19 (1906), 417–29.

19. Royal College of Physicians of Edinburgh minutes, 'Obituary of James Dunlop', 2 May 1944.
20. Dunlop, J.C., 'The Treatment of Weak-Minded Delinquents', *Scots Law Times* (1902), 29–31, at 31. The 85 cases included a microcephalic, itinerant traveller who was subject to mood swings; a woman of no fixed abode who survived on 'midden [bin] raking' and had been sentenced 26 times for breach of the peace; a woman who had been convicted of prostitution over 60 times, had eight illegitimate children and had been in poorhouses 38 times; and a former soldier who had taken to drink.
21. See, for example, Soloway, *Demography and Degeneration*, 11.
22. NAS, GRO 3/363/16, 'Report of the Census Board of the Royal Statistical Society, 1908/9', undated.
23. Stevenson, T.H.C., 'Suggested Lines of Advance in English Vital Statistics', *Journal of the Royal Statistical Society* 73 (1910), 685–713, at 696–9.
24. House of Commons *Debates*, 5th ser., 14 June 1910, col. 1252, *Census Bill*, Second Reading; House of Commons *Debates*, 5th ser., 24 June 1910, cols 642–5, *Census (Great Britain) Bill*, in Committee.
25. NAS, GRO 6/363/15, Dunlop, J.C., 'Memorandum on the Proposed Inclusion in the Census of a Study of the Fertility of Marriage', 26 November 1909.
26. Dunlop, J.C., 'The Fertility of Marriage in Scotland: A Census Study', *Journal of the Royal Statistical Society* 77 (1914), 259–99, at 259.
27. Dunlop, 'Fertility of Marriage in Scotland', 279–80.
28. Elliot, R., 'An Early Experiment in National Identity Cards: The Battle over Registration in the First World War', *Twentieth Century British History* 17 (2006), 145–76, at 155–6.
29. Craig, *History of the Royal College of Physicians of Edinburgh*, 670.
30. National Registration Act 1915, 5 & 6 Geo. V, c. 60.
31. Elliot, 'Early Experiment', 149–51.
32. Elliot, 'Early Experiment', 166–9.
33. TNA, RG 28/3, Bernard Mallet to Nash, secretary to the Reconstruction Committee, 2 August 1916; memorandum by Mallet, 17 May 1917.
34. TNA, RG 28/3, War Office circular with regard to arrangements for following the National Registration Act 1915, 26 July 1915; National Register (Landsdowne Committee), Interim Report, 3 September 1915.
35. NAS, GRO 5/1110/32, Dunlop, J., 'Memorandum on Pink Forms', 28 August 1915.
36. NAS, GRO 5/1110/38, Dunlop, J., 'Memorandum on English Proposals', undated.
37. See NAS, GRO 7/8, for related correspondence, including letter 23.1, 9 May 1916.
38. NAS, GRO 5/1236/1, S. Vivian to Patten MacDougall, 24 November 1917.
39. NAS, GRO 5/1236/26.1, Registrars Association of Scotland to Patten MacDougall, 6 February 1918.
40. 1 & 2 Geo. VI, c. 55.
41. 16 & 17 Geo. V, c. 48.
42. Glaister, J., 'Death Certification and Registration in Scotland: Its Present Defects and a Proposed Remedy', *Glasgow Medical Journal* 6 (1893), 241–60, at 248.
43. NAS, GRO 5/94, assistant secretary, Scottish Board of Health, to registrar general of Scotland, 8 May 1924.
44. NAS, GRO 5/93, secretary of registrar general for Scotland to R. Leach, clerk to the Guardians, Rochdale, 8 November 1912.
45. 'False Certificates of Stillbirth', *British Medical Journal* 1 (1909), 234–5, at 235.
46. Within this legislation, stillbirth registration was introduced as part of a broader measure that aimed to provide stronger safeguards against the concealment of crime in relation to the disposal of the dead.
47. NAS, GRO 5/887, assistant secretary, Scottish Board of Health, to James Dunlop, registrar general for Scotland, 25 April 1925.
48. NAS, GRO 5/887, James Dunlop to secretary, Scottish Board of Health, 10 April 1923.

49. Dunlop, 'Observations on Bill to Amend the Law'.
50. Rose, L., *The Massacre of the Innocents: Infanticide in Britain, 1800–1939* (London, 1986), 133.
51. Dunlop, 'Observations on Bill to Amend the Law'.
52. Dunlop, 'Observations on Bill to Amend the Law'.
53. That is, deaths within a year of birth per thousand live births. NAS, GRO 5/95, R.H., Department of Health for Scotland, to H. Scott, New Register House, 11 January 1938.
54. House of Commons *Debates*, 5th ser., vol. 332, 2 March 1938, cols 1116–19.
55. NAS, GRO 5/96, Booklet, 'Regulations and Instructions to Registrars, Registration of Stillbirths (Scotland) Act, 1938'; NAS, GRO 5/96, S. Vivian, registrar general for England, Somerset House, London, to J. Kyd, registrar general for Scotland, 10 November 1937.
56. House of Lords *Debates*, 5th ser., vol. 110, 5 July 1938, cols 513–15.
57. For a more comprehensive discussion of the factors behind the Registration of Stillbirths (Scotland) Act, see Davis, G., 'Stillbirth Registration and Perceptions of Infant Death, 1900–60: The Scottish Case in National Context', *Economic History Review* 62 (2009), 629–54.
58. The situation in England was similar, except that civil registration was introduced two decades earlier, in 1836, but there was no formal medical certification procedure until further legislation in 1874, which obliged English doctors to furnish a medical certificate gratis, under a 40s penalty.
59. NAS, GRO 5/621, A.K. Chalmers, medical officer of health, Glasgow, to John Houston, secretary of the Association of Registrars, 1 November 1922. Chalmers claimed that this practice was already in place in Aberdeen.
60. NAS, GRO 5/621, James Dunlop to A.K. Chalmers, 20 November 1922; Dunlop to Chalmers, 16 November 1922.
61. NAS, GRO 5/621, Dunlop to Chalmers, 19 December 1922. It was not until 1928, upon pressure from the Scottish Board of Health, acting on the recommendation of the Scottish Departmental Committee on Puerperal Morbidity and Mortality, that doctors were asked to make Scottish registrars aware not only of the fact of death, but specifically when that death occurred within four weeks of childbirth. See NAS, HH 1/327, J.C. Dunlop, registrar general for Scotland, to secretary, Scottish Board of Health, 9 August 1928.
62. NAS, GRO 5/219, W. Jones, secretary, Public Health Department, Glasgow, to Mr Andrew Froude, secretary, Registrar General's Office, 26 November 1928.
63. NAS, GRO 5/219, Froude to Jones, 3 December 1928.
64. NAS, GRO 5/219, memorandum by James Dunlop, 18 November 1932.
65. NAS, GRO 5/219, Froude to Jones, 22 November 1932.
66. Dunlop, 'Observations on Bill to Amend the Law'.
67. See, for example, NAS, GRO 5/528, J.C. Dunlop, registrar general for Scotland, to medical superintendent of a hospital in Edinburgh, 4 May 1922.
68. *Scotsman*, 30 July 1914.
69. NAS, GRO 5/334, internal correspondence, undated (c. August 1914).
70. NAS, GRO 5/963, internal correspondence, 7 January 1920.
71. NAS, GRO 5/814, 'Suggestions as to Death Certification', booklet prepared and issued by the registrar general for Scotland, August 1924.
72. *Evening Dispatch*, 29 July 1914.
73. The remit of this commission was 'to inquire into the prevalence of venereal diseases in the United Kingdom, their effects upon the health of the community, and the means by which those effects can be alleviated or prevented'.
74. NAS, GRO 5/971, evidence tendered by Dr J.C. Dunlop, superintendent of the Statistical Department in the Registrar General's Office, undated.
75. NAS, GRO 5/621, James Dunlop, superintendent of statistics, to a medical practitioner in the West of Scotland, 4 July 1916.

76. NAS, GRO 5/621, Registrar General's Office to registrar in Central Scotland, 24 February 1919.
77. NAS, GRO 4/7, James Craufurd Dunlop, Registrar General's Office, to Sir John Lamb, Scottish Office, Whitehall, 29 July 1930.
78. NAS, GRO 4/7, Confidential GROS Memorandum, 'Notes of the Duties Involved', August 1930.
79. NAS, GRO 4/2, Dunlop to the Treasury, 1 July 1927.
80. http://www.mrc-bsu.cam.ac.uk/BSUsite/Publications/Publications/web_biographies.doc [accessed 5 November 2010].
81. NAS, GRO 4/7, James Craufurd Dunlop to Sir John Lamb, 29 July 1930.
82. NAS, GRO 4/7, Andrew Froude, registrar general for Scotland, to Sir John Lamb, Scottish Office, 29 July 1930.
83. NAS, GRO 4/7, R.R. Scott, Treasury Chambers, to secretary, Department of Health for Scotland, 27 September 1930.
84. NAS, GRO 4/7, Froude to Lamb, 29 July 1930; A. Froude to H.L.F. Fraser, Department of Health for Scotland, 8 August 1930.

# 7

# Exploring the Myth of a Scottish Privilege

## A Comparison of the Early Development of the Law on Medical Confidentiality in Scotland and England

**Angus H. Ferguson**

## Medical Law and Medical Ethics

Medicine does not operate outside the law; and the law in the industrial period has been subject to sharp changes in response to economic and political demands. Eastern and Western states have put medical knowledge to many purposes, and have been able to implement this knowledge in a way which was impossible even to the most centralised bureaucracies of the ancient world. The rise of the medical expert, encouraged by modernising states, solved many technical problems, and raised many ethical ones.[1]

The close interaction of modern scientific medicine and the law is an established reality in the twenty-first century. From specialist academic texts through to the portrayal of forensic medicine in popular television programmes, there is a broad awareness of, and interest in, medico-legal affairs.[2] In recent decades historians have begun to trace the development of modern medico-legal inter-action. As Clarke and Crawford note, 'What is now usually termed "legal" or "forensic" medicine has at various times and places included not only what we know as clinical forensic medicine and forensic pathology, but also elements of medical law and ethics, "medical police", public health and poor-law medicine.'[3]

The extent to which each of these elements has featured in, or been a promi-nent part of, medical education and practice over the past two centuries, has been heavily influenced by the priorities, concerns and development of national juris-dictions. Thus, medico-legal relations developed differently under English and Scots law, and the place of legal medicine within the medical curriculum reflected this variation. While in England it remained a somewhat marginal area of interest, in Scotland, as White and Crowther have shown, during the course of the nine-teenth century forensic medicine and medical jurisprudence took deeper root.[4] They developed not only as areas of expertise for a cadre of specialists based at the Universities of Glasgow and Edinburgh, but also as an integral part of medical education and training in Scotland. While the emerging scientific approaches to forensic medicine and toxicology promoted the careers of university-based specialists, who were frequently called as expert witnesses in criminal cases, all doctors were aware that at some stage of their career they would have to interact with the law and might be called on to provide medical opinions in court.

In part this growing interaction reflected increased state interest in the medical affairs of the population during the course of the nineteenth and twentieth centuries. Legislation obliged doctors to notify cases of particular contagious or infectious diseases, or cases of criminal abortion.[5] However, medico-legal inter-action was not confined to statute and criminal law alone. As the civil courts, in particular the divorce courts, became accessible to a growing section of the population, doctors were often called upon to provide medical evidence during hearings. Therefore, as the opening quotation suggests, legal use of medical knowledge has facilitated both the civil and criminal processes, but, in so doing, has raised ethical problems. The purpose of what follows is to examine one such ethical problem posed by the rise of medico-legal interaction in the nineteenth and twentieth centuries, namely, the threat to traditional concepts of medical confidentiality.

Medical confidentiality is an ideal that has, at least theoretically, been associated with ethical medical practice since its inclusion within the terms of the Hippocratic Oath. The importance of confidentiality to the doctor–patient rela-tionship stems from the part it plays in promoting disclosure of all relevant information, by the patient to his or her doctor, in order to facilitate an efficient and effective diagnostic process. Although widely acknowledged as an integral element of medicine, in Britain medical confidentiality is not absolute. Since the late eighteenth century medical confidentiality has been subject to legal limita-tions. While it is generally recognised that doctors should not disclose information obtained in the practice of their profession, from the late nineteenth century onwards there have been recurring debates regarding exceptions to this rule.[6] The timing is significant, representing a period in which the medical profession began to emerge as a more coherent and recognisable body of practitioners, with an increasingly standardised body of knowledge. While arguably this contributed to their growing status and authority as a profession, the simultaneous rise of state concern over public health in the second half of the nineteenth century empha-sised a new set of agendas to medicine. The traditional ethic of protecting the confidentiality of private paying patients was juxtaposed with the demand that doctors prioritise the collective public interest, breaching patient confidentiality in order to prevent and control the spread of infectious disease or the practice of criminal abortion. Notification of abortion, along with public health concerns over the spread of venereal disease (VD), proved to be areas of continual controversy in the late nineteenth and early twentieth centuries, as the implications of keeping or breaching medical confidentiality were hotly contested by lawyers, doctors and civil servants. With a sharp rise in petitions for divorce, and government concerns over the importance of confidentiality to the success of state-backed VD treatment centres, the early inter-war years proved to be a period of particularly intense debate. From private meetings and correspondence between the minister of health and the lord chancellor, to public debates between representatives of the medical and legal professions, opinion was split over the implications of forcing doctors to breach patient confidentiality in court.

Frustrated by an apparent lack of regard for medical confidentiality within the courtroom, both the Ministry of Health and the British Medical Association (BMA) contemplated direct challenges to judicial authority on the issue. The ministry's taste for direct action was short-lived, satiated by its unsuccessful attempt covertly to encourage a medical witness to risk prison in the hope that this would provoke the law into a reconsideration of medical privilege.[7] Similarly, growing agitation amongst its membership over the treatment of doctors in court led the BMA to adopt an official policy of support for medical 'martyrs'. However, the senior members of the BMA council and central ethical committee had diminishing faith in the wisdom and practicality of such a policy. If high-level support for a direct challenge to the common law was waning, there was continued interest in an attempt at gaining medical privilege through statute law. In 1927, Ernest Gordon Graham-Little, MP for the University of London and a consultant dermatologist, introduced a private member's Bill aimed at providing a limited protection for medical confidences from disclosure in civil court cases. On the eve of the Bill's first hearing in November 1927, a joint meeting of the Bournemouth Legal Society and the Bournemouth division of the BMA was held to discuss the motion: 'Should communications to a medical man be privileged in legal procedure, both civil and criminal?'[8] In the course of this debate, one of the speakers in favour of the idea, Dr Lionel Weatherly, asserted that in Scotland medical privilege was recognised and that a doctor could be sued for slander if he broke a patient's confidence in court.[9] This chapter aims to examine Weatherly's claim by looking at the early development of the law relating to medical privilege in Scotland, focusing in particular on two relevant cases: *AB v CD* (1851) and *McEwan v Watson* (1904–5).

At the outset, it is important to distinguish between two forms of medical privilege discussed in what follows. The first refers to evidence given in the witness box. In this form, privilege protects a doctor from being sued as a result of giving relevant and accurate information during testimony in a court case. It is therefore a privilege aimed at protecting the medical witness.[10] The second form of privilege exempts information required during legal proceedings from disclosure in court on grounds that it was originally obtained in confidential circumstances. While in some countries the medical profession was granted the right to claim this form of medical privilege, in Britain the limitations placed on medical confidentiality in relation to legal proceedings have frequently been a source of debate.[11] Both forms of medical privilege will be discussed in what follows but the emphasis will be placed on the second form which has historically proven to be the more contentious of the two.

### Privilege to Maintain Confidentiality

The boundaries of medical confidentiality in Britain are not set down in statute law, and before concentrating on the position in Scotland, it is necessary to look at the earliest common law precedent for medical privilege in English law: the duchess of Kingston's trial (1776). Elsewhere I have argued that this case provides a questionable foundation for the law on medical confidentiality; however, it has had a lasting, and ongoing, effect in defining medical confidentiality and medical privilege in a number of jurisdictions around the world.[12]

Elizabeth Chudleigh, dowager duchess of Kingston, was brought to trial before the House of Lords, accused of marrying the duke of Kingston despite already being married to the earl of Bristol. Naturally, the trial of a duchess for the crime of bigamy attracted a great deal of attention, occupying many pages of print and providing a focal spectacle for upper-class society – for whom special galleries were constructed in the House of Lords. Pleading innocent to the charge, the duchess sought to maintain that her alleged secret marriage to the earl of Bristol had never taken place and that, consequently, her later marriage to the duke of Kingston was a legal act, which in turn meant that she was entitled to retain the wealth and estates which the duke had left to her in his will.

Amongst the many witnesses called to testify during the trial was Caesar Hawkins, serjeant-surgeon to King George III. As a friend of the duchess and her first husband, the earl of Bristol, Hawkins was asked to provide testimony regarding messages he had carried between them which made mention of the fact of their secret marriage. Standing in the witness box before a crowd of 5,000 onlookers, Hawkins responded: 'I do not know how far any thing, that has come before me in a confidential trust in my profession, should be disclosed, consistent with my professional honour.'[13] The question and answer were repeated. With Hawkins's reluctance to answer, the question was referred to the peers to decide, and there followed a lengthy statement by Lord Mansfield.[14] Responding to Hawkins's plea for privilege, Mansfield suggested that while a doctor had a duty of confidentiality to his patients, this did not apply when evidence was required in a court of law:

If a surgeon was voluntarily to reveal these secrets, to be sure he would be guilty of a breach of honour, and of a great indiscretion; but, to give that information in a court of justice, which by the law of the land he is bound to do, will never be imputed to him as any indiscretion whatever.[15]

Accepting this decision, Hawkins proceeded to give evidence; and ever since, the duchess's case has been cited as the benchmark precedent on medical privilege in English law.

Two aspects of the duchess's case are of particular importance to the question of medical privilege in Scotland. First, the case was a criminal hearing; and, second, it was heard in the House of Lords. While the House of Lords was regarded as the highest court of appeal in civil cases for both Scotland and England, it did not carry the same authority in Scottish criminal cases. The fact that the duchess of Kingston's precedent was not necessarily binding north of the Border left a question mark over the position of medical witnesses in Scotland regarding breach of medical confidentiality in court.[16] Perhaps reflecting this ambiguity, a number of key nineteenth-century Scottish jurists categorically stated in their textbooks that surgeons and physicians had no privilege to refuse to give evidence in a court of law, but cited no cases on the point.[17] One exception was William Gillespie Dickson, whose mid-nineteenth-century *Treatise on the Law of Evidence in Scotland* cited the duchess of Kingston's case as its earliest precedent.[18]

Another case to which Dickson paid particular attention was *AB v CD* (1851).[19] Heard in the Scottish Court of Session, the case involved a church elder, AB, in an undisclosed parish in Scotland, whose wife gave birth to a child six months after marriage. Having been informed of the birth by AB, and believing he intended to bring the child for baptism, the parish minister raised the matter at the next meeting of the kirk session. Thinking that the timing of the birth required some explanation, the kirk session decided to adjourn until AB could attend 'to afford such explanations and respectable medical testimony as he thinks fit, for the satisfaction of the session'.[20] Around the same time, the doctor, who was to become the defendant, CD, was called in to see AB's wife after her confinement. When it subsequently became clear that questions were being raised about the timing of the birth in relation to the marriage, the father, AB, referred the minister to CD, the doctor who had recently attended his wife, in the belief that he would be able to give an assessment of the age of the child. However, when approached by the minister, CD indicated that he had not examined the child in any detail during his previous visit to the mother.

Believing the child to be premature, and wishing to clear up any rumours of impropriety, AB then engaged CD and another doctor to determine whether the infant had been born at full term. The doctors did as asked and signed a report stating their opinion that the child was not premature. On receiving a copy of this report AB sent a letter to the kirk session resigning his position as an elder. However, in the meantime, CD, who had originally been unable to provide an answer to the minister, returned to him with the second copy of the report. As the minister was not at home when he called, CD left the report in an addressed envelope. On his return, the minister received the report in the belief that it was the medical evidence that AB had been asked to provide, and accordingly laid it before the next kirk session meeting. Consequently AB's letter of resignation was taken to be a confession of 'ante-nuptial fornication' and the medical report to be the accompanying evidence.[21] As a result, AB was declared to be no longer a member of the kirk session and the medical report was recorded in the official minutes of the meeting. While AB had originally referred the minister to CD for an informal opinion on the age of the child, he regarded the second consultation as a private engagement and therefore believed that CD had broken doctor–patient confidentiality in taking the report to the minister. With all made public, AB decided to sue CD for breach of confidentiality and slander.[22]

Mounting a defence for the doctor during the hearing in court, CD's lawyers argued that confidentiality could not be taken to be an essential element of the contract between a medical man and his clients as there were instances in which a doctor could be forced to divulge patient information. Their justification was the fact that a doctor could not claim privilege in court and they cited the precedent of the duchess of Kingston's case in support of this position. Perhaps unsurprisingly, the court rejected this argument and ruled that confidentiality *was* an integral part of the doctor–patient relationship, breach of which was sufficient grounds for an action for damages. However, this was not a rejection of the duchess's precedent but rather a refusal to interpret it in the rather obtuse manner that the doctor's defence sought. Lord Ivory emphasised the fundamental importance of confidentiality in the doctor–patient relationship, stating: 'If it could ever have been doubted that such a confidential relation subsists between a medical man and his employer, I think it high time that such a doubt should now be set at rest forever.'[23] Yet, as Lord Fullerton noted, the obligation of secrecy was not absolute: 'it may and must yield to the demands of justice, if disclosure is demanded in a competent court'.[24]

While such *obiter dicta* no doubt carried some unofficial authority on the question, medical privilege was not the point at issue in *AB v CD*. Influential as Lord Fullerton's thoughts were, other cases provide evidence that not everyone was as clear on the position of medical privilege in Scotland. The case of *McDonald v McDonalds* (1881) involved the confidentiality of medical records held by an insurance company.[25] The case arose from disentail of estates in Perthshire amongst a number of heirs. Under the terms of the Entail Amendment (Scotland) Act 1875, the second and third heirs to the estate sought to ascertain the value of their expectancy.[26] As part of this process, they sought information about the probable life expectancy of the first heir, Captain McDonald, from medical reports associated with his life insurance policy. The manager of the Scottish Equitable Insurance Company, one of the companies in possession of the relevant medical reports, refused to produce the documents on grounds that they were confidential and privileged. This protest was refused by the lord ordinary (Fraser), who ordered that the reports be located and produced.

As with *AB v CD*, this did not represent a clear-cut case of the court rejecting medical privilege, as the protest was not made by the doctor who had written the medical report, but by the insurance company who retained it. Nonetheless, the question of medical privilege was again discussed in a note to the published report of the case. This suggested that, while the English courts had rejected the idea that doctors could refuse to give evidence on grounds of privileged communications, these decisions had been 'regretted by later English judges, and none such have been pronounced hitherto by the Scottish Courts'.[27]

> If the present were a case where a communication made to a physician by his patient was sought to be recovered for a purpose antagonistic to the patient, the court would have to consider whether the English rule denying the protection should be followed, or whether the Scotch Courts, not being controlled by precedents, would create one the other way by ranking this within the class of privileged communications.[28]

While evidently some jurists seemed to be in favour of medical privilege, the law in England remained unchanged. In Scotland, although medical privilege continued to receive passing comment in cases relating to confidentiality, it appears that it was never the issue of immediate focus and therefore no specific ruling on the doctor's duty to break confidence in the witness box was made. Thus, even Wilkinson, in his late twentieth-century text *The Scottish Law of Evidence*, was forced to state that while there is no reported Scottish decision on the point, 'it is settled practice that he [a medical practitioner] may also be compelled to speak to communications passing between him and his patient'.[29] The case cited with this was *AB v CD*, suggesting that Wilkinson set store by Fullerton's endorsement of Mansfield's ruling in the duchess of Kingston's case. Wilkinson's work is cited, together with *AB v CD*, in connection with the absence of medical privilege in the witness box, by the current edition of *The Laws of Scotland: Stair Memorial Encyclopedia*.[30] In light of this it is evident that the duchess's impact in Scotland has been considerable.

## Privilege to Breach Confidentiality

In contrast to the absence of a Scottish precedent on the more controversial definition of medical privilege, there is a relevant precedent for the protection given to doctors to enable them to breach confidentiality in the course of legal proceedings without fear of subsequently being sued. The key case for this was *McEwan v Watson* (1904–5). Significantly the case involved two issues that provoked ongoing controversy in relation to medical confidentiality: abortion and divorce. While a sharp increase in divorce cases caused a crisis in confidence over the confidentiality of government-sponsored VD treatment clinics in the early 1920s, doctors were already confused over their role in notification of abortion by the late nineteenth century.[31] As an operation deemed illegal in all but a limited number of circumstances, abortion had been the subject of prominent medico-legal debate in the 1890s after the controversy sparked by the English case of *Kitson v Playfair* (1896).[32]

*McEwan v Watson* originated in the Scottish Court of Session, but was taken on appeal all the way to the House of Lords in 1905. In brief, the details of the case were as follows. Jessie McEwan (née Jones), daughter of James Jones, the managing director of the Dalmeny Oil Company, married Thomas McEwan, an electrical engineer, in 1900.[33] The marriage was not a success and in September 1901 she moved out of the marital home and instructed her lawyer that she was considering petitioning for divorce on grounds of her husband's cruelty.[34] With this in mind, in October 1901, she consulted and was examined by Sir Patrick Heron Watson, an eminent member of the Edinburgh medical elite and a renowned surgeon. Two-time president of the Royal College of Surgeons of Edinburgh, Watson also served for a number of years as the college's representative to the General Medical Council. In 1884 he was appointed as honorary surgeon to Queen Victoria in Scotland, an appointment which continued under King Edward VII.[35]

Jessie McEwan petitioned for divorce in December 1902, on grounds of ill-health as a result of her husband's cruelty. The proof hearing was started in July 1903 and then adjourned until October. Watson was not called to testify. It was later stated that Jessie McEwan and her father had not called Watson to testify during the divorce trial because he had

> most distinctly given both her and her father to understand that his opinion was not favourable to her view, and that he attributed her condition, not to the alleged cruel treatment by her husband, but to her own infirmity and bad state of health, produced or aggravated by the way in which she had for a long while been living – using opiates, and alcoholics largely and constantly.[36]

On 20 October 1903, Thomas McEwan's lawyers asked Watson to re-examine Jessie McEwan with a view to giving evidence on behalf of their client at the adjourned hearing. Watson agreed to the request and gave evidence on 24 October. He also passed over to Thomas McEwan and his lawyers the notes he had made at the time of his initial examination of Jessie McEwan in 1901. This was done without Jessie McEwan's consent, and, as her lawyers later stressed, 'in the knowledge that such consent would have been withheld if asked for'.[37] In these notes, Watson alleged that at the time of the 1901 consultation, Jessie McEwan had been 'bent upon inducing premature labour, so as to free her of any permanent reminder of her marriage with Thomas McEwan, meaning thereby that the pursuer was desirous criminally to procure abortion'.[38] He subsequently repeated the allegation when he appeared as a witness in court. It was this slur on her character that Jessie McEwan perceived as the reason for the subsequent failure of her divorce petition, leading her to bring an action against Watson for damages.

Four charges were laid against Watson, two relating to breach of medical confidentiality and two to allegations of slander. The issues for breach of confidentiality related to Watson's disclosure of the information that he had learned during his first examination of Jessie McEwan, when he was under her employment. Jessie McEwan's lawyers argued that by subsequently passing the information and notes made during this consultation to Thomas McEwan and his lawyers, and later volunteering the information in court, Watson had breached his professional obligation of confidentiality to Jessie. The remaining charges were for slander connected to his alleging, both during the precognition, and in the witness box, that Jessie McEwan had intended criminally to procure abortion.[39] Two elements of Watson's actions require further explanation. First, he indicated that when he was asked to examine Jessie McEwan in 1903, he did not initially realise that this was the same person who had sought his opinion two years earlier.[40] Second, the fact that he disclosed information about Jessie McEwan's state of health to her husband was not necessarily a controversial breach of confidentiality, as Thomas McEwan had a right and interest to be warned if his wife intended to seek criminal abortion. The controversial element was that Watson had passed on this information only two years later, when asked about the earlier consultation by Thomas McEwan in 1903. By this time, the child – who had evidently not been terminated – was in the custody of the father.[41]

In the first hearing, Lord Kincairney dismissed the two charges of breach of confidentiality and slander regarding Watson's testimony in the witness box, on the ground that these were *prima facie* privileged. A witness could not be sued for relevant information given under oath in court. As Lord Young subsequently phrased it,

it is in the interests of justice that he (a witness) should not give his
answers under any apprehension of being liable to an action for damages
should his evidence be defamatory to anyone, whether a party to the
action or not . . . It is in the interests of the public that the truth should be
ascertained in a Court of justice, and that witnesses should give their
evidence without such apprehension or fear.[42]

However, Kincairney upheld the two charges of breach of confidentiality and
slander relating to Watson's disclosure during conversation with Thomas
McEwan and his lawyers prior to his appearance in court. Kincairney based his
decision largely upon the precedent of *AB v CD* that confidentiality was an integral part of the doctor–patient relationship, breach of which was a suitable
ground for action.[43]

On appeal, Watson succeeded in having the outstanding allegation of slander
overturned due to its lack of specificity. As the Lord Justice-Clerk noted,

a pursuer proposing to take an issue should be most specific in putting in
issue the matters said to have been disclosed, of which it is alleged that the
disclosure was an actionable wrong. The form of the issue proposed in this
case is such as I have never seen. The question asked is only whether there
were disclosed 'matters relative to the pursuer and her state of health'.[44]

Evidently Jessie McEwan was reluctant to detail what she had considered to be
slanderous in Watson's statements, and, consequently, the court was unwilling
to allow her to pursue for damages on such a vague charge. Thus, after Watson's
first appeal, only the issue of breach of confidentiality outside the witness box
stood.

A further appeal to the House of Lords saw Lord Chancellor Halsbury and
the law lords unanimously conclude that this charge should also be disallowed.
The main reason for the decision was that if statements given to parties in preparation for a trial were not privileged, the process of justice would be made more
cumbersome as witnesses would have no opportunity to indicate what testimony they would give in the witness box. While the lord chancellor appreciated
that his interpretation of the law might lead to some potentially slanderous
information being given to a lawyer for a case which never came to trial, and
therefore was not privileged, this information would not be publicised and did
not, therefore, pose a sufficient threat to justify litigation:

Unless he [a witness] does give evidence in a Court of justice, in which
case he can be indicted for perjury if his evidence is wilfully false, nobody

knows anything about it – it slumbers, I suppose, in the office of the solicitor, and nobody hears or cares anything about it. Practically, I think that would be the answer.[45]

Thus, by its final stage, *McEwan v Watson* did provide legal recognition for medical privilege in the weaker of the two senses of the term, and in a manner which only reaffirmed the protection which ordinary witnesses enjoyed with regard to the testimony they gave in relation to legal proceedings.

## Implications for Medical Privilege in Scotland

So where does this leave Weatherly's claim, during the debate in Bournemouth in 1921, that medical privilege existed in Scotland? It could be argued that Weatherly was referring to the form of privilege confirmed in *McEwan v Watson*, but this is unlikely. As noted at the outset, the debate in Bournemouth took place on the eve of the introduction of a private member's Bill in the House of Commons which sought statutory protection for medical officers from publicly-funded VD treatment schemes called to give evidence in divorce hearings. The high profile breach, not only of professional codes of conduct, but also of a well-advertised government pledge that all proceedings at the clinics would be confidential, was a topic that sparked fierce debates throughout the 1920s. Given that it was the more controversial form of privilege that was the focus of debate, it is more likely that Weatherly had misinterpreted the ruling from *AB v CD* that confidentiality was an integral part of the doctor–patient relationship, breach of which was actionable under law, as being applicable even when the doctor was in the witness box. This interpretation may have been to the liking of some, but in the absence of a clear Scottish precedent, most adopted the approach taken in England. When, at the outset of the twentieth century, John Glaister, professor of medical jurisprudence and toxicology at the University of Glasgow, wrote what became a long-running and highly influential medico-legal textbook, he indicated that the absence of privilege for medical witnesses was the established law of the land. This, he stated, had been first laid down by Lord Mansfield in the duchess of Kingston's trial, from which he quoted at some length.[46]

Similarly, when the Ministry of Health made inquiries about the existence of medical privilege under other national jurisdictions in 1921, their lawyer, Sir Maurice Linford Gwyer, contacted the Scottish Office to ascertain the position of medical witnesses under Scots law. In replying, Miller-Gray of the Scottish Office informed him that, while there was no privilege for medical men in Scotland, it was felt that 'doctors should not be pressed to give evidence about their patients unless absolutely necessary'.[47] This informal compromise between legal and medical agendas was similarly advocated by key individuals in England when attempts at direct challenges to judicial compulsion of medical witnesses to give evidence were unsuccessful. Francis Crookshank, a doctor with a keen interest in medico-legal affairs, suggested that confrontation with the law was unnecessary:

> the medical witness, if he feels that the question cannot be answered without straining his conscience or grave risk of injustice or injury, should appeal quietly to the judge for relief. Such an appeal, when properly made, frequently leads to modification or suppression of the question by counsel, either spontaneously or at a hint from My Lord.[48]

However, judging by the continued unrest on the question in the late 1920s and 1930s, there was little evidence of such sensitivity and mutual understanding. In a letter to the *British Medical Journal* shortly after his contribution to the Bournemouth debate, Weatherly asserted:

> There can be no question that forty years ago judges and counsel were far more inclined to respect medical secrecy than they are today . . . The attitude of Bench and Bar has greatly changed since those days . . . hence the strong feeling of the medical profession, and the urging by them of some alteration in the law regarding medical privilege.[49]

No such alteration came. Graham Little's private member's Bill failed to make it through both Houses of Parliament in 1927, and, despite some evidence of both medical and legal support, a similar attempt at legislation in 1936 met with the same fate.[50]

In conclusion, doctors in Scotland did have medical privilege in so far as it related to them being protected from litigation arising out of evidence which they gave in relation to legal proceedings, a point clarified through the three stages of *McEwan v Watson*. With regard to the more controversial form of medical privilege, the case of *AB v CD* gave legal endorsement to the importance of confidentiality in the doctor–patient relationship but did not go so far as to endorse medical privilege. Similarly, the opinion expressed by the Scottish Office in 1921 recognised that medical confidentiality should be given a great deal of respect by the law but did not suggest that protection should be absolute. Despite the lack of a clear Scottish legal precedent on the issue, there seems to have been a general recognition that there was no medical privilege to decline giving relevant evidence in the witness box on grounds that it would breach doctor–patient confidentiality. In the absence of a specifically Scottish precedent on the point, Scottish jurists who did not remain silent on the point adopted Lord Mansfield's ruling from the duchess of Kingston's trial in conjunction with Lord Fullerton's endorsement of this position during *AB v CD*.

The fact that many Scottish jurists were silent on the point may be connected to the fact that the English courts were the main battleground for the high profile confrontations over confidentiality in the late nineteenth and early twentieth centuries. This can be interpreted in various ways. Given the importance of the civil divorce courts to the inter-war debate, it might reflect differences in Scottish and English laws on divorce. Or, as suggested by the views expressed by the Scottish Office, it may be that Scottish judges were more inclined to limit their demands for medical testimony without patient consent to cases where it was absolutely necessary, thereby minimising the likelihood of medical witnesses raising objection. If so, this greater judicial sympathy for the medical viewpoint, and medical co-operation with the law when required, might in turn reflect a mutual awareness and understanding of the relative professional agendas, arising from the greater emphasis on medico-legal study within the medical and legal curricula of Scottish universities compared to their English counterparts. While the prominence of controversy over medical confidentiality in the inter-war years differed between the two countries, the official legal position of medical witnesses was common to both. It would seem that, as with the more celebrated Scottish myths, it was easier to find an individual who believed in the existence of medical privilege in Scotland than it was to establish any objective evidence of the fact.

## Acknowledgements

This chapter stems from research undertaken during my PhD, which was funded by the Economic and Social Research Council.

## Notes

1. Crowther, M.A., 'Introduction', in Otsuka, Y. and Sakai, S., eds, *Medicine and the Law: Proceedings of the 19th International Symposium on Comparative History of Medicine – East and West* (Tokyo, 1998), xvi.
2. Examples of specialist texts include: McLay, W.D.S., *Clinical Forensic Medicine* (Cambridge, 2009); Cowan, S. and Hunt, A.C., eds, *Mason's Forensic Medicine for Lawyers*, 5th edn (Haywards Heath, 2008); Stark, M.M., ed., *A Physician's Guide to Clinical Forensic Medicine* (Totowa, 2000). The pervasion of forensic medicine into popular culture can be seen through mainstream and primetime American and British television programmes such as *CSI: Crime Scene Investigation* (CBS Paramount, 2000–present) as well as its offshoot programmes *CSI: Miami* (CBS Paramount, 2002–present) and *CSI: NY* (CBS Paramount, 2004–present); *Quincy M.E.* (Universal Studios, 1976–83); *Silent Witness* (BBC, 1996–present); *Waking the Dead* (BBC, 2000–present).
3. Clarke, M. and Crawford, C., 'Introduction', in Clarke, M. and Crawford, C., eds, *Legal Medicine in History* (Cambridge, 1994), 2.

4. White, B., 'Training Medical Policemen: Forensic Medicine and Public Health in Nineteenth-Century Scotland', in Clarke, M. and Crawford, C., eds, *Legal Medicine in History* (Cambridge, 1994), 145–63; White, B. and Crowther, M.A., *On Soul and Conscience: The Medical Expert and Crime* (Aberdeen, 1988); Crowther, M.A., 'Medicine and the Law in Nineteenth-Century Scotland', in Otsuka and Sakai, *Medicine and the Law*, 63–82.

5. What constituted an illegal as opposed to therapeutic abortion was a penumbral area of law. See Brookes, B., *Abortion in England 1900–1967* (London, 1988), 22–78; Brookes, B. and Roth, P., '*Rex v Bourne* and the Medicalization of Abortion', in Clark and Crawford, *Legal Medicine in History*, 314–43; Keown, J., *Abortion, Doctors and the Law* (Cambridge, 1988), 49–83.

6. For details on some of these debates see: Mooney, G., 'Public Health versus Private Practice: The Contested Development of Compulsory Infectious Disease Notification in Late Nineteenth-Century Britain', *Bulletin of the History of Medicine* 73 (1999), 238–67; Morrice, A.A.G., '"Should the Doctor Tell?": Medical Secrecy in Early Twentieth-Century Britain', in Sturdy, S., ed., *Medicine, Health and the Public Sphere in Britain, 1600–2000*, (London, 2002), 61–82; Pranghofer, S. and Maehle, A.H., 'Limits of Professional Secrecy: Medical Confidentiality in England and Germany in the Nineteenth and Early Twentieth Centuries', *Interdisciplinary Science Reviews* 31 (2006), 231–44.

7. For details of this see Ferguson, A.H., 'Speaking out about Staying Silent: An Historical Examination of the Medico-Legal Debates over the Boundaries of Medical Confidentiality', in Goold, I. and Kelly, C., eds, *Lawyers' Medicine: The Legislature, the Courts and Medical Practice, 1760–2000* (Oxford, 2009), 99–124.

8. *British Medical Journal (BMJ)*, Supplement, 3 December 1927, 215–16.

9. It should be noted that Weatherly had been asked to speak at very short notice, and while his views may have been influenced by his limited preparation, it is notable that no-one questioned or challenged his interpretation of the legal position in Scotland.

10. This form of privilege applies to all witnesses, medical and non-medical.

11. In the early 1920s the Ministry of Health drew up a memorandum comparing the boundaries of medical privilege in countries such as Canada, New Zealand and in many of the American states: ministry memorandum for cabinet meeting, June 1921: The National Archives, London (TNA), MH78/253.

12. For a detailed examination of this case see Ferguson, A.H., 'The Lasting Legacy of a Bigamous Duchess: The Benchmark Precedent for Medical Confidentiality', *Social History of Medicine* 19 (2006), 37–53.

13. *The Trial of Elizabeth Duchess Dowager of Kingston for Bigamy* (London, 1776), 119.

14. Lord Mansfield (William Murray) was a Scotsman. Born and raised in Scone in Perthshire, he received his early education at Perth Grammar School. He had a long and illustrious career at both the Scots and English bars, becoming renowned as a lord chief justice who significantly influenced English common law in the eighteenth century.

15. *The Trial of Elizabeth Duchess Dowager of Kingston*, 120.

16. For information on the influence of the House of Lords on Scottish Criminal Law see Mclean, A., 'The House of Lords and Appeals from the High Court of Justiciary, 1707–1887', *Juridical Review* (1985), 192–226.

17. Hume, D., *Commentaries on the Law of Scotland, Respecting Crimes*, 2nd edn (Edinburgh, 1819), vol. 2, 338; Burnett, J., *A Treatise on Various Branches of the Criminal Law of Scotland* (Edinburgh, 1811), 437; Tait, G., *A Treatise on the Law of Evidence in Scotland*, 3rd edn (Edinburgh, 1834), 387.

18. Dickson, W.G., *A Treatise on the Law of Evidence in Scotland* (Edinburgh, 1855), vol. 2, 1095. Repeated verbatim in the 1864 edition of the text.

19. *AB v CD* (1851) 14 D., 177.

20. *AB v CD* (1851) 14 D., 177.

21. *AB v CD* (1851) 14 D., 177.

22. During the course of the hearing the defendant offered to drop the second issue and focus solely on the breach of confidentiality.
23. *AB* v *CD* (1851) 14 D., 177.
24. *AB* v *CD* (1851) 14 D., 177.
25. *McDonald v McDonalds* (1881) 8 R., 357.
26. Entail Amendment (Scotland) Act 1875, 38 & 39 Vict., c. 61, section 5.
27. *McDonald v McDonalds* (1881), 8 R., 357. The suggestion of diverging opinions among English jurists may be a reference to Justice Buller in *Wilson v Rastall* (1792), *English Reports*, vol. 99, 1286; or Lord Chancellor Brougham in *Greenough v Gaskell* (1833), 1 M.Y. & K., 98, both of whom expressed less dismissive views on the idea of medical privilege.
28. *McDonald v McDonalds* (1881) 8 R., 357.
29. Wilkinson, A.B., *The Scottish Law of Evidence* (London and Edinburgh, 1986), 105.
30. *The Stair Memorial Encyclopedia* is a comprehensive collection of Scots law. Discussion of medical privilege is found in the section on Medical Law; sub-section 4: Issues Involving Medical Treatment; sub-section (4) Medical Confidentiality and Privacy; (d) Lawful Disclosure of Information: Exceptions to the General Principles of Confidentiality; section 313: No Privilege of Medical Confidentiality. In addition to citing both Wilkinson's text and *AB v CD* (1851), the section also includes a reference to *AB v CD* (1904) which was the first stage of the *McEwan v Watson* case discussed below.
31. Ferguson, 'Speaking out about Staying Silent'.
32. For details of this case see: McLaren, A., 'Privileged Communications: Medical Confidentiality in Late Victorian Britain', *Medical History* 37 (1993), 129–47.
33. *Scotsman*, 30 November 1904.
34. There was greater parity in the grounds for divorce for men and women in Scotland than existed under English divorce law at the time. See Phillips, R., *Putting Asunder: A History of Divorce in Western Society* (Cambridge, 1988).
35. As Crowther and Dupree note, Watson was an old friend of Lord Lister, though he did not share Lister's views on antisepsis and the danger of micro-organisms: Crowther, M.A. and Dupree, M.W., *Medical Lives in the Age of Surgical Revolution* (Cambridge, 2007), 111. For further information see Watson's obituary in the *Scotsman*, 23 December 1907.
36. Statement made by Lord Young during the proof hearing of the subsequent case relating to Watson's alleged breach of confidentiality: *AB v CD* (1904), Session Cases 7 F. (1904–5), 83. Although the initial hearing was reported as *AB v CD*, the subsequent appeal hearings were reported as *Watson v McEwan*.
37. *Watson v McEwan* (1905), Scots Law Times Reports, vol. 12 (Edinburgh, 1905), 249.
38. *Watson v McEwan* (1905), *Scotsman*, 29 July 1905.
39. Precognition is the process of establishing a potential witness's evidence prior to using his or her testimony during a court case. A written account of the precognition, often in narrative form, is normally kept.
40. *Watson v McEwan* (1905), Scots Law Times Reports, vol. 12, 601. The second consultation was carried out along with two other eminent medical men: Sir Henry Littlejohn, professor of forensic medicine at Edinburgh University and medical officer of health for Edinburgh; and Dr Joseph Bell, consultant surgeon at Edinburgh Royal Infirmary, and popularly understood to have been the individual on whom Arthur Conan Doyle modelled his fictional detective Sherlock Holmes. Entries for both Littlejohn and Bell are available in *Who Was Who*.
41. *Watson v McEwan* (1905), Scots Law Times Reports, vol. 12, 603.
42. *McEwan v Watson* (1905), Scots Law Times Reports, vol. 12, 600.
43. Indicating that *AB v CD* (1851) seemed to be the only Scottish authority on the point, the notes to the case also pointed to the emphasis placed on the importance of medical confidentiality during *Kitson v Playfair* (1896). See McLaren, 'Privileged Communications'.
44. *Watson v McEwan* (1905), Scots Law Times Reports, vol. 12, 599–600.

45.  *Watson v McEwan* (1905), *Scots Law Times Reports*, vol. 13 (Edinburgh, 1906), 341; *Session Cases* 7 F. (1904–5), 111.
46.  Glaister, J., *A Textbook of Medical Jurisprudence and Toxicology*, 2nd edn (Edinburgh, 1910), 44. This information is replicated in the subsequent editions of Glaister's book.
47.  Gwyer to Robinson, 17 June 1921: TNA, MH78/253.
48.  Crookshank, F.G., *Professional Secrecy* (London, 1922), 13. Crookshank was vice-president of the Medico-Legal Society and a member of both the BMA's central ethical committee and professional secrecy committee. Shortly before making these comments he resigned his position in protest at the confrontational policy that many in the BMA were adopting over the issue of confidentiality.
49.  *BMJ*, 3 December 1927, 1055.
50.  For more details on both attempts at legislation see Ferguson, A.H., 'Should a Doctor Tell? Medical Confidentiality in Interwar England and Scotland', PhD thesis, University of Glasgow, 2005, 154–89.

# 8

# Law, Medicine and the Treatment of Homosexual Offenders in Scotland, 1950–1980

## Roger Davidson

In recent years, the social politics and the legal and medical discourses surrounding homosexuality in twentieth-century Britain have attracted increasing attention from historians and social scientists. Within the growing literature, the medical perception and treatment of homosexuality and homosexual offences have been considered from a variety of standpoints. Many studies address the subject as a central aspect of the politics surrounding either the regulation of dangerous sexualities or the process of homosexual law reform.[1] Others, often from a social constructionist viewpoint, have focused on the competing sexological and psychoanalytical discourses surrounding homosexuality and their impact upon public policy.[2] Anecdotal evidence of medical attitudes and therapies is also scattered in the written and recorded testimonies of homosexuals.[3] However, with the notable exception of the oral history recently undertaken by King, Smith and Bartlett,[4] there has been little systematic primary research into the medical perception and treatment of male homosexuality that prevailed in the surgeries, clinics, courts and prisons of the land after the Second World War. This is especially true in relation to the Scottish experience, despite the distinctive traditions of law and medical practice north of the Border, as well as, arguably, Scotland's distinctive civic and sexual culture.

This paper seeks to begin to make good this omission by documenting the medical perception and treatment of homosexual offenders in Scotland in the period 1950–80, and the role that medical evidence played in the prosecution and sentencing of such offenders. Two main sources of evidence are explored. First, the verbal and written evidence of Scottish witnesses before the Wolfenden Committee is examined in order to identify how homosexual offenders were treated – or allegedly treated – in the 1950s. The Wolfenden Committee was appointed in 1954 in response to a moral panic surrounding an apparent escalation in urban vice, and with a remit to consider the law and practice relating to homosexual offences and prostitution. Secondly, a systematic analysis is undertaken of the medical reports on homosexual offenders submitted by psychiatrists and other doctors to Scottish High Court trials and appeals during the period 1950–80, and of their role in court proceedings. This will serve to throw important light on the degree to which medical views and practices pertaining to homosexual offenders in Scotland changed over the quarter century following Wolfenden and how far and in what ways they influenced the legal process.

## The View from Wolfenden

Scottish evidence to the Wolfenden Committee varied as to the extent to which medical considerations played a part in the sentencing of homosexual offenders in the 1950s. James Adair, former procurator-fiscal for Edinburgh and Glasgow, was of the opinion that: 'Some judges were very responsive to suggestions by medical men about treatment, while others agreed that these were not the concern of the judge.'[5] Certainly, under the Criminal Justice (Scotland) Act 1949, courts had explicit powers both to call for medical reports on offenders and to prescribe medical treatment (although not its specific nature) as part of a probationary sentence. Thus, an offender could, with his consent, be required under a probation order to undertake remedial treatment, either as a resident or non-resident of an institution or as a patient of a named doctor.[6] Some legal witnesses before the Wolfenden Committee considered that, compared with legal practice in inter-war Scotland,[7] there was an increasing trend in Scottish courts for medical reports to be used in cases involving homosexual offences, and that the practice was 'much more the custom in Scotland than in England'.[8] Dr W. Boyd, consultant psychiatrist to the Scottish Prison and Borstal Service, testified that he was: 'in charge of a Mental Health Service where both the Procurators-fiscal and the Sheriffs were willing to recognise that we could have cooperation, and many offenders were placed on probation on the condition that they attended hospital'.[9] Indeed, in Glasgow, whereas formerly the magistrates had tended to process homosexual offenders without any consideration of medical issues simply 'as men who were doing a dirty thing', and routinely to 'fine them a fiver each', in the 1950s such cases were increasingly remitted to the Sheriff Court to ensure some level of medical examination.[10]

In line with the recommendation of the Scottish Advisory Council on the Treatment and Rehabilitation of Offenders that psychotherapeutic and other medical treatment should be more widely available for convicted sexual offenders,[11] the Scottish Home Department had, it claimed, by the mid-1950s, begun to press for the provision of more psychiatric services within the Scottish prison system. The department recommended that all first offenders should have a full medico-psychological assessment prior to sentencing.[12] Further, it advocated that all male prisoners convicted of homosexual offences should be interviewed at some point by a psychiatrist and that, if the offender was suitable for treatment and was willing to undergo it during his sentence, he should be admitted to a psychiatric hospital as an in-patient or given treatment at a psychiatric clinic as an out-patient. Similar psychiatric examination and treatment was viewed as desirable for all male borstal inmates.[13]

However, despite such aspirations, Dr Inch, the medical adviser to the Scottish Prison and Borstal Services, maintained that the resources for treatment within Scottish prisons remained 'pitifully inadequate' and 'barely scratching the surface of the problem'.[14] With first offenders, who often served short sentences, at best only a 'few psychotherapeutic talks' were possible. Apart from Barlinnie, where a new medical psychiatric unit was being built, there were no special psychotherapeutic units in Scotland such as existed at Wormwood Scrubs and Wakefield, and many of the prisons were too small to justify in-house psychiatric provisions.[15] For any 'deep treatment', such as it existed, the Scottish Prison Service relied entirely on external psychiatric provisions within the National Health Service. Within the borstal system, treatment was, in practice, largely confined to casual, *ad hoc* advice conveyed by the governor, chaplain and psychiatrist to inmates, and to the enforcement of 'hard work and varied recreation, especially of an athletic nature' to counteract 'homosexual tendencies'.[16]

Scotland did vary from England and Wales in the type of medical treatment administered in prison to convicted homosexual offenders. According to the evidence of Scottish prison medical officers, no use was made of electro-convulsive therapy (ECT) in Scottish prisons. Narcoanalysis (psychoanalysis undertaken during a light phase of anaesthesia) had been used to a limited extent during the war but had been deemed unsuited to 'civil life'.[17] However, in contrast to England and Wales, where the practice had been discontinued as too dangerous, oestrogen treatment had been used in Scottish prisons on sexual offenders for some time (especially at Perth), largely inspired by the work of F.L. Golla at the Burden Neurological Institute in Bristol.[18] It was given only to prisoners who signed an agreement to the procedure and then only under strict medical supervision. According to Inch, oestrogen treatment had never been pushed 'to its limits – to the extent of producing atrophy of the testicles or even gynaecomastia [excessive enlargement of the male breasts] – but only to the point of eliminating or at least greatly reducing libido'.[19] The prime objective was to make the prisoners less anxious, more 'adaptable' and 'easier to handle', and to provide the 'small maintenance dosage that reliev[ed] tension' without producing any physical change in the patient. Significantly, such treatment regimes were not public knowledge. According to Inch, the Scottish Prison Service had 'never said anything'. 'We have,' he noted, 'just kept very quiet about it.'[20]

The fullest and most compelling Scottish evidence to the Wolfenden Committee in favour of homosexual law reform did come from medical witnesses. Perhaps the most influential evidence was that submitted by Drs Inch

and Boyd from the Scottish Prisons and Borstal Services.[21] Echoing the previous
recommendations of the Scottish Advisory Council on the Treatment and
Rehabilitation of Offenders, they aired serious doubts as to the value of imprisonment in reforming sexual offenders and favoured the decriminalisation of homosexual behaviour for consenting adults over 21.[22] In their view, a range of
alternative provisions was necessary. In accordance with Freudian interpretations, there needed to be more child guidance and child psychiatric clinics to
'treat deviation as early as possible before fixation occurred'. Courts should have
routine psychiatric reports on all homosexual offenders prior to sentencing,
supplied by a properly-staffed University or Regional Hospital Board clinic, and
more extensive use needed to be made of probationary orders for treatment of
first offenders under the 1949 Criminal Justice (Scotland) Act. For the homosexual recidivist or 'homosexual psychopath', there should be a separate psychopathic institute, as in Denmark. Finally, treatment regimes had to be more
effectively monitored and sustained by means of improved staff resources for
after-care and social work. Underlying their evidence was a belief that a less puni-
tive policy would in fact produce a more liberal and sympathetic attitude to
homosexuality in British society.

Evidence submitted by Drs Winifred Rushforth and W.P. Kraemer, respectively founder and medical director of the pioneering Davidson Clinic in
Edinburgh, established in 1940 to provide family therapy and psychoanalytical
treatment to the general public, also favoured the decriminalisation of homosexual behaviour between consenting adults as integral to changing social attitudes and to a refocusing of public debate onto issues of aetiology rather than
punishment.[23] In their view, in many cases, homosexuality was 'neither a disease
nor a matter of choice' but compulsive behaviour contingent on emotional
immaturity.[24] They stressed the value of psychotherapy in bringing some homosexuals 'into a more mature state' in which they could relate to women. They
considered that imprisonment merely reinforced the mental and social problems of homosexuals and should only be used for 'hardened offenders' who were
'a potential danger to young people'. They did not feel that prison predisposed
homosexual offenders to effective treatment, and viewed the existing prison
medical staff as unsuited to addressing sexual problems. At the very least, they
advocated the general introduction of group psychotherapy for offenders.
However, significantly, their evidence still identified homosexuals as fundamentally dysfunctional and anti-social and, in part, their opposition to legal coercion
was that it served merely to magnify not only the homosexual's sense of social
isolation but also his sexual ego. As Dr Kraemer testified, 'I feel that if we make
them into heroes and put them into prisons . . . it is not really doing very much
good, and it gives them a wrong idea of self-importance . . . [I]f you do that I feel

it is bad for society and for the character of these men, too.'[25] In his view, many of such 'young heroes want[ed] to suck forbidden fruit' and prosecution often served to fuel a neurotic compulsion for punishment.

In his contribution to the British Medical Association's evidence to the Wolfenden Committee, John Glaister, regius professor of forensic medicine at the University of Glasgow, also combined a somewhat pathological view of homosexuality with support for its limited decriminalisation. He was a vigorous supporter of coercive measures, including segregation in colonies, for 'the inveterate and degenerate sodomist, the debauchers of youth, and those who resort[ed] to violence to meet their desires'. Likewise, he endorsed a 'major attack by the law' on 'the confirmed invert and the male prostitute'. However, he did not feel that the incidence of homosexuality threatened the nation with 'racial decadence' and considered that consenting acts of adults in private (not including sodomy) were a matter 'of private ethics' and should be outwith the law. In his opinion, while society's disapproval was 'inevitable and desirable' and while homosexuality was certainly not something that should be encouraged, incarceration was not the answer in the majority of cases that involved minor offences. Glaister viewed prison as 'the last place for homosexual treatment'. On the contrary, he emphasised its propensity 'to incubate and foster homosexual tendencies'. Moreover, he also considered that the risk of prosecution often acted as an aphrodisiac for offenders. 'Many homosexuals,' he averred, 'feel that to flout the law is fraught with adventure due to possible detection, and to their peculiar make-up this may tend to add a fillip to their sex life.'[26]

At the same time, much of the evidence presented on the effectiveness of existing medical treatments for homosexual conditions was far from compelling. The experience of the Scottish Home Department was that, within the prison population, only a minority of homosexual offenders, some 30 per cent, were suitable for medical treatment and only 11 per cent prepared fully to co-operate with a course of psychotherapy.[27] In particular, it was claimed that short-term prisoners proved reluctant to agree to a course of treatment that might be prolonged beyond the date of their release. Nor were the medical staff of the Scottish Prison and Borstal Services at all certain of the outcome of their therapies. They insisted that it was never their aim to try and change the sexual identity of a homosexual, which they regarded as 'expensive, dangerous' and, almost certainly, impossible. Dr W. Boyd admitted that, although they might 're-direct' the energies of homosexuals and 'allow them to make a more adequate adjustment to their responsibilities', he did not 'for a moment suggest they could "cure" homosexuality'.[28] In his experience, it was not possible to treat homosexuals as sex offenders in prison and he recommended that hardened offenders should be treated in separate psychopathic institutes.[29] Even with the more limited aim of trying to reduce the levels of sexual urge and mental anxiety in homosexual offenders, the medical science was hazy. As Drs Inch and Boyd freely admitted, 'we do not know what may be happening so far as the endocrine treatment is concerned and what the ultimate result may be', and, although evidence suggested that in many cases it alleviated 'a most uncomfortable feeling of tension and guilt', and rendered patients more amenable to psychotherapy, they had never undertaken a controlled experiment 'to see whether aspirin would [have been] equally successful'.[30]

The evidence of the Davidson Clinic suggested that the scope for addressing homosexual behaviour by means of psychoanalysis was also limited. Although its staff claimed relatively high levels of success, this was clearly based on a relatively modest definition of 'success' and on extremely selective and long-term labour intensive therapy, exploring the patient's history right back into infancy and his or her earliest family relationships.[31] While it was argued that men in their late teens and twenties, who were still developing emotionally, might benefit from treatment, sexually active men who 'had extensively practised their perversion' were viewed as unsuited to analysis. For later age groups, the view of Rushforth and Kraemer was that 'if there had been little or no perverted behaviour', treatment might, at the most, free the patient from undue anxiety and enable him to find a less compulsive, and more 'discreet' and 'creative way of living' that was of value to himself and the community. In their opinion, a person who had been homosexual for any length of time, even if he adjusted by means of marriage, remained fundamentally homosexual. Moreover, the Davidson Clinic had found that homosexual patients referred by the police or social workers were especially unresponsive to psychotherapy.[32] Significantly, its analysts either would not or could not furnish the Wolfenden Committee with any recorded case where sexual reorientation had been effected.[33]

Such uncertainties merely fuelled the scepticism surrounding the medical treatment of homosexuality within the Scottish judicial and penal systems.[34] Thus, in evidence to the Wolfenden Committee, several sheriffs argued that, in many instances, homosexuality was an issue of criminal wilfulness rather than medical dysfunction and should be addressed accordingly.[35] In so far as they viewed it as a 'disease', they stressed its dysgenic impact upon the nation's health and demography and its essentially predatory and 'infectious' nature, with an initial sexual act engendering a cycle of addictive debauchery, often with ever-younger and more vulnerable partners.[36] Even where Scottish sheriffs and magistrates advocated greater recourse to medical treatment, they were insistent that it be part of normal criminal proceedings so that the element of deterrence remained and offenders could be compelled to comply with appropriate therapies.[37]

Significantly, the most influential attack on the 'medicalisation' of homosexuality came from James Adair, a member of the Wolfenden Committee, and former procurator-fiscal. His virulent critique, which effectively amounted to a minority report, and which echoed the prejudices and concerns of many within the Scottish legal and political establishment,[38] was scathing of the tendency of psychiatrists to sentimentalise the problem of homosexuality and to downplay its paedophilic aspects and damage to physical health. In his opinion, much of the evidence presented by 'mental specialists' was 'quite inexplicable and in not a few cases manifestly indefensible'. He considered that homosexuality had become the latest disease 'fashion' or 'craze' of 'medical men', and highlighted the uncertainties of medical and mental science 'and the limited knowledge and powers of the medical profession under existing circumstances to deal with homosexual patients'. According to Adair, a significant proportion of homosexuals seeking treatment were doing so only in order to evade the due process of law and were merely using medical therapy as a smokescreen for their perversion. Many, he argued, were already too old at 18 for treatment, with their sexuality and behaviour 'for all practical purposes immutable'.[39] Adair was especially concerned to elicit from witnesses the physical damage done by sodomy and was adamant that it should be retained as a separate offence with heavy penalties.[40] Indeed, in some ways, he displayed an obsession with anal intercourse reminiscent of the medical discourses surrounding the prosecution of sodomy in late nineteenth-century Britain.[41]

**The View from the High Court**

The extent to which the testimony submitted to the Wolfenden Committee accurately reflected the role of medical evidence in cases involving homosexual offences in Scotland in the 1950s, and the degree to which that role subsequently evolved, can in part be obtained from a study of court proceedings. A survey of cases brought in district courts under section 11 of the Criminal Law Amendment Act 1885, and under by-laws relating to public conveniences, does reveal an increasing use by offenders of medical arguments in written pleas to the court. Some emphasised that they were already seeking referral for psychiatric treatment;[42] others, especially those accused of contravening by-laws, increasingly proffered medical excuses for their behaviour, including hypertension, epilepsy, alcohol addiction and, most commonly, prostate and bladder problems.[43] However, in the lower courts, medical reports were rarely called for prior to formal summons or sentencing.[44] Limited and fragmentary evidence suggests that medical reports *were* deployed more regularly within the Sheriff Courts, but the absence of surviving case papers, coupled with issues of data protection, inhibits any systematic research in this area. This is the more disappointing in that it was before the Sheriff Courts that the bulk of prosecutions for 'homosexual offences' between consenting adults were tried.

What *have* been available to the author, under restricted access, are the psychiatric reports on defendants and convicted offenders submitted to the Scottish High Court and Court of Appeal over the period 1950–80 in all cases involving sodomy or contravention of the Criminal Law Amendment Act 1885, section 11. These reports form part of the judicial 'processes'; case papers in the proceedings before the court, including summonses, indictments and productions.[45] Inevitably, evidence drawn from such processes will be highly selective as the cases involved only the more serious crimes involving homosexual practices. None the less, they do convey some impression of the weight attributed within the legal process to psychiatric opinion.

An examination of High Court cases relating to homosexual offences suggests that, over the period, there was, quite apart from routine medical inspection under the mental health act in respect of fitness to plead, and forensic investigations of 'anal interference' where minors were involved, an increasing recourse to psychiatric evidence, commissioned both by the Crown and defence lawyers. By the 1970s, some 30 per cent of cases involved such medical evidence. This appears to have been especially so where the accused was a professional man such as a teacher or where he was socially well-connected.[46]

Broadly speaking, there are four treatment strategies for homosexual offences that can be detected in the medical evidence to the Scottish High Court in the period 1950–80. First, there were isolated cases where homosexual offences were diagnosed as primarily a function of mental deficiency and where the offender was deemed a danger both to himself and society. In such cases, admission to an 'institution or colony for mental defectives' – typically Carstairs – was recommended.[47]

Secondly, there was a group of offenders for whom medical treatment (predominantly psychotherapy but sometimes supplementary hormone therapy) was recommended with the aim of changing the direction of their sexual preference. These were cases in which, typically, the offender was either under 25 or deemed to be psycho-sexually immature for reasons of up-bringing, social conditioning, or the impact of random sexual advances or homo-erotic experiences. These were offenders whose homosexuality was regarded, primarily within a Freudian perspective, as 'transitional' rather than innate, with restrictive home environments and sexual ignorance impeding normal heterosexual development and outlets. However, even for this group, claims for the ability of medical treatment to secure a 'cure' or genuine sexual reorientation became more qualified as the period progressed. Thus, in the case of C.W.H., charged in Hawick in 1955 on two counts of contravening the Criminal Law Amendment Act 1885, the physician-superintendent of Dingleton Hospital, Melrose, was adamant that there was a 'recognised cure' for homosexuality, that there were cases of successful treatment 'within [his] own purview' and that the panel's homosexual tendencies could be 'cured and eradicated'.[48] Such unconditional claims were seldom, if ever, heard in medical testimony in the 1960s and 1970s. It should be added that, during the period 1950–80, in medical evidence to the High Court, aversion therapy using drugs or electric shocks was never explicitly recommended for this group of offenders.

Thirdly, there were offenders for whom medical treatment was recommended not to change their sexual orientation but to enable them to adapt better to their sexual problems and to life in general. Typically, these were cases where the accused was viewed as a latent homosexual who had successfully sublimated his urges over a long period but for whom an additional dysfunction such as alcoholism or marital stress had triggered overt homosexual behaviour, very often associated with acute anxiety and guilt. In such cases, 'latent homosexuality' was presented as 'an illness of the mind' and extensive psychotherapy, attached either to a probationary sentence or to admission to a psychiatric unit under section 55 of the Mental Health (Scotland) Act 1960, was often suggested as a means of enabling the offender to come to terms with his condition and to develop a self-awareness of social and other factors precipitating inappropriate urges and behaviours. A primary aim was to ensure that he did not remain socially isolated but was 'helped back into his place in society and to maintain his employment in the community'.[49]

Finally, there were medical offenders for whom medical treatment was advocated, often in association with a custodial sentence, as a means primarily of achieving greater continence and self-control. Typically, these were cases where homosexual behaviour was viewed as obsessive and/or predatory. By the 1970s, group psychotherapy, such as that available at the Douglas Inch Centre in Glasgow, a forensic out-patient clinic in Glasgow specialising in psychodynamic therapy, was increasingly recommended for such offenders, but the predominant treatments advanced were aversion and sex-suppressant therapy. Thus, in the case of T.P., tried before the High Court in Glasgow in 1968 for contravention of section 11 of the Criminal Law Amendment Act 1885, the physician-superintendent of Dingleton Hospital recommended that, in addition to his prostate gland being investigated, the panel should be referred to the Royal Edinburgh Hospital for aversion therapy. In his view, 'It might be that some kind of negative conditioning, like electric shocks, in relation to homosexual stimulation might turn him against this form of sexual activity.'[50] In other cases, such as that of A.H.L., tried for a series of offences against teenage boys in 1977, supervised drug therapy, such as the use of Anquil, designed 'to curb his sex drive', was recommended.[51]

In assessing the impact of psychiatric evidence on sentencing for homosexual offences in this period, the picture is complicated by the fact that many such offences were part of wider charges involving the sexual assault or corruption of young children. Indeed, one of the more notable features of such trials was the conflation of homosexual offences with what would now be regarded as paedophilia. Moreover, due to the severity of the charges brought in the High Court, its proceedings inevitably exclude many cases in which medical evidence may have contributed to more lenient, non-custodial sentences being passed.

In general, where an offence was deemed sufficiently serious to warrant a prison sentence, the duration of such a sentence was not determined on thera-peutic grounds. However, there *was* a small but increasing number of cases where medical evidence does appear to have elicited the use of section 3 of the Criminal Justice (Scotland) Act 1949 to impose probationary orders with asso-ciated psychiatric treatment.[52] In many such instances, the younger, the more self-reflective and co-operative the defendant, the less fixated his sexual behav-iour, and the less protracted the recommended treatment,[53] the more likely it was that such evidence would affect sentencing.

Thus, in the case of H.C.M.,[54] accused in 1953 of sodomy and lewd and libidi-nous practices with soldiers from Redford barracks, medical testimony for the defence stressed the panel's self-awareness that there was 'something far wrong with him psychically', and his willingness to leave the country after treatment to go for further 'special' therapy in Denmark.[55] No treatment, it was alleged, would be forthcoming within the Scottish prison system.[56] It was also argued that, as a 'passive homosexual', in medical circles, the defendant would be viewed as having 'a definite constitutional disease' rather than the criminality often diagnostic of the 'active homosexual'.[57] In the event, H.C.M. was sentenced to three years' probation on condition that he entered Moray Royal Institution at Perth for treatment for 12 months as a voluntary boarder.

In the case of T.A., convicted in 1954 of eight charges of gross indecency and three of attempted sodomy in Hawick, under section 11 of the Criminal Law Amendment Act 1885, the defence also requested a psychiatric report with a view to mitigating sentence.[58] Despite the involvement of males below the age of 21, again the willingness of the panel to 'have himself put right' and to co-operate in treatment was decisive, as was his awareness, in the view of the psychiatric witness, that homosexual relations would always be intrinsically unfulfilling and 'accompanied by feelings of shame and disgust'. T.A. was put on three years' probation, subject to spending 12 months in a mental hospital. Subsequently, a revised court order requiring attendance only as an out-patient was issued on the grounds of his responsiveness to oestrogen treatment and psychotherapy.

Similarly, in the case of R.H., tried in 1956 at the High Court in Edinburgh on charges of sodomy and lewd and libidinous practices, mitigating evidence in favour of treatment as a voluntary boarder in a mental hospital was submitted both by Professor Sir David Henderson, physician-superintendent of the Royal Edinburgh Hospital, and Dr William Boyd, consultant psychiatrist to the Scottish Prison Service. The panel was portrayed as the victim of predatory and precocious male teenagers, and not, given his previous heterosexual relationships, as a 'true homosexual'. His sexual proclivities were seen as a function of his deprived upbringing – sharing a bed throughout adolescence with his brother – and his dysfunctional relations with girls, rather than a deep-seated fixation, indicating a likely positive outcome for treatment. Accordingly, R.H. was remitted to Hawkshead Hospital for residential treatment for a year under a three-year probationary order. As with T.A., treatment proved so effective that this was duly revised in favour of out-patient therapy.[59]

A fourth case illustrates that, by the end of the period, medical options were being deployed even in cases involving younger male adolescents. In the case of I.S.N., charged with sodomy and lewd and libidinous practices in 1979,[60] a number of considerations were advanced by a consultant psychiatrist of the Douglas Inch Centre: that the behaviour was immature rather than predatory; that a custodial sentence would not be in the long-term interests of society; that progress in therapeutic techniques had considerably increased the chances of effecting behaviour modification; and that such techniques were available at the centre. Accordingly, sentence was deferred while the panel attended the centre for group therapy and individual counselling. Although, after six months, psychiatric reports could not report any 'dramatic change in his personality [or] sexuality', the accused was eventually admonished and dismissed so as to enable him to 'continue to work on his problems and consolidate his gains'.[61]

However, such attitudes were often contested by psychiatric witnesses for the prosecution. In the case of H.C.M., after he had breached his probation order and reoffended, the Lord Justice Clerk endorsed the view of Sir David Henderson that 'lenient treatment' having failed, a 'stringent penalty of imprisonment' was called for. In his opinion, 'a little severity just for once might put him in a proper frame of mind' for benefiting thereafter from therapy. The defence counsel's plea that the panel should 'be allowed to leave the country in order to his undergoing treatment in a foreign clinic for his mental condition' was summarily dismissed.[62]

The medical case for the prosecution also prevailed in the case of J.G., tried before the High Court in Edinburgh in 1973 for sodomy and attempted rape. The defence psychiatrist from Woodilee Hospital pressed for a sentence of compulsory admission to a psychiatric unit for two to three years under the Mental Health (Scotland) Act 1960, on the grounds that his 'personality disorder . . . associated with sexual deviation of a homosexual nature', could be expected to respond to treatment. However, Dr H.G., consultant in charge of Stobhill General Hospital and clinical lecturer in psychological medicine at the University of Glasgow, while conceding that homosexuality amounted to 'mental illness', did not regard the panel as a suitable case for treatment, given 'the long duration of his homosexual orientation'.[63] A sentence of four years' imprisonment was imposed. Similarly, in the case in of I.N., the consultant psychiatrist giving evidence on behalf of the procurator-fiscal was dismissive of any recourse to medical treatment in sentencing. While he conceded that the defendant's behaviour might be modified, he considered it unlikely that his sexual orientation would be changed since 'he [was] not genuinely disposed to change it':

> He is talking of treatment at present because he wishes to avoid prison . . .
> I do not think it would help his prospects of learning to conform to
> society's wishes if, having thoroughly broken the law because he believes
> it is a bad law, he were to be encouraged to view medical treatment as a
> means of escaping punishment. If convicted, he would do best to thole his
> assize and seek help at a later date out of a genuine wish to change.[64]

In a variety of other cases, also, favourable psychiatric evidence signally failed to affect sentencing, especially where minors were involved. In the case of J.B., tried before the High Court in Dundee in 1961 on charges of sodomy and lewd and libidinous practices, extensive psychiatric evidence was produced relating to the impact of his previous imprisonment in Japanese prisoner-of-war camps, his vulnerability to blackmail from adolescent boys, and his willingness to enter a mental hospital for treatment, but a sentence of three years' imprisonment was imposed.[65]

Likewise, in the case of P.C., charged at the High Court in Perth in 1965 with sodomy and lewd and libidinous practices, the presiding judge was not disposed to delay sentencing for a psychiatric report.[66] He rejected the argument of defence counsel that such a report might be useful in determining the effects of different terms of imprisonment, on the grounds that, in his opinion, the offender would receive treatment in prison anyway. A sentence of six years' imprisonment was duly delivered.[67]

A similar fate befell W.T.M., convicted in 1971 for a range of homosexual offences with males between the ages of 14 and 22. When the case had been initially heard before the Sheriff Court, strong evidence in favour of a non-custodial sentence, conditional on a two-year period of treatment, had been submitted by Dr H.G. In his opinion, W.T.M.'s homosexuality was 'a mental illness' and 'require[d] and [was] susceptible to treatment', but did not justify detention under a hospital order. A further report from Dr J.M. of Riccatsbar Hospital, Paisley, was even more supportive of a probationary sentence. In his view, the fact that the panel was bi-sexual and had previously enjoyed satisfactory heterosexual relationships, that 'his basic personality' and 'motivation towards normal behaviour' was 'good', and that he was 'very willing to co-operate', made the prognosis for treatment very hopeful. However, when, because of the nature of the charges, the case was remitted to the High Court in Edinburgh, a sentence of three years' imprisonment was imposed.[68]

The views of the judiciary with respect to psychiatric evidence were sometimes most clearly articulated during appeal proceedings. In the appeal by C.W.H. in 1955 against conviction for contravention of section 11 of the Criminal Law Amendment Act 1885, the transcript of the original trial clearly reveals that, despite the evidence of the physician-superintendent of Dingleton Hospital that the panel's homosexuality was a mental disease with 'a pathological origin' and susceptible to treatment (including drug therapy), the sheriff was disposed to view the offences as a function of a 'moral' rather than 'psychological' defect. He reported to the Appeal Court that he was not satisfied that the offender's mental condition was abnormal or that 'it required, or would be susceptible to, medical treatment'. The appeal against a one-year prison sentence was accordingly dismissed.[69]

Similar sentiments were expressed by the presiding judge in his report to the Court of Appeal in the case of A.H.L. in 1977 against a seven-year prison sentence.[70] Psychiatric reports had emphasised that A.H.L.'s offences against young boys were due to his homosexual proclivities and could possibly be treated as a mental illness, preferably by attendance at a psychiatric clinic. In the view of Lord Wheatley, the priority was to take the offender 'out of circulation', whether or not effective treatment might be available in prison. He added a pointed postscript that the suggestion by psychiatrists that probationary treatment might be an option was wholly 'unrealistic' and merely served to raise 'unjustifiable hopes and corresponding disappointment'; something he recommended that psychiatrists submitting evidence in court should firmly take on board.[71] Although in this case the psychiatric reports were forwarded on to the prison authorities, application to appeal was refused.[72]

## Conclusion

It is problematic to draw firm conclusions from this overview of merely two perspectives on the medical perception and treatment of homosexual offenders in Scotland in the period 1950–80. Evidence to the Wolfenden Committee was arguably driven as much by concern to justify departmental procedures as to capture an accurate picture of contemporary medical and legal practices. In addition, not only may the evidence from the High Court be far from typical, but also the use of trial processes and appeal papers, as with all legal records, pose a range of methodological challenges.[73] It could be argued, for example, that due to the closure of High Court precognitions, I have accorded the narratives derived from medical reports undue priority and lacked due regard to 'the multiple texts that make up a legal record'. Finally, the evidence presented here was very much shaped and informed by legal discourses and desiderata. The exploration of clinical records and of gay archives and recollections may well reveal alternative narratives of how law and medicine interacted over homosexual issues.

None the less, some tentative conclusions can perhaps be drawn. First, it is clear that, in testimony to the Wolfenden Committee, the evidence of medical and legal witnesses from Scotland reflected the more general ambivalence towards medical strategies for homosexual offences articulated in its proceedings and final report. While many witnesses did embrace the need for the medical treatment and rehabilitation of offenders, and appear to have been increasingly sympathetic to more psychodynamic forms of psychotherapy, their mindset remained heavily rooted in taxonomies of deviance shaped by established notions of sexual pathology rather than in more progressive ideas of sexual expression and inclusion. Cure or sublimation, with their implications of self-rejection or self-denial, remained at the basis of therapy.

Secondly, an analysis of court records suggests that the impact of medical evidence on trial proceedings for homosexual offences was complex. From the 1950s, such evidence did play an increasing role in cases, and psychiatric reports figured ever more prominently in trial processes. However, medical testimony was by no means monopolised by the defence and could also be mobilised very effectively by the Crown Office. The evident lack of consensus over the aetiology of homosexuality and the efficacy of medical treatment further ensured that medical evidence was often marginalised within legal proceedings. Indeed, many cases reflected enduring tensions between medical conceptions of homosexual behaviour 'as a pathology or intrinsic condition' and judicial conceptions of it as embodying 'criminal sexual "acts" rather than identities'.[74] As a result, psychiatric issues continued to be framed within legal discourses that often reflected broader moral assumptions and concerns surrounding homosexuality within Scottish civil society, the very same assumptions and concerns that were to delay homosexual law reform north of the Border until 1980.[75]

### Acknowledgements

I am greatly indebted to the Wellcome Trust whose financial support made possible the original research upon which this article is based. I also wish to thank the Lord Justice General for permission to consult and cite selected

Scottish High Court trial processes and appeal papers held at the National Archives of Scotland. This chapter was originally published in Goold, I. and Kelly, C., eds, *Lawyers' Medicine: The Legislature, the Courts and Medical Practice 1760–2000* (Oxford, 2009) and I am indebted to Hart Publishing for permission to reprint it for the purposes of this volume.

## Notes

1. See, for example, Weeks, J., *Sex Politics and Society: The Regulation of Sexuality since 1800*, 2nd edn (London, 1989), chapters 6, 8; Higgins, P., *Heterosexual Dictatorship: Male Homosexuality in Post-War Britain* (London, 1996), 51–8; Davenport-Hines, R., *Sex, Death and Punishment: Attitudes to Sex and Sexuality in Britain since the Renaissance* (London, 1990), chapter 8. For an overview of the social politics of homosexual law reform in Scotland, see Davidson, R. and Davis, G., '"A Field for Private Members": The Wolfenden Committee and Scottish Homosexual Law Reform, 1950–67', *Twentieth Century British History* 15 (2004), 174–201; Davidson, R. and Davis, G., 'Sexuality and the State: The Campaign for Scottish Homosexual Law Reform, 1967–80', *Contemporary British History* 20 (2006), 533–58.

2. See, for example, Waters, C., 'Havelock Ellis, Sigmund Freud and the State: Discourses of Homosexual Identity in Interwar Britain', in Bland, L. and Doan, L., eds, *Sexology in Culture: Labelling Bodies and Desires* (Oxford, 1998), chapter 10; Waters, C., 'Disorders of the Mind, Disorders of the Body Social: Peter Wildeblood and the Making of the Modern Homosexual', in Conekin, B., Mort, F. and Waters, C., eds, *Moments of Modernity: Reconstructing Britain 1945–1964* (London and New York, 1999), 135–51; Crozier, I.D., 'Taking Prisoners: Havelock Ellis, Sigmund Freud, and the Construction of Homosexuality, 1897–1951', *Social History of Medicine* 13 (2000), 447–66; Houlbrook, M., *Queer London: Perils and Pleasures in the Sexual Metropolis, 1918–1957* (Chicago and London, 2005), 195–8, 257–62.

3. See, for example, Jivani, A., *Its Not Unusual: A History of Lesbian and Gay Britain in the Twentieth Century* (London, 1997), 122–8; Cant, B., ed., *Footsteps and Witnesses: Lesbian and Gay Lifestories from Scotland* (Edinburgh, 1993), 49; Davidson, T., ed., *And Thus Will I Freely Sing: An Anthology of Gay and Lesbian Writing from Scotland* (Edinburgh, 1989), 154–9.

4. King, M., Smith, G. and Bartlett, A., 'Treatments of Homosexuality in Britain since the 1950s – An Oral History: The Experience of Patients', *British Medical Journal*, 21 February 2004, 427; King, M., Smith, G. and Bartlett, A., 'Treatments of Homosexuality in Britain since the 1950s – An Oral History: The Experience of Professionals', *British Medical Journal*, 21 February 2004, 429.

5. The National Archives, London (TNA), HO345/9, Proceedings of the Wolfenden Committee on Homosexual Offences and Prostitution (PWC), summary record of 21st Meeting, March 1956. On the issue of variance in judicial practice, see also *Report of the Wolfenden Committee (RWC)*, Parliamentary Papers, Cmnd. 247 (1956–7), XIV, 63, paragraph 182; Henderson, D.K., *Society and Criminal Conduct* (Edinburgh, 1955), 25.

6. TNA, HO345/9, CHP/108, PWC, evidence of Faculty of Advocates, March 1956; National Archives of Scotland (NAS), HH60/268, evidence of Scottish Home Department, October 1954.

7. Evidence suggests that, prior to the Second World War, the police and judiciary in Scotland were often extremely hostile to the efforts of psychiatrists to secure medical treatment rather than imprisonment for their clients. See, for example, Merrilees, W., *The Short Arm of the*

*Law: The Memoirs of William Merrilees OBE: Chief Constable The Lothians and Peebles Constabulary* (London, 1966), 121–2. This attitude was strongly reinforced by the judgement of the Lord Justice Clerk in the case of *HM Advocate v M.* in March 1944. M. had been charged on indictment in the Sheriff Court of the Lothians and Peebles at Edinburgh with a number of homosexual offences under the Criminal Law Amendment Act 1885. The sheriff had been sympathetic to sentence being deferred until the likely response of the panel to psychotherapeutic treatment under a probationary order had been assessed. However, the Lord Justice Clerk determined that it was not the court's prerogative merely to approach such cases 'from the purely medical standpoint', and with a 'single eye to the possible rehabilitation of the offender'. Instead, he ruled that 'the duty of the Court was to give effect to the law which punished such offences as crimes' without delay, and he imposed a sentence of eighteen months' imprisonment: NAS, ED15/109, note by Scottish Home Department, 18 March 1946.

8.   TNA, HO345/15, CHP/TRANS/42, PWC, evidence of K.M. Hancock, director of the Scottish Prison and Borstal Services, 1 November 1955; TNA, HO345/16. CHP/TRANS/60, evidence of Association of Sheriffs Substitute, 9 April 1956. See also, Moran, L.J., *The Homosexual(ity) of Law* (London and New York, 1996), 116. It was obligatory to have a medical report on any person under the age of 21 involved in such cases.

9.   TNA, HO345/15, CHP/TRANS/41, PWC, evidence of W. Boyd, 1 November 1955.

10.  TNA, HO345/16, PWC, evidence of Magistrates of Corporation of Glasgow, 9 April 1956.

11.  Scottish Advisory Council on the Treatment and Rehabilitation of Offenders, *Psycho-Therapeutic Treatment of Certain Offenders with Special Reference to the Case of Persons Convicted of Sexual and Unnatural Offences* (Edinburgh, 1948), 6–9.

12.  NAS, HH60/268, PWC, memorandum by Scottish Home Department, October 1954. In the opinion of Dr T.D. Inch, medical adviser to the Scottish Prison and Borstal Services, offenders who were mentally defective, neurotic or psychotic should be hospitalised and the 'homosexual psychopath' subjected to an indeterminate sentence within a 'special institution or colony'. The routine provision of medical reports was also advocated by some magistrates, but not by the Crown Agent: TNA, HO345/16, evidence of Magistrates of the Corporation of Glasgow, 9 April 1956; evidence of L.I. Gordon, crown agent, 9 April 1956.

13.  NAS, HH60/268, PWC, memorandum by Scottish Home Department, October 1954.

14.  NAS, HH57/1287, PWC, note by T.D. Inch, 13 October 1955. On the scarcity of psychiatric resources in Britain, see also *RWC*, 62, paragraph 180; Westwood, G., *Society and the Homosexual* (London, 1952), 89.

15.  TNA, HO345/15, CHP/TRANS/41, PWC, evidence of W. Boyd, 1 November 1955. In view of this, the policy of the Scottish Home Department, in direct contrast to that of the Home Office, was to integrate the prison medical service with mainstream and psychiatric medicine within the National Health Service. The lack of adequate resources for the implementation of probationary treatment for sexual offenders in Scotland was an enduring problem. In 1959, a Glasgow psychiatrist reported that, due mainly to a shortage of qualified staff, provisions were still 'ludicrously inadequate . . . The usual treatment is to administer some drugs and to perform a little elementary psycho-analysis': *Scotsman*, 6 June 1959. See also Henderson, D.K. and Batchelor, I.R.C., *A Textbook of Psychiatry for Students and Practitioners*, 9th edn (London, 1962), 206; Wardrop, K., *Psychiatry and Probation* (London, 1971), 8.

16.  NAS, HH57/1287, PWC, note by Scottish Home Department on Scottish Prisons and Borstal Institutions, October 1955.

17.  NAS, HH57/1287, PWC, note by Scottish Home Department.

18.  For Golla's use of hormone treatment, see Golla, F.L. and Hodge, R.S., 'Hormone Treatment of the Sexual Offender', *Lancet*, 11 June 1949, 1006–7.

19.  NAS, HH57/1288, memorandum by T.D. Inch, 'Sexual Offenders: Treatment in Prisons'; TNA, HO345/15, CHP/TRANS/42, PWC, evidence of T.D. Inch, 1 November 1955.

More routinely, homosexual offenders suffering from anxiety states were treated with Langactic and Sodium Amytal: NAS, HH57/1288, H.S. Walter, psychiatric clinic, Aberdeen Royal Infirmary, to G.I. Manson, medical officer, HM Prison, Peterhead, 3 December 1957.

20. TNA, HO345/15, CHP/TRANS/42, PWC, evidence of T.D. Inch, 1 November 1955. The subsequent disclosure by the Wolfenden Committee of the use of hormone therapy produced some colourful headlines. See *Sunday Pictorial*, 16 February 1958: 'Sex Pills for Scots in Jail'.

21. See NAS, HH57/1287, note by T.D. Inch for PWC, October 1955; TNA, HO345/15, CHP/TRANS/42, PWC, evidence of T.D. Inch and W. Boyd, 1 November 1955.

22. Significantly, this was not a view shared by many Scottish prison medical officers: TNA, HO345/15, CHP/TRANS/42, PWC, evidence of T.D. Inch and W. Boyd, 1 November 1955.

23. See, TNA, HO345/7, CHP/36 and 345/16, CHP/ TRANS/62, PWC, evidence of W. Rushforth and W.P. Kraemer, 10 April 1956. In 1956, the clinic was staffed by five medically-qualified therapists and six lay therapists. Both medical and lay therapists underwent a period of training during which they themselves had to undergo 'a complete and successful personal analysis'. The clinic employed a mixture of Freudian and Jungian techniques, with drugs used 'only exceptionally as an adjunct to treatment'. Its practice was heavily influenced by the work of Melanie Klein, the pioneering Viennese psychoanalyst. In evidence, it was claimed that the clinic was the only 'analytical group' then operating in Scotland. The clinic accepted in the region of 100 new patients a year, of which about 10 per cent were 'overt homosexuals', largely referred by the police, a minister, or a general practitioner. The lay therapists, who were unpaid during their training, were not formally recognised within the Edinburgh medical establishment or by the university.

24. TNA, HO345/16, PWC, evidence of W.P. Kraemer, 10 April 1956.

25. TNA, HO345/16, PWC, evidence of W.P. Kraemer.

26. British Medical Association (BMA) Archives, B/107/1/2, memorandum by Professor John Glaister, 30 June 1955.

27. The reasons listed for unsuitability for treatment were: not recommended by specialist (44.7 per cent); too dull or inadequate character (23.4 per cent); absence of any anxiety over sexual practices or of any real wish to change (8.5 per cent); denial of tendency or tendency not apparent (17 per cent); too old and unadaptable or practice too well established (4.3 per cent); belief that conviction has cured offender (2.1 per cent): TNA, HO345/9, CHP/88, PWC, evidence of Scottish Home Department, 30 October 1955; TNA, CAB129/66, Cabinet memorandum, sexual offences, Secretary of State for Scotland, 17 February 1954. For comparative data for England and Wales, see *RWC*, 66, paragraph 197.

28. Professor Glaister also considered the likelihood of cure for 'innate inverts' as utopian. He felt it likely that 'there will always be a nucleus in our midst, just as we have other groups of handicapped persons': BMA Archives, B/107/1/2, memorandum by Glaister, 30 June 1955.

29. TNA, HO345/15, CHP/TRANS/42, PWC, evidence of W. Boyd, 1 November 1955.

30. TNA, HO345/15, CHP/TRANS/42, PWC, evidence of K.M. Hancock and T.D. Inch, 1 November 1955; evidence of W. Boyd, 1 November 1955. Evidence on the outcome of treatment was also compromised by the lack of follow-up surveillance of released prisoners. Inch testified: 'As regards the after effects, certainly none of them have yet come back to us but we do not know, and we have no means of knowing, whether they continue treatment afterwards or not . . . I am unfortunately quite unable to say what the permanent end result is.' TNA, HO345/15, CHP/TRANS/42, PWC, evidence of K.M. Hancock and T.D. Inch, 1 November 1955; NAS, HH57/1288, Departmental minute, 5 December 1957.

31. TNA, HO345/7; 345/16 PWC, evidence of W. Rushforth and W.P. Kraemer, 10 April 1956.

32. TNA, HO345/7; 345/16 PWC, evidence of W. Rushforth and W.P. Kraemer. They anticipated that group psychotherapy might prove more effective but predicted that bringing together a group of homosexuals within the clinic would provoke a public outcry.

33. Indeed, Winifred Rushforth considered that the primary role of the clinic was *not* to try and alter sexual orientation, but to facilitate the patient's understanding of his homosexual feelings and anxieties.

34. Sir David Henderson attributed the failure of psychiatrists to 'gain the complete confidence of the legal profession' in homosexual cases to this lack of any clear evidence of a 'cure'. See Henderson, *Society and Criminal Conduct*, 25. This disparity between medical and legal expectations also prevailed south of the Border: see Westwood, *Society and the Homosexual*, 90.

35. Thus, according to Sheriff Hamilton, 'It [was] fashionable to say that homosexual offenders [had] a "mental kink" and require[d] treatment but apart from the odd case of physical ailment such as prostate gland enlargement, the only "treatment" which [might] be beneficial [was] such as [would] strengthen the willpower to resist offending': TNA, HO345/8, PWC, memorandum prepared by Association of Sheriffs-Substitute, 1955.

36. Thus Sheriff-Substitute Middleton of Dunfermline and Kinross challenged the committee as to whether there was ever a homosexual case 'where the relationship [was] confined to two individuals, and there [was] no danger to other members of society': TNA, HO345/16, evidence on behalf of Association of Sheriffs-Substitute, 9 April 1956.

37. TNA, HO345/8 and 16, CHP/44 and CHP/TRANS/60, PWC, evidence of Association of Sheriffs-Substitute, March 1955, 9 April 1956; TNA, HO345/16, PWC, evidence of stipendary magistrate, Glasgow, 9 April 1956.

38. For a discussion of the broader debate over homosexuality in Scottish society, see Davidson and Davis, '"A Field for Private Members"'.

39. See especially, *RWC*, 117–21; TNA, HO345/12 and /16, PWC, 15 October 1954, 10 April 1956; HO345/2, J. Adair to W.C. Roberts, 4 October 1956; HO345/10, note on WC discussion meetings, 11 and 12 September 1956.

40. See TNA, HO345/9, PWC, minutes of 21st meeting, March 1956.

41. See Crozier, I., '"All the Appearances were Perfectly Natural": The Anus of the Sodomite in Nineteenth-Century Medical Discourse', in Forth, C.E., and Crozier, I., eds, *Body Parts: Critical Explorations in Corporeality* (New York and Oxford, 2005), 65–84.

42. See, for example, Edinburgh City Archive (ECA) Burgh Court Papers, case of W.B.A., letter of defendant to clerk of court, 25 May 1960. Significantly, some 36 per cent of the patients attending the Jordanburn Nerve Hospital in the 1950s for problems relating to homosexuality, for whom medical correspondence survives, were referred either by solicitors or general practitioners in relation to criminal proceedings: Lothian Health Services Archive, Edinburgh University Library, LHB7/CC1, Royal Edinburgh Hospital medical clinic and out-patient letters, 1950–8.

43. ECA, district court papers for 1960 and 1970.

44. This lack of medical investigation was one of many criticisms of the judicial system levelled by the Scottish Minorities Group (SMG) in their campaign for homosexual law reform: National Library of Scotland, miscellaneous pamphlets of the SMG, *The Case for Homosexual Law Reform in Scotland* (1973).

45. Although previously in the public domain, because of their sensitive nature, in accordance with the Data Protection Act 1998, these records are now closed for 75 years unless special access is granted by the High Court of Justiciary.

46. See, for example, NAS, JC9/36, 38; JC26/1956/65, trial papers of H.C.M. On the correlation of class and medical evidence, see also Higgins, *Heterosexual Dictatorship*, 160–1.

47. See, for example, NAS, JC9/37; JC26/1954/145, trial minutes and papers relating to J.H.

48. NAS, JC34/4/189, appeal papers relating to C.W.H., report of proceedings at Sheriff Court, Hawick.

49. See, for example, NAS, JC26/1962/90, trial papers relating to J.J.T., report by Dr M.A.E.S., Eastern District Hospital Psychiatric Unit, 26 October 1962; NAS, JC26/1973/293, trial papers relating to J.G.

50. NAS, JC9/57; JC26/1968/216, trial minutes and papers relating to T.P. For reference to the use of aversion therapy, see also JC26/1970/204, trial papers relating to R.C. In such cases, aversion therapy was clearly perceived as suppressing anti-social behaviour rather than effecting a genuine reorientation of sexual preference.

51. NAS, JC26/1977/386, trial papers relating to A.H.L. For the use of drug therapy, including oestrogen therapy, see also NAS, JC26/1956/65; JC26/1979/402; JC26/1979/200.

52. In the view of two leading Scottish psychiatrists, Sir David Henderson and Ivor R.C. Batchelor, by 1962 improving relations between the medical and legal professions had 'led to a greater emphasis on treatment and rehabilitation rather than on an arbitrary prison sentence': *Textbook of Psychiatry*, 194.

53. Sir David Henderson, who had given evidence in Scottish trials over many decades, reported that, where psychoanalysis had been recommended, once its duration and uncertain outcome had been explained, the court usually took the view that treatment should be undertaken only after a prison sentence had been served: Henderson and Batchelor, *Textbook of Psychiatry*, 206.

54. NAS, JC9/36, JC9/38, JC26/1956/65, trial minutes and papers relating to H.C.M.

55. Specifically, oestrogen treatment under Dr Christian Hamburger, the Danish endocrinologist. 'An institution in Ireland' was also recommended.

56. Significantly, the Lord Justice General declined to have this point elaborated, interjecting that: 'I think I know the position in prison.' Evidence in other cases suggests that this was in fact the situation in the 1950s. See, for example, evidence of C.W.F.W., a habitual homosexual offender, to the effect that he was promised treatment but 'as soon as I have got into prison nobody has in any way been concerned with the matter except that I should serve the sentence . . . I have been compelled to be my own doctor in this matter': NAS, JC34/4/209, appeal papers relating to C.W.F.W.

57. Medical evidence for the defence was submitted by Dr A.P. Cawadias, an endocrinologist, author of *Hermaphroditos: The Human Intersex*, and former vice-president of the Royal Society of Medicine. In practice, there is some evidence that law officers viewed the 'active' partner more leniently and perceived the 'passive' partner as the 'real' transgressor' in bringing another man to orgasm. See Bancroft, J., *Human Sexuality and Its Problems* (Edinburgh, 1989), 714. This viewpoint was undoubtedly reinforced by the medical discourse surrounding the increase in sexually transmitted diseases, which identified passive homosexuals as major 'reservoirs of infection'. See Davidson, R., *Dangerous Liaisons: A Social History of Venereal Disease in Twentieth-Century Scotland* (Amsterdam and Atlanta, 2000), 251.

58. NAS, JC9/37, trial minutes relating to T.A.

59. NAS, JC9/39; JC26/1956/122, trial minutes and papers relating to R.H.

60. NAS, JC26/1979/194, trial papers relating to I.S.N.

61. This is in marked contrast to the case of T.F. the same year, charged with similar offences before the High Court in Edinburgh. In this instance, psychiatric reports stressed that the panel had long-standing predatory paederastic tendencies, that he regarded his casual sexual acts with adolescent males as socially acceptable, and that, given his previous convictions, it was not considered that 'psychiatry ha[d] anything to offer as an alternative to imprisonment': NAS, JC9/82; JC26/1979/402, trial minutes and papers relating to T.F.

62. NAS, JC26/1956/65, trial papers relating to H.C.M.

63. NAS, JC26/1973/293, trial papers relating to J.G.

64. NAS, JC26/1979/194, trial papers relating to I.N. See also JC/34/9/184, trial papers relating to J.R.; JC34/21/230, appeal papers relating to R.M.K.W.

65. NAS, JC26/1961/3, trial papers relating to J.B.

66. The possible conflict between the need for prompt sentencing and for adequate medical evidence was an issue that had been raised by the Wolfenden Committee. See *RWC*, 64.

67. NAS, JC34/11/42, appeal papers relating to P.C., transcript of trial in Sheriff Court. See also JC26/1966/67, trial papers relating to C.E.J.T.

68.   NAS, JC9/66; JC26/1971/344, minutes and trial papers relating to W.T.M.
69.   NAS, JC34/4/189 appeal papers relating to C.W.H.
70.   NAS, JC9/78; JC26/1977/386; JC34/26/300, minutes, trial papers and appeal papers relating to A.H.L.
71.   This very much echoed the views of the Wolfenden Report. See *RWC*, 61–2.
72.   Such a case resonated with earlier warnings by the psychiatrists, David Henderson and Ivor Batchelor, that a co-ordinated approach to cases involving sexual anomalies would 'never be accomplished so long as angry judges thunder[ed] moralistic platitudes from the Bench, and indiscreet psychiatrists indulge[d] in optimistic theorizing': Henderson and Batchelor, *Textbook of Psychiatry*, 207.
73.   On these challenges, see especially, Robertson, S., 'What's Law Got to Do with It? Legal Records and Sexual Histories', *Journal of the History of Sexuality* 14 (2005), 161–85.
74.   On this tension, see Cook, M., 'Law', in Cocks, H.G. and Houlbrook, M., eds, *The Modern History of Sexuality* (Basingstoke, 2006), 79.
75.   The Sexual Offences Act 1967, which decriminalised male homosexual acts in private in England and Wales between consenting adults over the age of 21, did not apply to Scotland. Similar provisions for Scotland had to await the Criminal Justice (Scotland) Act of 1980. For details of the constraints operating in Scotland after 1967, see Davidson and Davis, 'Sexuality and the State'.

# 9

# 'Boy' Clerks and Scottish Health Administration, 1867–1956

## Ian Levitt

In late 1953, Sir George Henderson, the secretary of the Department of Health for Scotland was due for retirement and senior officials in the Scottish Office and Treasury began to consider his successor.[1] Constitutionally the selection of a successor was the responsibility of the prime minister on the advice of the Scottish secretary, but in practice, possible names were considered first by these officials. Henderson had been secretary since 1943 and had been heavily involved in the introduction of the National Health Service, as well as the post-war housing programme. Choosing his successor proved not an easy task. One of the under-secretaries was regarded as too close to retirement, whilst another was a 'nice old thing', who had long since 'treaded water'. The third, a recent appointment, was deemed to lack the breadth of experience such a post required. In the event the nomination went to Harold Smith, the Scottish Office London liaison officer (an under-secretary position), who had served previously in the Department. The nomination did not go without some concern, the Treasury noting that Smith had originally been appointed as an assistant solicitor before transfer to the administrative class in the general reorganisation of emergency services immediately before the war.[2] After some hesitation the Treasury finally agreed the nomination, but, within official circles, it highlighted the acute concern about the Department's ability to meet the challenge surrounding the nationalised health service and the ancillary areas of housing and town planning. The problem of succession and the Treasury's hesitation was principally the fact that the Department and its predecessor bodies had been staffed through the recruitment of 'boy clerks' – those that had entered service immediately on leaving school, rather than university.[3] Characteristically, government departments were headed by those appointed after university through open competition, successful candidates being offered vacancies in departments based on how well they had performed, with posts in the Treasury, Colonial Office and Home Office considered amongst the 'top rank'. This chapter will seek to examine the structure of the Department of Health for Scotland, and critically assess how far staff capabilities may have inhibited or otherwise affected the quality of health and related services north of the Border. In recent years there has been renewed interest in the evolution of twentieth-century government machinery and its ability to implement policy consistently and over a wider social and economic field than previously.[4] There has also been continued interest in the development of Scottish health policy.[5] Although such accounts have looked closely at the evolution of policy and suggested structural problems concerning funding and institutional resistance to state intervention, they have typically been less interested in the capacity of Scottish departments to advise ministers and implement decisions effectively. Thus the chapter will look first at the origins of the administrative structure and its implications for the effective management of Scottish public health in the period before 1919. It will then assess its subsequent adaptation when faced with post-war 'reconstruction' and, after 1921, the subsequent restriction on public expenditure. Finally, it will provide an assessment of official reaction to the Department's capacity to manage the broader collective provision embedded in the post-war welfare state.

## The Board System and Local Health Supervision, 1867–1919

As an administrative system Scottish health services began after the passing of the Public Health (Scotland) Act in 1867. Implementing the Act was the responsibility of the Board of Supervision for the relief of the poor, constitutionally a sub-department of the Home Office, but in reality a board that operated semi-independently in terms of its administration. Immediately after the Act was passed, the Treasury agreed to the appointment of 'minor' staff clerks to lead a public health branch (which contained other more junior clerks) within the Board.[6] The Board itself had a full-time chairman and a number of unpaid other members, some of whom held other legal appointments within the Scottish justice system. In comparison to other Whitehall departments, the Board was very much unique in its *modus operandi*, especially after the reform of the civil service to ensure competitive entry into its ranks. The chairman and secretary were Crown appointments, but all junior appointments were left to Board members; they considered 'nominations' and interviewed those they thought most appropriate. In essence employment by the Board was based on patronage.

In the period immediately after the 1867 Act such an attitude probably mattered little in terms of implementing policy. Uniformly, if they had not attended university, the clerical staff were educated at secondary schools until at least 16 years of age. Such did not imply that they were, or had to be, Scots. A 'boy copyist', C. Cleveland Ellis, who eventually became an outdoor inspector, was from Malvern, his main claim for the post apparently being his family's boarding house for retired military and other suitably connected retired annuitants.[7] The Board's chairman came from a military family, as did several of the senior officers. Irrespective of the nature of the appointments, the Board's duties were primarily inspectorial, ensuring that local authorities implemented the infectious diseases and scavenging sections of the Act, and auditing the various statistical returns that were required. Board activity was thus highly routinised and although, on occasion, it instructed local authorities to take action to close polluted wells and offer appropriate medical care during epidemics, its primary duty was not the preparation of new legislation. In Scotland responsibility for such action lay with the lord advocate in conjunction with the home secretary, and after the Secretary for Scotland Act, 1885, the Scottish secretary. The Board's epistolary style was well known.

The Conservative government's decision in 1889 to reform local government, introduce democratically elected county councils (householder franchise) and compel the appointment of county medical officers of health, ushered in a new tempo in local administration.[8] The Board of Supervision, with its part-time medical officer (appointed in 1872), who, on instruction, responded to break-downs in local administration, was clearly an anachronism where public health was regarded as an imperative guiding local action. County medical officers of health could not be dismissed without the support of the Scottish secretary and such officers were soon pronouncing with authority on such matters as the closure of schools as a result of local epidemics. The Treasury's action refusing the regrading of Board clerical salaries in 1891, unless a more competitive entrance examination was set, represented the first onslaught at reforming the Board, the Treasury official noting that 'we cannot, I think, let this go on'.[9] After lengthy correspondence, in which the Treasury noted that 'the entrance examination in force scarcely exceeds what is in most Government Departments required from persons of the Messenger Class', the Board agreed a system of open competition.[10]

The incoming Liberal government of 1892 was further committed to local government reform and as a result of the Local Government (Scotland) Act of 1894 democratically elected parish councils took the place of the heritor-appointed parochial boards. More pertinent for health policy, the Board of Supervision was replaced by the Local Government Board for Scotland (LGB(S)), which was placed directly under the control of the Scottish secretary (there had been constitutional doubts about his ability to compel the Board of Supervision to take action). To facilitate this control the Scottish Office's under-secretary, based in London, was made an ex-officio member of the LGB(S), whose members also contained the solicitor-general and three Crown appointments – a chairman, a legal member (an advocate of seven years' standing) and a full-time medical member. The primary purpose of this reform was to ensure that the Scottish secretary could take action, if felt necessary, to ensure the implementation of the Public Health Act on the direct advice of the

Board or by issuing minutes for the Board to implement. The Public Health
(Scotland) Act of 1897 and the Burgh Police (Scotland) Act of 1902 were very
much the result of the increased politicisation of the health agenda. These Acts
redefined the duties of local authorities, compelling them to take more preventative action and to implement the instructions of the Scottish secretary in cases
where he felt that they had been in default in their duties. Burghs generally
improved local facilities such as sewerage and street cleansing: for example,
Falkirk, which had once been described as the 'dirtiest' town in Scotland, was
soon noted for its paved and well-kept streets.

    Despite the subsequent legislation, the 1894 Act contained two weaknesses
impacting on health surveillance. First, the constitutional position of a board
based in Edinburgh, reporting to a minister at Westminster, remained. Thus the
LGB(S) was not constructed on the basis of other UK departments such as the
Home Office, or even the 'Scotch' Education Department (SED). In these departments, first-division clerks, usually graduates appointed in open competition,
headed up blocks of work. (The SED's clerks were usually ex-schoolteachers and
hence graduates.) LGB(S) members were meant to combine an appreciation
of Scottish opinion and deal with all but the most political issues directly in
Edinburgh, and to manage Board work accordingly. Thus, there was no constitutional imperative to reorganise the clerical branches on the basis of an administrative structure. This second weakness was soon recognised by the Scottish
secretary. In 1895 he sought the appointment of an assistant secretary, but in the
face of Treasury opposition on the grounds that the Board's staffing had been
established on a clerical basis, accepted the suggestion of the post of chief clerk.[11]
(At that time the salary of LGB(S) members was between £1,000 and £1,400 per
annum, with the secretary earning between £700 and £1,000 and a head of branch,
a staff clerk, receiving £250–£350. By comparison, senior clerks at the Scottish
Office received between £450 and £600, the assistant under-secretary £1,000 and
the permanent under-secretary £1,500. The differential in salary between the clerical and administrative officers was quite clear, even taking into account a London
'allowance'.) The clerk's purpose was to manage the branches on a day-to-day
basis, leaving the secretary greater freedom to work more directly with the
LGB(S). Two branches remained much as they had been since 1867 – poor law
and public health – but in consequence of the 1894 Act, local government was
added to the statistical branch and a further branch, audit, was established to
review local authority finance. Ultimately, the LGB(S) operated very much in
subsidiary form to the English Local Government Board, looking to it for the
formation of new policy and draft legislation, which the LGB(S) could adapt for
Scottish purposes. It would be incorrect to suggest that the LGB(S) operated to
manipulate Scottish opinion to English thought – for example, the notification of

tuberculosis as an infectious disease in 1905 throughout the UK appears to have been a Scottish initiative – but it ultimately meant that Scottish civil servants operated in a climate that stressed 'fusion' in health policy, unless there were exceptional circumstances. Industrial Scotland was not dissimilar to industrial England (or Wales) and thus, apart from the operation of Scots law and certain municipal traditions (for instance on building control), industrial workers were entitled to receive the same level of protection in public health matters north and south of the Border. It meant that the LGB(S) remained staffed on a clerical basis – primarily 'boy' clerks appointed on leaving school. These included George Henderson, who in 1907 joined the Board of Education and then transferred to the Scottish Board, becoming a second division clerical officer in 1918.

The Treasury's attitude towards the LGB(S) was effectively stereotyped by the decision in 1867 to reaffirm its clerical basis. A full-time medical inspector was agreed in 1901 (the part-time medical officer could not investigate all the post-1897 Public Health (Scotland) Act inquiries), but other requests were confined to additional clerical appointments in consequence of new measures such as the Unemployed Workmen Act of 1905.[12] The LGB(S) sought a more serious review of its staffing in 1909, partly in response to clamant demand by the miners' union for better control of sanitary conditions, but also because of the greatly increased number of financial audits and local inspections, which, in turn, increased the flow of 'remedial' action required. Again the Treasury pointed out that policy matters were the remit of the Board members and not the clerical branches.[13] It was not the function of a branch head clerk to become too 'specialised' and stray into policy matters; it was the Board's duty to review any serious local maladministration and issue minutes for the various branches to execute. The expected protocol was for the legal or medical member of the LGB(S) to consider an issue, send a minute to the other and then to the chairman for onward issue to the solicitor-general and Scottish Office permanent undersecretary, who would, if necessary, obtain the views of the Scottish secretary. In that respect the Treasury's attitude was correct. In relation to the equivalent English department, on a proportional basis of population (or even by applying the 'Goschen' formula used to distribute education grants) the LGB(S) salaries exceeded those of equivalent senior staff south of the Border.

To assuage the Scottish secretary, in 1909 the Treasury agreed that the chief clerk could be called 'assistant secretary', but without an increase in salary (£500–£600 per annum).[14] With some additional minor clerks to handle routine work, the Treasury had conceded little. In 1913 the LGB(S) returned again to the distribution of its work, principally in relation to implementing the Town and Country Planning Act of 1909 and the political pressure to take action in the field of housing. There was no suggestion that the Board was seeking any sizeable government grant for subsiding house building, but it did see the necessity for firmer action to ensure more sanitary housing. This time the Treasury relented and agreed a second assistant secretary.[15] A town and country planning branch was established and the public health branch divided into two (the second dealing more directly with housing matters). At the outbreak of war in 1914, although Scottish health administration had increased its supervisory role, it was still founded on the assumption that the clerks were 'executive' officers, and were to carry out instructions and not provide or develop policy for consideration of ministers. At best the assistant secretaries might seek to influence LGB(S) policy, if their advice was requested. In any case matters of 'high policy' were discussed directly with the Scottish secretary by the permanent under-secretary. Other Scottish Office administrative staff liaised with the LGB(S) as appropriate, especially in matters concerning legislation, estimate debates and prospective legislation. In particular, the Scottish Office, not the LGB(S), held primary responsibility for local government taxation, as well as the Highlands and Islands (the 'Congested Districts').

   To what extent did the LGB(S)'s clerical basis impact on Scottish policy? Undoubtedly provision in the Highlands and Islands required special considera-tion, but grant aid to assist the road network, the ferries and the telegraphic system had been provided under the supervision of the Scottish Office. Distance to hospital and immediate medical care remained an issue, but with improved communication was less severe than previously. In the industrial south matters were different. Scottish health indicators in the late nineteenth century were little different from those in England, but it was becoming evident that the infant and maternal mortality rate was declining less swiftly. Occasionally an epidemic swept through an area with devastating consequences, which the health services found difficult to control. Most notably was not the bubonic plague which broke out in Glasgow in 1901 – the local authorities were quick to react and introduce isolation measures – but the outbreak of measles in 1907. This outbreak came close to demonstrating the limits of the city's control. The demand for isolation facilities as a result of slum overcrowding resulted in hospital over-crowding, which in turn facilitated the spread of the disease. Equally, unlike England which had established voluntary hospitals in the majority of urban areas outside of the cities that held teaching hospitals, the access to consultants in Scotland was very much predicated on the facilities available at the four universities – Glasgow, Edinburgh, Dundee and Aberdeen. Although there was nothing to suggest that the Scottish teaching hospitals lacked comparable facilities to those in England – the universities received a proportionately higher level of government medical grants – it meant that the Scottish population was much more dependent on those hospitals than the English.[16] In that respect, an administrative system based on a semi-judicial supervisory 'eye' supported by clerical officers appeared less relevant to the emerging exigencies.

## The Clerk, the Interventionist State and Scottish Subsidiarity 1919–39

At the end of the First World War Whitehall departments were reorganised on the basis of an assistant secretary managing divisions which contained discrete areas of work, assisted by two or more principals of administrative rank. The general increase in government activity meant a revision to both the nature of advice given to ministers and the overall supervision of policy subsequent to legislation or ministerial decision. The Scottish Office was reorganised on such a basis, as was the SED. However, the government's decision in 1919 not to create a Scottish Ministry (or Department) of Health, but a Scottish Board of Health (SBH), meant that the pre-war administrative arrangements in health and social welfare remained, albeit with the new Board subsuming the functions of the LGB(S), the Scottish National Health Insurance Commission (established in 1912) and the Highlands and Islands Medical Board (established in 1913). (These were similarly established on a clerical basis.) The SBH contained six permanent members drawn from the previous boards and commission (two of whom were medical practitioners), plus one woman, but the newly created parliamentary under-secretary of health (as vice-president) replaced the solicitor-general. The Scottish Office's permanent under-secretary was not made a member, the assumption being that the parliamentary under-secretary would provide a political, rather than administrative link with the Scottish secretary, who was named as president. Below the Board there was a secretary and seven 'divisions': national health insurance (approved societies, exemptions and employment regulations); local health administration (insurance committee medical services and local authority infectious diseases provision); 'community' health services (Highlands and Islands and nursing health services, and maternity and child welfare, including the medical inspection of schoolchildren); local health and welfare benefit supervision (public health, non-contributory OAPs and parish councils); housing and town planning; establishment; and finance and audit. An assistant secretary headed each division (the previous branches), but despite adopting the nomenclature of a Whitehall department, these officers were paid on the same basis as before reorganisation.[17] Except housing (see below) it meant that the clerical basis of the SBH remained a small group of members supported by executive branches. As the Treasury noted, the issue was not solely of the nature of the work that was undertaken but the officers' character and education, stating on one occasion in a somewhat condescending language that, 'the University Education of Class One men in London offices makes him more generally efficient and adaptable; the staff clerk in Edinburgh who has worked his way up and steeped in the Acts of Parliament and practice of his office is probably quite as useful a man at his particular job'.[18] A proposal to promote the clerks was rejected; being 'useful' was not enough. Interestingly the parliamentary under-secretary's private secretary was not drawn from the SBH, but from the Scottish Office, a reflection that such a position required an administrative officer (usually of principal rank) who held a greater command of the parliamentary process and of the work of other London-based departments. In day-to-day matters a minister could not be advised by a clerical officer, but in practice the Scottish Office official, unlike his Ministry of Health counterpart, had little background in health administration. At the same time the exclusion of the SBH officials from this post meant that the SBH held little experience in the day-to-day work of ministers and liaison with other Whitehall departments.

As a result of the report of the Royal Commission on Scottish Housing and the coalition government's commitment towards a post-war state-aided programme, a housing directorate was established within the SBH.[19] (The deficit in Scotland was estimated at 125,000 houses.) Its first director, paid on a scale equivalent to a Board member, was John Jack. Jack, a solicitor by training and Dunfermline's town clerk, had impressed Scottish ministers with his administrative abilities on the wartime scheme to house Rosyth's dock workers, and they felt that knowledge of local government procedures was an essential requirement to ensure the implementation of the Housing (Scotland) Act of 1919. It was also an acknowledgement that the SBH clerical staff could not supply the necessary skill. In housing matters Jack reported to the SBH chairman, who, in turn, represented Scottish interests on official committees in London.[20] At best this was a fragile administrative link, seen most succinctly in July 1921 when the Scottish secretary was unaware 'officially' that the UK housing programme was to be suspended with immediate effect. Neither officials in the Treasury nor in the Ministry of Health had kept the SBH clerical staff informed of the change in policy; there had been discussion of a gradual reduction in the programme. (The Scottish secretary would have known informally through his private office, but this did not mean that he could be briefed, as appropriate, by the SBH ahead of the cabinet.) Although the SBH chairman was able to obtain some amelioration of the suspension, the matter was repeated at the end of 1922 when the incoming Conservative government's minister of health promulgated a new subsidised scheme that was uneconomic in Scottish conditions. North of the Border proportionately fewer houses were built.[21] After 1925 subsequent governments accepted that Scottish conditions required special financial assistance. Much of this was the result of the lobbying of back-bench Labour Clydeside MPs rather than the SBH's ability to apply administrative pressure on inter-departmental discussion.

The structure of the SBH and its office procedures were the subject of considerable correspondence between the Board, the Scottish Office and the Treasury for much of the 1920s. An attempt was made in 1921 to increase the salaries of SBH members on the basis of their increased 'responsibilities' and comparative 'efficiency'.[22] (A review of the salaries of senior officials elsewhere had been adjusted in the light of the post-war programme of 'reconstruction'.) The Treasury resolutely rejected the claim, stating that in their view the responsibility of SBH members was of 'a different character' from that of the senior officials in the Ministry of Health, adding that they did not 'have the same arduous life and volume of work that fall to many of the [administrative] assistant secretaries in London. They are far removed from the actual seat of Government, and a great many of their major problems are settled for them in England. Moreover many of the questions they consider are finally "vetted" by the Scottish Office.'[23] It was a powerful rebuff, which highlighted the view that the SBH belonged to the inferior 'Class IV' group of departments like the Royal Mint and Stationery Office, those that held little influence in policy formulation.

The early part of the period also saw the SBH seek to integrate the previous three separate administrations into one (as indicated above), but with the public expenditure cutbacks after 1921, the Treasury insisted that to increase administrative 'efficiency' the number of assistant secretaries (executive officers) should be reduced on retirement or resignation. As a consequence the number of divisions was reduced from seven to five, the work being reallocated as thought appropriate, though housing and national insurance remained as before. The SBH, whose membership was reduced to four by 1922 (due to retirement) certainly understood that its assistant secretaries handled similar work to the Ministry of Health, but, as constituted, accepted that its members were responsible for matters of 'principle', its organisational manual stating that

> each Division is in the charge of a Committee consisting of two or three members of the Board with an Assistant Secretary as its executive head. Questions involving principles that have already been settled by the Board are disposed of by Divisional Officers. Questions of more importance are submitted to the Convenor of the appropriate Committee and either disposed of by him or brought before a formal meeting of the Committee. Meetings of the Board and Divisional Committees are held weekly.[24]

As such it was not appropriate for a clerical officer to meet and discuss policy with administrative officers based in London. At best, the secretary could take matters up, if SBH members themselves were not available. This was seen most succinctly in two areas of health policy: tuberculosis control and the voluntary hospitals. In 1922 the same financial restriction that applied to housing also impacted on tuberculosis control and the SBH was informed that no further new sanatoria would be sanctioned. As it turned out, English authorities, somewhat richer in terms of rateable value, had not utilised all the grant aid available, and with proportionately more sanatoria beds available for those afflicted with tuberculosis, the impact of the restriction was not immediately apparent. In Scotland the position was more serious: with higher levels of overcrowding, the need for sanatoria isolation was greater. It was left to the SBH's chairman and secretary to press the Scottish case after the Ministry of Health and Treasury had agreed future policy. Eventually the Treasury accepted that some amelioration was required and on the basis that the allocation to the English programme had not been fully utilised agreed to transfer a part of the funding, so long as the total did not exceed the total reduced allocation to the UK.[25]

The government had established a Voluntary Hospitals Commission in the immediate aftermath of the war to assist the hospitals adjust financially to a return to 'normal' economic conditions. In early 1924 the Commission proposed an inquiry into future funding in the light of increased demand for hospital treatment, and in the context of a period when voluntary hospital finance had come under severe pressure. The Commission's primary aim was to ensure the voluntary hospitals' independence in an era of a general increase in state-sponsored welfare and the threat of local authority encroachment. In Scotland, ministers (during Labour's first minority government) sought a separate inquiry with a remit that also covered 'ancillary' services, an acknowledgement that local non-teaching hospitals could not meet needs on a scale demonstrated south of the Border. The Treasury had already agreed the UK inquiry and objected to a possibly more sweeping inquiry north of the Border, which might embarrass both its ministers and those at the Ministry of Health, but were reassured that it was unlikely that the inquiry would lead to 'an indictment of the voluntary system'.[26] In the event the Scottish inquiry recommended a one-off government grant to cover deficiencies in voluntary provision, but otherwise supported the *status quo*, that is the local authorities and Poor Law authorities should not encroach on the traditional ground of the voluntary hospitals and more particularly the teaching hospitals. The recommendations were considered by the SBH, which, in fact, could not reach a unanimous decision on the future of Scottish hospital policy.[27] The Scottish secretary, Sir John Gilmour, an erstwhile traditional Conservative, regarded the lack of unanimity as demonstrating the SBH's fundamental weakness in the control of policy. It confirmed the view of two previous Scottish secretaries (Robert Munro and Lord Novar) that a board system was too deliberative in its proceedings and, despite its knowledge of Scottish conditions, operated contrary to the rapid response that ministers desired. In terms of hospital policy the Scottish position was further confounded. An initiative to seek voluntary hospital grant aid was turned down by the Treasury on grounds of public expenditure restraint (and impact on England), which, in turn, was followed by objections from voluntary hospitals when the SBH sought to encourage local authority initiatives in general medicine. Ultimately the lack of 'clarity' within the SBH reflected an administrative system that had been geared for a different era – supervision of the local authority – and a civil service that operated on an executive basis, rather than seeking to 'control' of blocks of work to avoid ministerial embarrassment and loss of public confidence.

Discussion on the future of Scottish health administration had first raised the issue of the board/clerical system in March 1922 when Munro responded to the retrenchment in public expenditure by proposing a cut in SBH membership. The minister did not consider seriously an alternative structure, but his successor Lord Novar (1922–4) initially proposed converting the SBH into a directorate.[28] It was not clear what Novar intended below the level of the director, but it proved too radical for the Conservative government's managers and the amending legislation was quietly dropped. (The proposal implied an element of authoritarian rule.) Gilmour had no qualms about what he wanted. During Stanley Baldwin's second government (1924–9) he faced severe pressure to contain the expansion of welfare (public spending reduced private productive investment and led to inflation), but in Scotland he faced increasing all-party pressure for ameliorative provision, from additional subsidies on housing to grant aid for hospitals and poor relief. Although there had been some real growth in public expenditure after 1923, the Scottish health budget remained at approximately 10 per cent below the 1921 level.[29] Gilmour knew that he required, on the one hand, an administration that could assist the government to 'mould' Scottish opinion towards caution in welfare policy, and, on the other, one that could influence Whitehall more effectively on Scottish imperatives.

The Treasury did not object to Gilmour's proposed reform, converting the Board into a department.[30] Neither did the Cabinet, nor Parliament. However, translating a board into an administrative department overnight was not something that could be achieved easily within the traditions of the British civil service. Two SBH members retired in early 1928 and a third was due for retirement soon after. The issue was not the Board members, but the fact that it was impossible to recruit administrative officers from Whitehall departments to take over the senior posts within the Department. Even if individuals had been willing, they had no experience of Scottish conditions or the structure of local government – and if they had been English, the government knew it could expect an outburst of parliamentary 'nationalism' from Scottish MPs, already uneasy over a perceived ending of the semi-autonomous Board tradition. (The Scottish Office itself was small, containing fewer than a dozen administrative class officers, all of whom could not be transferred for the lack of suitable replacements.) Gilmour was forced to accept that some of the clerical officers should be promoted into administrative positions in a department of four divisions.[31] One of the SBH members, Muriel Ritson, took over the national insurance division and Jack the public assistance, general local government services and establishment division (it was expected that his background in local government service would be particularly useful in the control of policy after local authority reorganisation in 1929). The Board's secretary, John Jeffrey, became the Department's secretary (he did have a university education, at King's College, London), but the public health and housing divisions were held by previous clerical officers, Henry Fraser and Alex McKinna. (Fraser, the son of a tea planter, was university-educated and had entered the civil service as a clerical officer in the Scottish National Insurance Commission, via local government service. McKinna had been the senior clerical officer responsible for housing under the SBH.) The structure underneath them remained dominated by clerical officers, unlike the Scottish Office in London, where assistant secretaries were supported by university-educated principals. Its latest recruits were Stuart Murrie (Edinburgh and Balliol, Oxford) and Charles Cunningham (St Andrews), both later to hold departmental secretaryships (Murrie in the SED and Scottish Home Department, and permanent under-secretary of state, Scotland; Cunningham in the Scottish Home Department, and permanent under-secretary of state in the Home Office). Other Scottish Office officials who entered service shortly afterwards and who succeeded to departmental secretaryships included John Anderson and Bruce Fraser. In that respect there was little immediate change to Scottish health administration: in the eyes of Whitehall it remained an inferior department, short of the capabilities that other ministries took for granted. This was confirmed in the salaries that the Department attracted. Ritson and Jack retained their previous salaries on a personal basis, but the other assistant secretaries were not paid at the administrative level. The Treasury deliberately agreed a scale somewhat below that offered to Whitehall assistant secretaries, even allowing for London 'weighting', to avert 'friction' with others initially appointed either on an administrative or clerical basis. Officers underneath them similarly failed to attract the salary of administrative principals; there was no evidence of increased responsibility.[32] Gilmour may have ensured a department that was constituted to support a minister more directly, but it was assumed to remain subsidiary to the Ministry of Health in the development of UK policy.

The most pressing issues affecting the Department of Health after 1929 concerned public assistance, slum clearance and hospitals. After the establishment of the Unemployment Assistance Board in 1935, the Department's interest in the former was confined to the remnants of the Poor Law, but the same could not be said of the health services and housing. In the health services the expected local authority interest in establishing general hospitals failed to materialise. Hostility from the voluntary movement combined with the financial pressures on local authorities confined developments to Edinburgh and Aberdeen, where the teaching hospitals took advantage of previous Poor Law institutions. In fact, in response to the lack of interest the Department reduced its complement of medical officers, expanded on the expectation of greater liaison work.[33] Fraser also resigned to take a post in local government. His replacement, John Vallance, WS, was the Department's solicitor; none of the other clerical officers was considered suitable. (Harold Smith filled the vacancy in the Department's legal section as a result of other promotions.) In housing the position was equally discouraging. Despite the grants available and the national government's decision in 1932 not to cut housing subsidies in Scotland as much as south of the Border, the pace of building slowed. The ministerial view was one of despondency, partly in a belief that additional grants would be necessary, but also because of a view that the Department lacked the administrative capacity to pressurise local authorities and the industry into effective action.

Jeffrey was promoted to permanent under-secretary of state at the Scottish Office in 1933. Although approaching retirement (he was 62), his 'knowledge and long experience' of Scottish affairs was sufficient to convince the Scottish secretary and the prime minister that his candidacy was preferable to that of the assistant under-secretary, who happened to be English and was not noted for his communication skills. The prime minister, Ramsay MacDonald, had become greatly concerned about the effectiveness of Scottish administration in incorporating Scottish opinion into the government's policy of 'sound' money and modest social intervention.[34] In Scotland this led to inquiries into the Scottish health services and maternal health and morbidity. John Highton, who had been the chief insurance inspector, was promoted to departmental secretary. Although it was known that he was in poor health, he had obtained a reputation of deep concern over unemployment and housing.[35] Highton, from Glasgow (but half-English), was another 'boy' clerk, though he had undertaken a university degree (through the Royal Technical College) by evening class.

Highton moved quickly to strengthen the Department's administration. In June 1934, he sought Treasury approval for the introduction of Class 1 administrative assistant secretaries and principal officers to deal with the pressure of the new work.[36] The Treasury agreed to the promotion of the existing assistant secretaries, but on condition that only those heads of branch who had demonstrated administrative class potential would be redesignated as principals and that any deficiency would be filled by transfers from other departments. Six of the existing clerical heads were redesignated (there were eight) and a principal, Murrie, transferred from the Scottish Office in London. It also agreed to separate local government services division from establishment matters. The reorganisation took effect in August 1935.[37] At the same time the Scottish secretary insisted on the creation of a 'flying squad' of officers who could work more closely with local authorities in delivering a higher target of housing completions.[38] Henderson, who was then an outdoor inspector and had earned ministerial note for supervising the evacuation of St Kilda, was drafted to lead the 'squad'.[39] (Murrie was designated to work in the branch that dealt with housing for agricultural workers. The Housing (Rural Workers) (Scotland) Act of 1938 provided additional grant aid beyond the Housing Acts.) This was followed by the recruitment of the Department's first administrative assistant principal, Douglas Haddow, a Cambridge wrangler, soon to be followed by other administrative officers, including Norman Graham.

Highton noted the success of the 'flying squad' at increasing the rate of housing approvals (they doubled), but it was evident that unless greater grant aid was provided under more direct departmental supervision, Scottish housing conditions would continue to remain inferior to those in England. The lower rateable value of the majority of industrial local authorities, and hence their fiscal capacity, precluded an enlarged building programme to combat the slums. Highton proposed to ministers the establishment of a state-owned housing corporation to build in areas of greatest need and was instructed to work out plans in more detail, but in 1936 due to his illness, the planning was put into abeyance. On recovery, Highton was promoted to permanent under-secretary of state following Jeffrey's retirement.[40] In turn, William Douglas was appointed departmental secretary. Douglas, an administrative class official (and an Edinburgh graduate), had served in the Ministry of Labour, including a spell as divisional controller for Scotland, but, although reputedly excellent at communication with staff, had little direct experience of housing or health matters. As Walter Elliot, the Scottish secretary, informed the Treasury, he was not able to recommend any of the assistant secretaries, though 'the Department had a number of the younger officers of great promise'. [41]

Douglas's immediate task was to assist ministers to put forward the case for a state-directed housing corporation, which they now supported. The Treasury remained unimpressed by the proposal, which they argued could create a precedent and, in financial terms, was out of step with the government's policy of non-inflationary social expenditure. At a meeting with the chancellor of the exchequer (John Simon) in July 1938, the Scottish secretary (John Colville) was informed that the proposal was unacceptable, given other demands on the Exchequer. The Scottish secretary and the Department left the meeting despondent, but on the advice of the minister's private secretary, Charles Cunningham (a Scottish Office principal), the Scottish secretary immediately wrote to the chancellor, ignoring the decision and stating that he would put forward revised plans for the Association in the autumn.[42] The tactic worked, but it again indicated that Scottish ministers required much shrewder officials who appreciated the mechanics of Whitehall argument. Ultimately Cunningham, who as private secretary to the Scottish secretary had had close liaison with other Whitehall departments and had witnessed their approach to the Treasury, understood that Chamberlain's national government itself was only superficially 'tough'. The housing association and additional grant aid measures slipped though the Cabinet in the aftermath of the Munich crisis; Chamberlain needed his ministers.

A key issue that emerged during the housing association and other discussions was the detachment of ministers in London from departmental day-to-day support and the apparent lack of detailed appreciation of the Scottish interest in the formation of UK policy. The process, of course, worked in the reverse: Scottish officials based in Edinburgh were not necessarily fully aware of what could be achieved by a carefully prepared brief written in the meticulously crafted Whitehall style. Following Highton, Scottish ministers pressed the case for a comprehensive review of Scottish health issues, with the aim of greater state support, but were again turned down.[43] What was evident from the correspondence was that much greater preparation was required to establish any special Scottish 'case', with the kind of 'acumen' displayed by Cunningham. The moral argument, based on an occasional or even weekly visit by Edinburgh-based officials, who knew little of their opposite number in the Treasury or Ministry of Health, was not sufficient. In 1938, to obviate these difficulties, the Treasury agreed to Douglas's request that a principal should be stationed in London to assist 'liaison' on a permanent basis.[44] The officer would represent the Department at conferences and committees and only when absolutely necessary seek attendance from a senior official in Edinburgh. Murrie became the first liaison officer and was 'on hand' when the Scottish secretary sought Cabinet support for a state-aided emergency hospital programme, ostensibly to secure accommodation in case of war casualties, but in practice built in locations with severe shortage of civilian hospital provision.[45] Douglas himself moved to the Treasury in early 1939 and was replaced by William Fraser, a principal assistant secretary at the Treasury. This transfer was intended to strengthen again the Department's presentation of its 'Vote'. As the Treasury noted, the decade had witnessed a subtle alteration in attitude towards subsidiarity. It was no longer assumed that Scottish policy should automatically follow that south of the Border or that it could not make separate claims. However, as one official wrote, to enable the Scottish secretary to argue his case more effectively, much would depend on further 'recruitment direct from the Administrative Class examination and by the infiltration of experienced officers from elsewhere'.[46]

## Needs-Based Collective Provision and the Administrative Officer, 1939–56

The outbreak of war in 1939 brought some considerable revision to the Department's administration. The initial thrust was to speed the emergency hospital programme and by early 1940 a number of new divisions were established to cope with the expected casualties.[47] Although the volume of casualties was not on the scale predicted, it was evident that the hospitals would be required for specialist medical care associated with military wounds and for civilians affected by aerial bombardment, and generally for maintaining civilian morale at a time of compulsory labour. Again the Department encountered significant difficulties in promotion to assistant secretary level and was obliged to recruit a recently retired colonial servant, Sir James Dunnett, and to take staff seconded from the SED. Another ex-colonial civil servant was recruited towards the end of the war and remained in service well beyond the usual age of retirement of 60. The position was eventually eased with the promotion of administrative class officers, like Haddow, James McGuinness and Norman Graham, but until 1950, the Department's four senior officers (secretary and deputy secretaries) as well as the majority of assistant secretaries had not been appointed through Class 1 competition.[48] Fraser had moved to another Whitehall department in 1943.

## Conclusion

To what extent did the administrative structure impact on Scottish health administration? The exigencies of the Second World War meant that virtually all government activity suffered undue stress; evacuation, aerial bombardment and the virtual cessation of house building meant considerable temporary adjustments to provision.[49] However, the reconstruction era, particularly Labour's immediate post-war reform of health care and the provision of enhanced housing subsidies, meant that arguments over the Scottish interest in Treasury discussion was less prominent than previously. The 1945 election had been fought on the issue of needs-based collectivism. The issue resurfaced after 1947 with the first cut-back in the housing programme (following the dollar crisis), reducing the Scottish programme to little more than keeping pace with replacement, followed two years later with a ceiling imposed on the NHS budget, reaffirmed when the Conservatives regained power in 1951. It was 'administrative' politics as usual. In Scotland's case, the detail of the NHS reform had been 'headed-up' by Haddow, who took the overall health brief in 1949 (hospitals, primary care and local health administration). (The Scottish secretary was complimented by the prime minister (Attlee) on securing the reform with less contentious medical acrimony than south of the Border.) Undoubtedly his 'tough' management of hospital board budgets did much to restore confidence that a free health service at point of access could be maintained. The fact that he held a 'sharp tongue' and 'suffered fools badly' was not regarded an impediment within Treasury circles.[50] It was this qualitative difference in conduct that differentiated the Treasury view of the 'clerical' class of officer from those whom they knew could raise arguments above the commonplace, and the commonplace argument had failed to prevent the reduction of the Scottish housing programme in 1947, despite the higher level of overcrowding. It also led to the suspension of further new town development to deal with Glasgow's 'over-spill', the Abercrombie plan. As far as the Treasury was concerned, in a period when domestic politics were dominated more than ever by issues concerning collective provision it was inconceivable that a Cabinet minister should not have the advice of officers of the highest quality, irrespective of potential embarrassment to 'orthodox' administration. The Treasury may have objected to the additional claims (and usually did), but it did expect 'innovative' arguments.

Managing Scottish health administration changed qualitatively between the late nineteenth and mid-twentieth century. A central issue that Scotland faced in securing recognition in housing and health needs related to inheriting an administration that had been established to support a different form of government, supervising the local authority. Whatever the clerical competence of the individual officers, they faced a UK civil service that had been built on a clear division of responsibility between policy advice to ministers and executive management of tasks, once ministerial instruction was issued. The decision to establish the Scottish Board of Health, rather than a ministry, in 1919 was probably a ministerial error. It delayed the reconstruction of Scottish health administration on the lines adopted by Whitehall ministries for nearly a decade and it was not until well into the 1930s that administrative class officers recruited through open competition were appointed. As such it meant that officers from that group did not reach the degree of expertise considered necessary for promotion for another decade. For much of the inter-war period, arguing the Scottish case in Whitehall was undoubtedly impeded by the 'class' system that operated deep within the civil service code, one that could dismiss the intellectual ability or 'experience' of senior officers with apparent ease. Smith, who died unexpectedly in 1956, was replaced by an administrative entrant transferred from the Scottish Home Department with little experience of either health or housing. But that did not matter: with nearly a decade as a deputy secretary dealing with crime, prisons and 'penumbra' matters, he was 'mature' and thus knowledgeable. 'Boy' clerks may have been 'useful', but belonged to a different era.

178                              *Ian Levitt*

## Notes

1. Some information on this chapter has derived from interviews with retired Scottish Office and Treasury civil servants, but sadly some have died since the research began.
2. The National Archives, London (TNA), T/273/125, minute, Sir E. Bridges, 23 July 1953.
3. One of the three under-secretaries had been first appointed as a 'boy' clerk aged 16, in 1912: TNA, T/1/12392, minute, 23 May 1919. His duties were primarily that of an abstractor, i.e. tabulating material from various local authority returns.
4. For instance, Alford, B.W.E., Lowe, R. and Rollings, N., *Economic Planning 1943–51: A Guide to Documents in the Public Record Office* (London, 1992); Land, A., Lowe, R. and Whiteside, N., *The Development of the Welfare State 1939–51: A Guide to Documents in the Public Record Office* (London, 1992); Cantwell, J.D., *The Second World War: A Guide to Documents in the Public Record Office* (London, 1993); Bridgen, P. and Lowe, R., *Welfare Policy under the Conservatives: A Guide to Documents in the Public Record Office* (London, 1998); Levitt, I., 'Scottish Air Services 1933–75 and the Scottish New Towns 1943–75: A Guide to Records at the National Archives of Scotland', *Scottish Archives* 5 (1999), 67–82; Hennessy, P., *Whitehall* (London, 1989); Hennessy, P., *Never Again: Britain 1945–1951* (London, 1992); Cairncross, A. and Watts, N., *The Economic Section 1939–61: A Study in Economic Advising* (London, 1989); Webster, C., *The Health Services since the War* (London, 1988); Levitt, I., *The Scottish Office 1919–59* (Edinburgh, 1995); Peden, G., *The Treasury and British Public Policy* (Oxford, 2000); Theakston, K., *Leadership in Whitehall* (London, 2000).
5. For instance, McCrae, M., *The National Health Service in Scotland: Origins and Ideals 1900–1950* (East Linton, 2003); McLachlan, G., *Improving the Common Weal; Aspects of Scottish Health Services 1900–1984* (Edinburgh, 1987); Jenkinson, J., *Scotland's Health 1919–1948* (Oxford, 2002); Crowther, M.A., 'Poverty, Health and Welfare', in W.H. Fraser and R.J. Morris (eds), *People and Society in Scotland, Volume II: 1850–1914* (Edinburgh, 1990), 265–89.
6. TNA, T/160/7, 'Blue Notes – Board of Supervision', 1887–8. The nomenclature of such officials varied over the period, but the status remained.
7. TNA, T/8603b, letter, 5 January 1891.
8. TNA, T/165/13, 'Blue Notes', Local Government Board for Scotland, 1895–6.
9. TNA, T/8603b, letter, 9 January 1891.
10. TNA, T/101/5, letter, 2 February 1893.
11. National Archives of Scotland (NAS), E/824/23, minute, 19 March 1895.
12. For example, NAS, E/824/18, letter, 11 October 1905.
13. TNA, T/1/11041, 29 January 1909.
14. NAS, E/824/24, minute, 12 July 1909.
15. TNA, T/165/43, 'Blue Notes', Local Government Board for Scotland, 1914–15; NAS, E/824/29, minute, 14 January 1913.
16. *Report of the Committee on Scottish Universities*, Parliamentary Papers, Cd. 5257 (1910).
17. NAS, E/824/43; TNA, T/12392, Treasury letter authorising staffing, 29 April 1919; TNA, T/165/47, Scottish Board of Health, 'Blue Notes, 1920–21'. There were two secretaries until the previous Local Government Board's secretary retired in 1921.
18. TNA, T/1/12392, minute, 9 April 1919.
19. Treasury permission to create a directorate was given in March 1918, but the administrative scheme was recast to meet the expected exigencies of the proposed Housing (Scotland) Bill; TNA, T/1/12392, memorandum, 22 February 1919.
20. The Treasury had wanted the housing commissioner to be a member of the SBH, but the Scottish secretary rejected the proposal on the grounds that it would have effectively created a department within the SBH and contradicted the general purpose of the Board of Health (Scotland) Act: TNA, T/1/12392, letter, 29 April 1919.

21. The SBH's chairman resigned in October 1922 and his replacement had less interest in housing. Much of the 'liaison' work was left to Jack, working directly with ministers.
22. TNA, T/162/23, letter, 30 March 1921.
23. TNA, T/162/23, minute, 21 April 1921.
24. TNA, T/162/101, 'Scottish Board of Health: Organisation', 29 March 1924.
25. TNA, T/161/118, letter, 28 February 1922.
26. TNA, T/161/230, chairman's letter, 16 May 1924.
27. NAS, HH/45/65, Sir J. Lamb, permanent under-secretary of state, Scottish Office, 1921–33, memorandum, 10 February 1937. A similar lack of unanimity emerged over clerical salaries and grades: TNA, T/162/355, minute, 25 June 1925.
28. Politically, Novar was a National Liberal and somewhat contemptuous of reconstruction collectivism: NAS, HH/45/51, minute, 5 January 1923.
29. TNA, T/165/56, 'Blue Notes', Department of Health for Scotland, 1929.
30. NAS, DD/1/31, minute, 14 February 1929.
31. NAS, DD 1/31, Scottish Board of Health letter to Treasury, 24 November 1928.
32. TNA, T/162/355, minute, 18 December 1928 and letter, 28 February 1929.
33. TNA, T/165/60, 'Blue Notes', Department of Health for Scotland, 1933.
34. TNA, T/162/418, Treasury minute, 2 September 1933.
35. *Scotsman*, obituary, 27 March 1937.
36. NAS, DD/1/12, minutes, 26 June 1934, 26 January 1935.
37. NAS, DD/1/21, minute, March 1936.
38. TNA, T/162/355, Highton's letter, 12 March 1934.
39. TNA, T/162/998, departmental chart, July 1934.
40. Highton died shortly after taking up the post and was replaced by the transfer of the permanent under-secretary at the Board of Trade, who was Scottish only by descent.
41. TNA, T/162/398, letter, 28 November 1936.
42. NAS, DD/6/1092, minute, 29 July 1938.
43. TNA, T/161/854, letter, 10 February 1938.
44. TNA, T/162/998, letter, 2 January 1938. The intention was also 'to afford some measure of relief' to the Scottish secretary's private office: TNA, T/162/476, minute, 25 September 1937.
45. TNA, T/160/880, Emergency Hospital and Evacuation (Scotland) Estimate, June 1939. Of the £2.24m., £1.5m. was set aside for hospital construction.
46. TNA, T/161/524, minute, 25 February 1938.
47. NAS, DD/1/21, minute, 23 January 1940.
48. Because Jack took early retirement in 1941, Henderson, although English, faced little competition for the secretaryship nomination.
49. TNA, T/165/135, 'Blue Notes', Department of Health, April 1950.
50. TNA, T/273/125, T. Padmore, minute, 15 February 1956. Nor was it regarded as an impediment to his appointment as permanent under-secretary of state in 1964; the then Scottish secretary wholeheartedly endorsed his appointment.

# 10

# Central Policy and Local Independence: Integration, Health Centres and the NHS in Scotland 1948–1990

## Marguerite Dupree

In her history of the workhouse system in England from 1834 to 1929, Anne Crowther showed how the workhouse combined functions of social welfare and medical treatment for many years, and how emerging difficulties led the state to create the specialised institutions which eventually replaced the workhouse. She also pointed out that 'the poor law offers a striking example of central policy contending against local independence'.[1] This chapter explores one of the institutions that replaced the workhouse system – the National Health Service (NHS) – and an attempt to integrate functions in one part of it – the health centre. Health centres also provide an opportunity to examine central policy and local independence with regard to the distinctiveness of health services in Scotland and within different areas of Scotland.

Charles Webster's official history of the NHS in Britain gives a comprehensive overview of the advent of the NHS in terms of national policy formation and implementation, but inevitably it gives a top-down view.[2] The variations in experiences of the introduction of the NHS in different localities are beginning to be explored systematically, though there is a tendency to focus on the regional hospital boards, the main administrative innovation of the new service and subject of reorganisation in 1974, and to pay less attention to general practice and local authority provision.[3] This examination of health centres is part of a wider study of the NHS in the West of Scotland which attempts to explore regional variation in the implementation of national health policy and delivery of medical services in Britain, focusing on all branches of the NHS and how these changes were shaped and experienced in particular locations. The importance of a regional or local perspective is clear from John Pickstone's work, which shows how local concerns and initiatives produced a distinctive, innovative pattern of development of psychiatric units in district general hospitals in Manchester around 1950, 'not in response to national policy but because of the way new regional decision-makers reacted to peculiar problems in the provision and staffing of mental health services'.[4] This chapter focuses on the distinctive history of health centres generally in Scotland and on two contrasting initiatives in the 1960s and 1970s – one in Livingston, near Edinburgh; the other in Glasgow. This will, I hope, illuminate both regional variations within Britain and between areas of Scotland and the difficulties and possibilities of integration of the tripartite structure of the NHS.

## The Tripartite Structure of the NHS

When the British NHS emerged on the Appointed Day, 5 July 1948, it had a tripartite administrative structure. There were different forms of administration for hospitals, public health and independent contractor services as can be seen in the organisational chart for the NHS in England and Wales in figure 10.1.

The dominant and most original feature of Aneurin Bevan's scheme lay in the nationalisation and regionalisation of the hospitals (shown in dotted lines on the left-hand side of figure 10.1). It made possible the integration of all types of hospital (apart from teaching hospitals) under Regional Hospital Boards appointed by the minister and responsible for the application of government policy, overall strategic planning, budgetary control and some specific duties such as the development of specialities and appointment of hospital consultant doctors. The municipal hospitals were taken away from the local authorities, but, through their medical officer of health, the local authorities (shown in dashed lines on figure 10.1) remained in charge of functions such as maternity and child welfare, domiciliary midwifery, health visiting, home nursing, home helps, vaccination and immunisation and other activities connected with public health and health education. They were also responsible for health centres (shown in a bold line on figure 10.1). Finally, the scheme also allowed for the separate administration of services provided by independent contractors, i.e. general medical practitioners, general dental practitioners, opticians and pharmacists (shown in dot-dash lines on figure 10.1). At the local level, executive councils, essentially renamed committees inherited from the previous panel system under the 1911 National Insurance system, administered their services. The executive councils in the main followed the geographic pattern of the local health authorities, but there were longstanding tensions between the two as the general practitioners (GPs) adamantly resisted any suggestion that they become salaried employees of the local authorities.

The NHS in Scotland was introduced on the Appointed Day under separate legislation and although the administrative structure in Scotland was basically the same as in England and Wales, there were some differences (figure 10.2). For example, the minister and department responsible for the service was the secretary of state for Scotland and the relevant department in the Scottish Office[5] rather than the minister of health and his department; the teaching hospitals were under the Regional Hospital Boards in Scotland while those in England went directly to the minister; also, there was a difference in responsibility for health

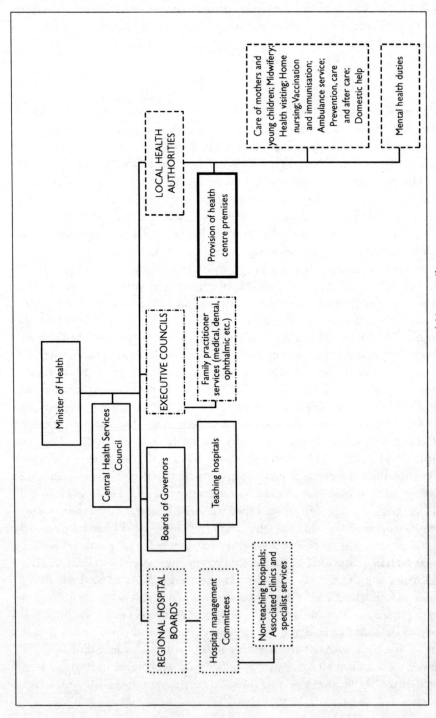

Figure 10.1 National Health Service, England and Wales 1948, Organisation chart (abbreviated)

**Source:** Adapted from Ross, James Stirling, *The National Health Service in Great Britain: An Historical and Descriptive Study* (London, 1952), 393.

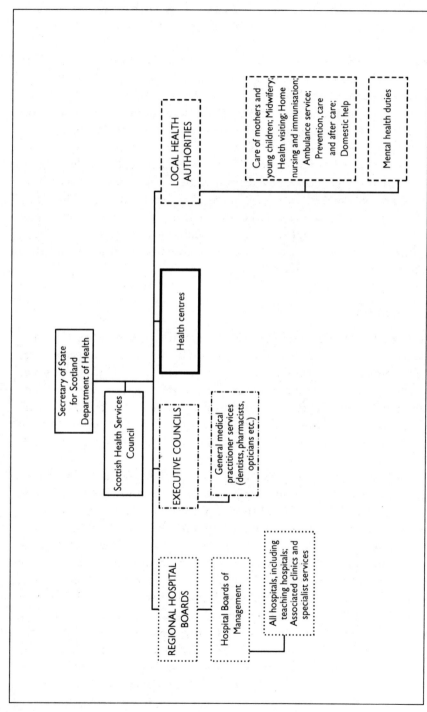

Figure 10.2 National Health Service, Scotland 1948, Organisation chart (abbreviated)

**Source:** See figure 10.1.

centres (shown in a bold line on figure 10.2). In England they were the responsibility of local authorities; while in Scotland they were a direct responsibility of the
Scottish Office.

Both contemporaries and historians have pointed to fragmentation of the
provision of health services as a major problem before the NHS. Co-ordination,
co-operation and integration were major policy aims of policy-makers in the
inter-war years and leading up to the NHS. Although there was an unprecedented amount of restructuring achieved with the NHS Acts, the tripartite
administrative system risked creating a series of parallel, unequal, incompatible
and unco-ordinated health services. This was counteracted centrally both by
promises of active intervention on the part of the minister and by high expectations of a complicated system of central consultative committees, and locally by
the provision and maintenance of health centres intended to house both local
authority staff and independent contractors. Thus, health centres played a highly
important role in the initial plans for the NHS and had a different administrative
position in England and Scotland.

### Health Centres

The concept of a health centre has a variety of meanings. A report for the World
Health Organisation in 1972 attempted 'to clarify the various meanings of
"health centres"' and review the literature on their evaluation as a means of
delivering health services and improving health in the developing countries. The
author pointed out that for over 50 years health centres had been advocated,
built and operated, but they had many different purposes, functions, staffing and
administrative patterns in different countries and in different contexts within
the same country.[6]

In the United States George Rosen and more recently William Rothstein have
reminded us of the widespread movement between 1910 and 1940 and again in
the late 1960s and early 1970s when local public health departments or private
agencies established centres providing health services on a local basis. These
neighbourhood centres were aimed at the urban poor. In New York City the
neighbourhood health centres grew out of milk stations and the bureaucratic
problem of what to do with school nurses in the summer. Hitherto most nurses
had specialised in a particular medical problem, such as maternity, infant care or
tuberculosis; in the health centres a nurse provided all the health care for a
number of families. Like many local authority health services in Britain, the
health centres in the United States generally emphasised prevention. Yet,
although most medical care concerned with diagnosis and therapy remained
outside their sphere of activity, they treated diseases considered public health

problems such as tuberculosis, venereal diseases and fever, which constituted the major health problems of the poor, and as a result they were able to provide the main types of health care required in the neighbourhoods they served. By 1939 the public health department in New York City had established 30 health centres. They focused on families, holding family record cards, and integrated social services as well as health services in buildings serving districts of about 250,000 residents each.[7]

In Britain in the 1920s a different idea of health centres emerged. They were designed to foster more integrated and active citizens through new approaches to health care delivery. The Pioneer Health Centre at Peckham in London was established with voluntary funding and embodied a conception of positive health, personal responsibility and the family unit; it encouraged a healthy lifestyle, individual responsibility and provided a family social centre to promote community integration.[8]

At the same time on the other side of London the new, Labour-controlled council in Finsbury in 1934 planned and built a health centre as part of a wider programme to improve health services and build housing to 'demonstrate what a socialist model of welfare could be'.[9] The council commissioned a building which 'could house under one roof municipal health services which included a dental clinic, chest clinic, a solarium for ultra-violet ray treatment, a cleansing station for verminous people, disinfecting stations, a mortuary and a laboratory . . . office space, a reception area and waiting room and a lecture theatre'.[10] It did not, however, offer GP services, or hospital specialist services. While in both cases health centres were part of larger plans to improve the urban environment, one historian recently characterised Finsbury as embodying a 'statist, curative and inculcating model', in contrast to Peckham's 'preventative, voluntarist and facilitating' model of health care.[11]

A still different concept of a health centre appeared in 1920 in the Dawson Report, sponsored by the Ministry of Health, which described the health centre as the future direction of primary health care provision. Health centres were a means to integrate preventative and curative medicine. The medical practitioners were central to Dawson's view of the health centre, which was local but had little sense of mass participation beyond the view that the people themselves should be in large part responsible for their own health, with responsibility fostered through on-going health education. Dawson's report advocated 'primary health centres' which included a few beds and consultant clinics to link general practice with 'secondary' specialist hospital services.[12]

Later planning documents took up the idea of health centres. For example, the British Medical Association (BMA)'s Medical Planning Commission Report in May 1942 saw general practice as group practice from publicly provided health centres, where preventative and curative work would be concentrated, though it did not include the link with specialist care in hospitals.[13] Another contemporary report suggested that

> health centres should have between six and twelve doctors with a room each, a small operating theatre, x-ray room, pathology room and dispensary, and accommodation for home nurses and midwives and health visitors. The health centre would undertake all maternity and child welfare and school medical services, linked with the local hospital which would supervise the pathology and x-ray work. There would be assistant doctors on six to twelve month appointments, and there might be two dentists.[14]

Health centres featured in the controversies surrounding proposals for the health service after the Beveridge Report in 1942, and in the Willink plan of early 1945 they became an experiment only. However, Bevan's legislation reinstated them with a key role.[15] Dawson's concept of health centres is cited as the precursor to the NHS, but in the context of the NHS health centres came to have different, yet still varied meanings.

### Health Centres in Scotland 1946–60: The Department of Health for Scotland Programme

Despite the key role assigned to them in Bevan's legislation, accounts of the implementation of the provisions for health centres in the NHS Acts emphasise the very small number of them opened and the lack of enthusiasm of the government health departments.[16] This appears to have been the case in England where responsibility for health centres rested with local authorities. However, a close look at Scotland, where the responsibility was the secretary of state's, reveals that the Department of Health for Scotland tackled the provision with energy and determination, developing an experimental programme and adapting it when expenditure cuts required. Eventually it was thwarted by the Treasury, the costs of the Korean war, and the priority given to hospitals.

In just over a year – beginning in August 1946 when the legislation to establish the NHS was still under consideration and ending in September 1947, many months before the Appointed Day – the Department of Health for Scotland produced a comprehensive memorandum setting out an experimental programme for the provision and maintenance of health centres, complete with an architect's plans of a typical health centre that could be adapted to varied situations in light of experience.[17] Anticipation of its new responsibilities and pressure from the 'planning people' for guidance for planning health services for new towns spurred the Department into action. In the process it had to create a new planning mechanism to carry out its responsibilities, as it found there was no alternative to taking on the planning and implementing of the initial programme itself as the alternatives – local authorities, the new hospital boards and the Ministry of Works – were unsuitable.

The plan for the typical health centre (figure 10.3) was carefully thought through. Although the department took powers to include all three parts of the service, the typical centre combined only GP and local authority services. In figure 10.3 the entrance is in the centre, the GP consulting rooms are in the left wing and the local authority rooms are in the right wing. It was not to be a mini-hospital that would make GPs into consultants.[18] Instead, unlike the Finsbury health centre, the plan aimed 'to maintain the personal and intimate character of the best type of present-day general practice. The characteristic relationship between the family doctor and his patients must be preserved and extended as far as possible'. This set a limit for the size of the building and variety of services. The aim was to include 'all the services which contributed immediately to the domiciliary health services and [to resist] the inclusion of other valuable services such as day nurseries and recreational facilities which should be provided elsewhere'.[19]

The plan considered the content and layout of a health centre in detail, specifying, for example, that there should be a separate waiting room for each doctor and each consulting room should have a separate exit so patients did not go out through a waiting room (figure 10.3, enlarged view). In this way it attempted to 'preserve as far as possible the intimacy of the private consulting room and by providing separate waiting rooms for each part of the service to avoid any congregation of patients in waiting halls'.[20] It set out staffing and accommodation for health centres in a new township with five units each serving a population of 10,000. Each health centre would have four GPs, four dentists and one pharmacist who were independent contractors, as well as child welfare, maternity services and health visitors from the local authority. There would be no provision for day nurseries, out-patient departments of hospitals or full-time specialists. Where a clinic centre was being set up in a new town, the hospital accommodation would probably be so situated in relation to the town as to make such provision unnecessary. But hospital provision was not ruled out in areas where hospitals were not conveniently situated.[21]

The Department proposed an initial experimental programme of four health centres, each in a different type of area. By the Appointed Day in 1948 one site, Sighthill in Edinburgh, had been selected, consultations begun, and hopes raised for the start of building in 1949. Building did not begin until 1951 and it was opened in 1953. Though the trade unions urged the secretary of state to speed up the programme, financial constraints had begun to set in by the Appointed Day

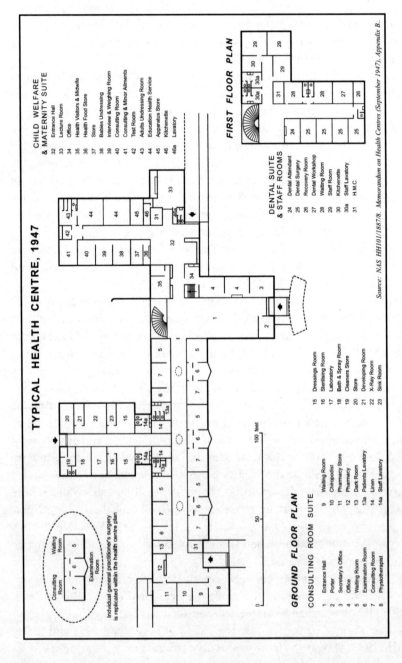

Figure 10.3  Scottish Health Department Health Centre Plan, 1947.

**Source:** NAS HH101/1887/8: Memorandum on Health Centres (September 1947), Appendix B (re-drawn by M. Shand)

and it was becoming clear that a health centre at the level of cost of Sighthill, £140,000, could not be repeated, so the Department adapted its plans and brought forward a proposal for a centre at Stranraer costing only £20,000 which was accepted, and plans for several more at that level were in hand. However, in the early 1950s, in a financial climate determined by the costs of British involvement in the Korean war and with priority given to expenditure on hospitals, the Treasury objected to any subsidy of rents for the GPs in the centres and would not agree to a continuing programme. They calculated the economic rent at Sighthill at around £900 per annum while the GPs paid only £300; at Stranraer the economic rent was estimated to be £526 while GPs paid £200.[22] This effectively blocked the Department's programme including one health centre plan it had already approved and others waiting in the wings. Officials searched for ways to fill the gap, including reducing costs further and approaching charitable foundations, for example the Nuffield Trust which had helped finance health centre experiments in England at Harlow, Corby and Manchester,[23] but without success. Thus, the Department built no more health centres until the 1960s – not because it lacked the expertise and machinery to plan and implement the centres, nor due to lack of demand, but because of the Treasury's intransigence, the inability or unwillingness of GPs to pay economic rents, and the priority given to building up the hospital services.

**Resurgence in the 1960s and 1970s**

The mid-1960s saw an upsurge of interest in health centres among both GPs and the Scottish Office, and the beginning of a major programme. Table 10.1 shows the increase in the number of health centres in Scotland between 1962 and 1990, with the most rapid increase from the mid-1960s until the mid-1980s. In 1967 two new centres were opened and forty-eight others were at various stages of consideration. Capital expenditure rose from £10,000 in 1966–7 to £159,000 in just one year and continued to rise. By 1982 there were 166 health centres in operation in Scotland and another 56 were at various stages of construction or planning. Almost 33 per cent of GPs were practising from health centres which varied in size and facilities according to local circumstances, catering for between one and thirty-six practitioners.[24] In England there was a similar rehabilitation of the idea of health centres, but it began later than in Scotland.[25]

**The Livingston Experiment – Initiative from the Top**

Among the many features that account for this programme and Scotland's lead[26] were the coming of more pro-active officials into the central departments and the

**Table 10.1 Number of health centres in Scotland, 1962–1990**

| Year | Number of health centres in operation |
| --- | --- |
| 1962 | 2 |
| 1963 | 3 |
| 1964 | 3 |
| 1965 | 4 |
| 1966 | 4 |
| 1967 | 6 |
| 1968 | 11 |
| 1969 | 14 |
| 1970 | 18 |
| 1971 | 34 |
| 1972 | 39 |
| 1973 | 62 |
| 1974 | 67 |
| 1975 | 80 |
| 1976 | 92 |
| 1977 | 110 |
| 1978 | 117 |
| 1979 | 127 |
| 1980 | 137 |
| 1981 | 144 |
| 1982 | 166 |
| 1983 | 173 |
| 1984 | 175 |
| 1985 | 181 |
| 1986 | 183 |
| 1987 | 184 |
| 1988 | 184 |
| 1989 | 192 |
| 1990 | 194 |

**Sources:** Scottish Home and Health Department, Annual Reports, 1963–74; Hospitals and Health Services Yearbook 1975–92

particularly close relationship in Scotland between officials and leaders of the professional organisations. A clear illustration is the innovative Livingston scheme which established health centres in the new town of Livingston near Edinburgh and was initiated by the Scottish Home and Health Department in the mid-1960s. John Brotherston became chief medical officer (CMO) in Scotland in 1964. Brotherston trained in Edinburgh and in the United States, particularly at Johns Hopkins University with a Rockefeller Fellowship in preventive medicine, and taught in London, before becoming the professor of public health and dean of medicine at Edinburgh University where he built up a diverse academic department of public health and social medicine over the nine years before his appointment as CMO.[27] He was critical of the breakdown of communication between GPs and hospitals, citing the need for 'leadership and planning' and calling the structure in 1963 'syndicalist anarchy'.[28] He believed that 'the tripartite structure of the Health Service with its administrative and financial separations might be acting as a barrier to change and development in the delivery of healthcare'.[29] He was a man of great energy who made the integration of health services his main aim during his 13 years as CMO for Scotland.[30] Brotherston and the small number of departmental officials and leading figures in the profession frequently travelled to London by train or plane and were subject to considerable delays. As one leading GP later remarked in his autobiography,

> one of the opportunities that came with flying to and from London . . . [was] the chance . . . to have forward looking discussions with . . . James Hogarth from the Scottish Office and . . . John Brotherston. There are at least three projects that I can remember as being born at Heathrow . . . The second item of airport waiting time gestation was a blue-print for a Scottish Home and Health Department funded study in the New Town of Livingston, where a GP would also hold a part-time appointment in a major local hospital.[31]

The joint appointments of GPs based in health centres as part-time hospital specialists worked well enough at Livingston where a new district hospital was planned at the same time as the health centres, but it was not generally copied.

A Scottish Home and Health Department (SHHD) paper written in July 1964 shortly after Brotherston became CMO outlined the proposal for an 'experiment' to establish an integrated health service within the context of existing administrative and financial arrangements in Livingston New Town; it was never financed by any special *ad hoc* fund of money. Established in 1962, the New Town of Livingston offered an opportunity in circumstances which the SHHD thought were likely to be favourable: there was no established township; the population was sparse with only very limited existing medical services; and there was an intention to build a new district hospital to replace the existing general hospital. The experiment to provide a fully integrated area health service, which was centred around a hospital and health centres, was introduced under the auspices of six authorities working through a joint advisory committee, a device used to introduce health centres in other areas in Scotland, as there was no one authority which had responsibility to plan in each community for its total requirements. In early summer 1965 the minister, Judith Hart, announced the decision to go ahead with the project; the Health Services Joint Advisory Committee for the Livingston Area (JAC) was established and held its first formal meeting at the end of April 1966. Deciding it needed an executive officer to advise, develop and carry out plans, the JAC created the administrative post of principal medical adviser and added these responsibilities to the vacant post of medical superintendent of the local general hospital. After overcoming initial disagreements over the job description and agreeing joint finance for the post, the principal medical adviser took up his duties on 1 October 1967. The report on the first five years of the experiment covers the period from this date to 30 September 1972.

From the outset the most innovative feature of the Livingston experiment was the work to integrate hospital and primary care, consultants and GPs. In part this was a response to the anxiety about a 'brain drain' from the emigration of young doctors from the UK to other countries due to the increasingly sophisticated training of doctors who could see no future in the hospital and specialist services, but who were not interested in entering general practice under the conditions prevalent in the UK. Brotherston and the SHHD saw the Livingston experiment and the Scottish health centre programme in general as ways to enhance the work opportunities of general practice, providing the 'doctor with greater diagnostic and therapeutic back up and team support' through health centres. In Livingston this also involved joint appointments for GPs with sessions in the hospital. Each GP's list was limited to 1,500 patients; for the patient the doctor provided the full range of general medical services and the patients were seen in the health centres by appointment or in their own homes as necessary. The other part of the doctor's conjoint appointment was five sessions with the Regional Hospital Board as a medical assistant in a speciality, with the doctor being a full member of the appropriate consultant team. The scheme proved very attractive with 50 applications for each of the vacancies advertised in Livingston during the first five years, an area which had previously had difficulty attracting GPs to practice vacancies. The plan was to build four health centres each catering for the population of a district eventually reaching roughly 20,000 people. The first health centre, Craighall, located in the first area of housing to be built and inhabited was opened in January 1969, and it catered for a population of about 10,000 by 1972. Its staff included six doctors, four dentists, eight nurses, nine secretarial staff and part-time physiotherapy, chiropody and dietetic staff.[32]

Reorganisation of the NHS under legislation for Scotland in 1972 created area health boards, to be implemented on 1 April 1974. Brotherston and the SHHD had to decide whether to continue the Livingston 'experiment' and fund it specially.[33] Criticism emerged from a BMA committee report which did not want the joint appointments to become a widespread model, arguing the New

Town, with its young age structure and underdeveloped local authority services, did not provide a model applicable to non-New Towns, while some specialities, e.g. psychiatry, were more amenable to joint appointments than others, such as surgery.[34] The SHHD agreed that the joint appointments would not be a proto-type for health centres in other areas, though they would remain in Livingston with the agreement of the new Lothian Health Board which would oversee Livingston in the future. Livingston was now organised on an area basis so, like health centres elsewhere in Scotland, it no longer needed a JAC; however, the SHHD hoped that its other innovation, joint appointments, would continue.[35] The report on the Livingston project after ten years suggests they did.[36]

**Glasgow – Initiative from GPs**

The Livingston 'experiment' was one pattern; more common was the initiative of GPs found in Glasgow. However, while it is generally recognised that much of the initiative for the renewed popularity of health centres came from repre-sentatives of GPs, in Glasgow – a major industrial city with a population of over a million and notorious overcrowding – the reasons arose from particular local circumstances, namely a uniquely large urban redevelopment programme. And it resulted, not in individual *ad hoc* initiatives, but in a plan for Glasgow as a whole, which brought together representatives of the three parts of the health service and the University of Glasgow.

In October 1964, joining the vogue for 'experiment', William Fulton, a GP and secretary of the Local Medical Committee responsible for the administration of general practice in Glasgow, wrote a memorandum entitled 'An Opportunity to Experiment in Glasgow' approved by the Local Medical Committee. The memo-randum argued that financial incentives for individual practitioners to provide group premises, which had become the policy in place of health centres since the early 1950s, was not appropriate in Glasgow where a huge urban redevelopment programme was going forward and required planning. In the redevelopment areas all (or nearly all) the buildings would be demolished and the whole area rebuilt with a much lower density of population. Doctors in these areas would lose their surgeries, and as yet there were no plans for replacements despite ten years of consultation between Glasgow Corporation and the Executive Council which administered the local health services and no lack of goodwill; also even-tually fewer doctors would be required in Glasgow as a whole. The memorandum argued that this was the time for the central authority to act to plan and build a number of health centres and take the opportunity to carry out an experiment that could revolutionise general practice in Glasgow. The planning would not be difficult because it could be aligned with the hospital plan in which Glasgow was divided into five sectors, and the provision of general medical services could follow this pattern. The premises could take a variety of forms, but the three parts of the NHS were complementary and the needs of the patient would be better served if they were available under one roof.

The memorandum stressed that it should be the responsibility of central government to undertake the planning and building of the new premises, retaining GPs' longstanding opposition to local authority, responsibility for centres. It argued that there was no doubt that local opinion would favour central government action rather than the local authority, as the cost would not fall on the rates. Nor would the relation of the patient to the individual GP change. Each patient had a personal doctor who had continuous responsibility for seeing him or her through all illnesses. It would not be a polyclinic where a group of doctors shared a common responsibility for large blocks of patients. The aim of better organisation was to enable doctors to waste a minimum of time on non-essentials from the medical point of view and to provide a better and more personal service for their own patients over a wide range of clinical and social aspects of their health.

The LMC released the memorandum to the press and there was wide coverage and approval in the newspapers.[37] The *Scottish Daily Express* suggested that the estimated cost of the centres of £1 million was a 'drop in the bucket' compared with the planned expenditure for hospital expansion.

By the end of January the SHHD indicated that it viewed the proposals favourably and invited the Glasgow Executive Council formally to submit their plan, though it stressed that the relevant bodies needed to agree to work together. It called for immediate detailed planning for two health centres in redevelopment areas and for long-term planning to identify the next areas requiring attention. This approval from the centre made it possible for a joint committee in Glasgow, known as the Joint Medical Services Committee, including representatives of the GPs, local authority, hospital services and University, to be set up in 1965, and it went on to plan the future provision of health centres in the city.

By 1970 there were four centres under way, and the Department was asking the LMC to prioritise further areas for health centres in Glasgow. The 'Opportunity for Experiment in Glasgow' had become the 'Glasgow Health Centre Programme'.[38] The first health centre in Glasgow, the Woodside Health Centre, opened in June 1971.

Joint Medical Services Committees on the Glasgow model were also set up in other Scottish cities to plan health centres, including Dundee, Dumbarton and Stirling.[39] In April 1974 the reorganisation of the health services brought the local authority health services, the Regional Hospital Boards and the Executive Committees together under the authority of 15 Regional Health Boards. As we saw above in Livingston, this involved disbanding the Joint Medical Services

Committees and handing the planning and operation of health centres over to the new Regional Health Boards. As the legislation for Scotland had passed in 1972 before that for England and Wales, and there was general agreement in favour of the reorganisation in Scotland,[40] there was time to plan the handover of health centres, like that of the other previously separate parts of the service, and sort out remaining issues, such as whether the SHHD would continue to own the Livingston health centres and when the Joint Medical Services Committees would disband.[41]

The growth of the number of health centres in the areas of the Regional Health Boards in Scotland after 1974 is shown in table 10.2. One striking feature of the pattern of development is the relatively slow growth of the number of health centres in Glasgow, despite the initiative of William Fulton and the Executive Committee and continuing pressure from Fulton and Labour MPs. The number reached 18, but only in the late 1980s. Several local features account for the delay. The primary reason was the difficulty the Joint Medical Services Committee and subsequently the Regional Health Board had in obtaining suitable sites from Glasgow Corporation.[42] For example, in the interest of moving ahead the Joint Medical Services Committee accepted a site in the new development at Easterhouse on a difficult slope, and in the redeveloped area of Bridgeton with an awkward shape that did not allow for enough car parking spaces to meet the Scottish Office Design Department's guidelines without utilising the ground floor; this in turn raised the costs, because lifts would be necessary to allow access for the elderly and disabled. The local authority education department had falling enrolments, so there were empty school buildings which the Joint Medical Services Committee tried to obtain, but without success. One school on Church Street adjacent to the Western Infirmary would have provided facilities for training medical students as well as services adjacent to the hospital for easy referral for patients. The education authority before 1974 would give up the site only if the SHHD paid for a replacement swimming pool, and the situation did not ease after 1974 despite the merging of planning departments within the new local authorities in 1975.

While there was enthusiasm among GPs for health centres in redevelopment areas or new developments within the city, another reason for the relatively slow growth in numbers of health centres in Glasgow was the reluctance of GPs in established practices in stable neighbourhoods to move. This reluctance stemmed in part from concern for their patients' views and circumstances; and their fear of losing patients and money they had already spent refurbishing their premises.

Patients appear to have been absent from the planning process for health centres in Glasgow. As we have seen, not only the Scottish Office, but also Joint Medical Committees with representatives of Executive Councils, local

Table 10.2 Number of health centres in Scotland by region, listed in descending order of 1974 ranking, 1974–1990

| Health board | Year | | | | | | | | | | | | | | | | |
|---|---|---|---|---|---|---|---|---|---|---|---|---|---|---|---|---|---|
| | 1974 | 1975 | 1976 | 1977 | 1978 | 1979 | 1980 | 1981 | 1982 | 1983 | 1984 | 1985 | 1986 | 1987 | 1988 | 1989 | 1990 |
| Lothian | 11 | 13 | 15 | 16 | 17 | 17 | 20 | 20 | 24 | 24 | 26 | 26 | 28 | 27 | 27 | 28 | 28 |
| Lanarkshire | 10 | 12 | 12 | 12 | 12 | 12 | 13 | 12 | 15 | 17 | 17 | 17 | 18 | 19 | 19 | 19 | 19 |
| Grampian | 7 | 10 | 13 | 13 | 15 | 20 | 20 | 21 | 21 | 21 | 21 | 22 | 22 | 22 | 20 | 20 | 20 |
| Fife | 7 | 10 | 12 | 13 | 14 | 16 | 17 | 17 | 19 | 19 | 19 | 19 | 19 | 19 | 19 | 19 | 19 |
| Forth Valley | 7 | 8 | 9 | 9 | 10 | 10 | 10 | 13 | 13 | 12 | 12 | 13 | 14 | 15 | 15 | 15 | 15 |
| Greater Glasgow | 5 | 5 | 5 | 5 | 6 | 6 | 7 | 8 | 13 | 15 | 15 | 15 | 16 | 16 | 16 | 18 | 18 |
| Argyll and Clyde | 5 | 6 | 6 | 9 | 9 | 9 | 12 | 12 | 13 | 12 | 12 | 13 | 12 | 12 | 12 | 12 | 13 |
| Dumfries and Galloway | 5 | 5 | 5 | 5 | 6 | 6 | 6 | 6 | 6 | 6 | 6 | 6 | 6 | 6 | 6 | 6 | 6 |
| Highland | 4 | 4 | 7 | 7 | 7 | 8 | 8 | 8 | 8 | 9 | 9 | 11 | 11 | 11 | 11 | 11 | 11 |
| Tayside | 2 | 3 | 4 | 8 | 8 | 10 | 11 | 12 | 13 | 14 | 14 | 15 | 15 | 15 | 15 | 16 | 16 |
| Borders | 2 | 2 | 2 | 4 | 4 | 4 | 4 | 5 | 10 | 12 | 12 | 12 | 9 | 9 | 10 | 14 | 15 |
| Shetland | 1 | 1 | 1 | 1 | 1 | 1 | 1 | 1 | 1 | 2 | 2 | 2 | 2 | 2 | 2 | 2 | 2 |
| Orkney | 1 | 1 | 1 | 1 | 1 | 1 | 1 | 1 | 1 | 1 | 1 | 1 | 1 | 1 | 1 | 1 | 1 |
| Ayrshire and Arran | 0 | 0 | 0 | 6 | 6 | 6 | 6 | 7 | 8 | 8 | 8 | 8 | 9 | 9 | 10 | 10 | 10 |
| Western Isles | 0 | 0 | 0 | 1 | 1 | 1 | 1 | 1 | 1 | 1 | 1 | 1 | 1 | 1 | 1 | 1 | 1 |

Source: *Hospital and Health Services Yearbook 1975–1992*

authorities, Regional Hospital Boards and universities planned health centres. However, patients were not entirely without influence. No health centre was built on the western side of Glasgow, nor is there one now. One was proposed to be located on the site of Gartnavel General Hospital off Great Western Road in the centre of the district. However, in October 1973 at a meeting of GPs in the area with SHHD officials, GPs with surgeries along Dumbarton Road, whose patients were poor, opposed it, because public transport to Gartnavel was indirect and costly and would be difficult for their patients. As a result of the meeting the health centre idea for this part of Glasgow was dropped. The dean of medicine at Glasgow University described the meeting in a letter to the principal:

> The meeting was conducted mainly by Dr W.W. Fulton who displayed a large map of the area in which all surgeries and consulting rooms had been marked. He had obviously done a lot of homework on this and was able to point to any given pin and say 'this is a three-man practice and they have a second consulting room at . . .' and show us where this other one was. In the western area there are somewhat over forty practitioners and the majority of the surgeries lie in Anderston and along Dumbarton Road. Gartnavel is central to the area with roughly half the practices on either side but there are no consulting rooms anywhere near it. For example, there is not a single one in the entire Kelvinside/Kelvindale area. The same is true of the northwest part of the area, around Anniesland Cross and Knightswood. After this map had been shown the Chairman asked me to speak as the university had been the main body supporting the idea of a centre at Gartnavel. I said that I thought at least as much of the pressure had come from the Regional Board as from the University and that both bodies were really far more interested in a centre built on the Church Street triangle if only the time element could be overcome. I added that we were still negotiating with the Glasgow Corporation.
>
> Dr Fulton did say to the meeting that he, personally, did not favour a centre at Gartnavel but apart from this made no effort to lead the discussion which was of a very open and indeed interesting nature. There were about 40–50 GPs present coming from all over the area and I think that they could be regarded as representative.
>
> At an early stage in the proceedings it became very clear that they were divided into two groups and that no one was really thinking of the area as one block. It is divided into two almost equal parts (both with reference to area and to number of practices) by a line running northward from the Dumbarton Road end of Balshagray Avenue. Both groups of doctors, however, were united in saying that they feared a large loss of patients if

they were to move their practices to Gartnavel. Those from the western
sector pointed out that most of their patients arrived by car, while those
from the eastern side thought that, with the very high fares for Corporation
transport, Gartnavel would present a problem to many of theirs. A vote
being taken, Gartnavel was not supported by a single person.

    After this the practitioners from the western sector were asked about
their views as to where a health centre might be sited in their area. They
made it very clear that they were not really interested in having a health
centre at all. Most of them said that they had spent considerable sums in
equipping and furnishing their surgeries and consulting rooms and felt
that they would lose a good deal were they to transfer to another locality.
The practitioners from the eastern group, while rejecting Gartnavel,
showed a good deal of interest in the idea of a centre at Church Street and
a vote taken among them showed a good number in favour . . . I feel that
we may consider the Gartnavel project as dead.[43]

    If patients did not have a direct input into the planning process, there were
surveys in the 1970s of patients' attitudes to health centres, including one of
patients attending the health centre at Clydebank before and after it opened; by
1976 it was the largest health centre in operation with 32 GPs providing services
for 66,000 patients.[44] The results of the survey of Clydebank patients are not available, but there is evidence from England. A survey of patient attitudes in England
suggested general approval of health centres. Patients commented on the importance of privacy at the reception counter and in treatment rooms and keeping
large piles of records out of view. While patients approved of appointment systems
at health centres, they complained about difficulties in making appointments and
the attitudes of some receptionists. Also, the surveys found that patients lacked
knowledge of the range of services available at health centres.[45]

    The uncertainty of patients is not surprising as the range of services available
at health centres in 1976 varied greatly and continued to do so fifteen years later,
as did the size of the populations that health centres covered. By 1991, nearly
half (45 per cent) the Scottish population had access to a health centre, a large
increase over the 20 per cent of the population in 1976.[46] The coverage in the
Borders (80 per cent) and Forth Valley (65 per cent) was particularly high,
while that in Ayrshire and Arran (21 per cent) and in Dumfries and Galloway
(27 per cent) was particularly low; and the size of population covered by
individual health centres varied from 99 of the total of 188 health centres with
population coverage below 10,000 to the 14 health centres that served more
than 30,000 patients in 1991. Specialist services with a community orientation
were located in many health centres, but there was considerable variation

in coverage. For example, psychiatry was the most commonly provided, with 79 of the 188 health centres served, while 54 of the health centres had specialist obstetric clinics and smaller numbers had specialist paediatric and ophthalmic clinics.[47]

## Conclusion

The idea of health centres was not new in 1946 and 1947 when the legislation passed establishing the NHS in Britain, but its meaning varied, and health centres had a special integrating role in the scheme for the NHS. The general failure to establish health centres in the early years of the NHS left little to counteract the administrative separation of the three branches. The alternatives to health centres pursued in the 1950s were limited financial incentives, such as interest-free loans, to individual practitioners to build the new premises and to encourage group practice, but even if fully funded, the GPs in Glasgow realised that these had limitations, particularly in redevelopment areas. The resurrection of health centres in the mid-1960s relied on the initiative of GPs and on co-operation at the local level. As we saw in the plan of the 'typical' health centre at the outset of the NHS, the GPs were not trying to build their own mini-hospitals, but were trying to recreate the advantages of the family doctor in more collaborative surroundings. By the mid-1970s after the reorganisation of the NHS in 1974, the concept of health centres as a way to integrate the tripartite administrative structure gave way to their becoming a place where primary care services developed as a 'fully integrated element of the total system of health care'.[48]

 The revival of health centres from the mid-1960s highlights the importance of looking at the history of the NHS from the bottom up. Even though in the early stages of the NHS in Scotland the Department of Health for Scotland showed itself capable of planning and building health centres, initiative from the top down in the Scottish Office in the mid-1960s was limited to Livingston. Yet, Scottish Office support was still essential for the revival of the health centres and implementing local initiatives, and the initiatives and central government backing for health centres in the mid-1960s came first in Scotland in part because of the close collaboration between the medical profession and the SHHD. As William Fulton, the Glasgow GP and medical politician, commented,

we were so often first to be organised in Scotland. It is a small country and we know and trusted each other well enough to get agreement. We did not need long-drawn out negotiations as was so often the case in the South. It was common for senior officers in the Health Department to hold office in [medical organisations] . . . We hardly needed formal liaison Committees in these days.[49]

Yet, despite its separate statutory basis and organisation, and differences between Scotland and England in working relationships between officials in the Scottish Office and the medical profession, the Treasury was still able to thwart or encourage initiatives such as health centres. The National Health Service in Scotland was distinctive, but it was still British.

## Acknowledgements

I am grateful to the Wellcome Trust for the funding that made the research for this paper possible. Previous versions of this chapter have been presented at conferences in Boston and Glasgow, and I would like to thank the audiences for their comments and suggestions.

## Notes

1. Crowther, M.A., *The Workhouse System 1834–1929: The History of an English Social Institution* (London, [1981] 1983), 3, 6.
2. Webster, C., *The National Health Services since the War* (2 vols, London, 1988 and 1996); Webster, C., *The National Health Service: A Political History* (Oxford, 1998).
3. See, for example, Ham, C., *Policy-Making in the National Health Service: A Case Study of the Leeds Regional Hospital Board* (London, 1981).
4. Pickstone, J., 'Psychiatry in District General Hospitals' in Pickstone, J., ed., *Medical Innovations in Historical Perspective* (Basingstoke, 1992), 185–99.
5. The name of the relevant department was changed from the Department of Health for Scotland to the Scottish Home and Health Department on 1 June 1962.
6. Roemer, M.I., *Evaluation of Community Health Centres* (Geneva, 1972), 7, 9.
7. Rosen, G., 'The First Neighborhood Health Center Movement: Its Rise and Fall', in Numbers, R. and Levitt, J.W., eds, *Sickness and Health in America: Readings in the History of Medicine and Public Health* (Madison, [1971] 1985), 185–200; Rothstein, W.G., 'Bureaucratic Creativity and Professional Conservatisim: Neighborhood Health Centers in New York City 1900–1980', paper delivered at the annual conference of the American Association for the History of Medicine, Boston, 2 May 2003.
8. Beach, A., 'Potential for Participation: Health Centres and the Idea of Citizenship c.1920–1940', in Lawrence, C. and Mayer, A.-K., eds, *Regenerating England: Science, Medicine and Culture in Interwar Britain* (Amsterdam, 2000), 203–30; Scott-Samuel, A., ed., *Total Participation, Total Health: Reinventing the Peckham Health Centre for the 1990s* (Edinburgh, 1990); Darling, E., *Re-forming Britain: Narratives of Modernity before Reconstruction* (Abingdon and New York, 2007), 54–71.
9. Darling, *Re-forming Britain*, 73.
10. Darling, *Re-forming Britain*, 74.
11. Darling, *Re-forming Britain*, 80.
12. Webster, C., 'The Metamorphosis of Dawson of Penn', in Porter, D. and Porter, R., eds, *Doctors, Society and Politics: Historical Essays* (Amsterdam, 1993), 212–28.

13. Pater, J., *The Making of the National Health Service* (London, 1981), 39–40. See also Hall, P., 'The Development of Health Centres', in Hall, P., Land, H., Parker, R. and Webb, A., *Change, Choice and Conflict in Social Policy* (Aldershot, [1975] 1986), 277–310, at 278–84.

14. Pater, *Making*, 42.

15. Pater, *Making*, 172–4; Webster, C., 'The Politics of General Practice', in Loudon, I., Horder, J. and Webster, C., eds, *General Practice under the National Health Service 1948–1997* (Oxford, 1998), 20–44, at 20–1.

16. Hogarth, J., 'General Practice', in McLachlan, G., ed., *Improving the Common Weal: Aspects of Scottish Health Services 1900–1984* (Edinburgh, 1985), 162–212, at 193. Webster, 'Politics', 22; Hall, 'Health Centres', 278.

17. National Archives of Scotland (NAS), HH101/1887/8, September 1947.

18. For the opposite view, regarding England, see: Bosanquet, N. and Salisbury, C., 'The Practice', in Loudon et al, *General Practice*, 45–64, at 55.

19. NAS, HH101/1887/8, September 1947, 4.

20. NAS HH101/1887/8, September 1947, 7.

21. NAS, HH101/1988/16, October–November 1946.

22. NAS, HH101/1887, 28 February 1957.

23. *Nuffield Provincial Hospitals Trust: Report 1948–1951* (London, 1951), 35–47. I am grateful to George Gosling of Oxford Brookes University for bringing this report to my attention.

24. Hogarth, 'General Practice', 200, 206.

25. Webster, 'Politics', 32; Hall, 'Health Centres', 277–310.

26. Including, for example, the upturn in the economy in the 1960s, a new government in 1964, the feeling that it was the GPs' turn for capital investment after the ten-year plan for hospital building was launched in the early 1960s, and increasing self-confidence among GPs with the Doctors' Charter of the mid-1960s.

27. 'Sir John Brotherston', *The Times*, 16 May 1985. John Howie Flint Brotherston (1915–1985) served as chief medical officer for Scotland from 1964 to 1977. He played a key role in the reorganisation of the Scottish health service and the associated legislation of 1974. He was knighted in 1972.

28. 'Family Doctor Now a Rarity, Medical Dean Declares', *The Times*, 21 October 1963.

29. Brotherston, J.H.F., 'Preface', in Duncan, A.H., ed., *The Livingston Project: The First Five Years* (Edinburgh, 1973), v.

30. 'Sir John Brotherston', *The Times*, 16 May 1985.

31. Kuenssberg, E.V., *Transplant* (memoir printed privately, 1993), 252–3. I am grateful to his son, Nick Kuenssberg, for allowing me to read his father's autobiography.

32. The preceding two paragraphs are based on the articles in Duncan, *Livingston Project*, esp. v–32. See also NAS, HH101/3632/22, Sir John Brotherston, 'Comments on Dr Duncan's Second Draft: *The Livingston Project – the First Five Years*', 25 August 1972.

33. NAS, HH101/ 3632/9A, The Livingston Project – Note of a Meeting held at St Andrew's House on 14 June 1972; NAS, HH101/3632/23, Memorandum from W.P. Lawrie, 23 January 1973.

34. NAS, HH101/3632/42, British Medical Association (Scottish Office) Report of Livingston Working Party. Brotherston believed the BMA report and publicity surrounding it misrepresented the Livingston experiment. See NAS, HH101/3632/82 and HH101/3632/88.

35. NAS, HH101/3632/68, Note of Meeting held on Wednesday 5 June [1974] . . . in St Andrew's House; NAS, HH101/3632/78, The Livingston Experiment – Note of Meeting between Representatives of the SGMS Committee and SHHD on Friday 5 July 1974.

36. Munro, H.D.R., ed., *The Livingston Scheme: A Ten Year Review* (Edinburgh, 1982), vii, ix, 1–14.

37. The *Glasgow Herald*, the *Scotsman, The Times* and the *Scottish Daily Express* all carried articles on 23 October 1964.

38. Greater Glasgow Health Board Archives (GGHB), HB100/6/1/3, P. Mackay to T.H. Souter, 10 April 1970; T.H. Souter to P. Mackay, 13 April 1970.

39. NAS, HH101/3493/27, Health Centre Provision, March 1969.
40. Webster, 'Politics', 35–6.
41. Brotherston, 'Comments on Dr Duncan's Second Draft'; NAS, HH101/3632/23, W.P. Lawrie, 'Health Centre Planning – Joint Advisory Committee', 23 January 1973.
42. NAS, HH101/3582 and 3853 reveal the frustration of the Glasgow Executive Council at the delays in the programme and the problems finding sites in the redevelopment areas.
43. GGHB, HB55/REG/12/HC/0/B, Health Centres – General Correspondence, vol. 1: September 1973–July 1975. 10 Oct 1973 A.J. Haddow (administrative dean, Faculty of Medicine, University of Glasgow) to the principal, University of Glasgow. Report of a meeting of GPs concerning health centres in western Glasgow, 9 October 1973.
44. Macgregor, I.M., Patterson, J.S., Drummond, D.C. and Slater, B.C.S., 'Health Centre Practice in Scotland – Part 2' *Health Bulletin* 38 (1980), 5–22, at 18. See also: Cammock, R., *Health Centres Reception, Waiting and Patient Call* (London, 1973).
45. Patterson, J.S., 'Patients' Attitudes to Health Centres', *Health Bulletin* 33 (1975), 52–7.
46. Macgregor et al., 'Health Centre Practice in Scotland – Part 2', 18.
47. Milne, R.G., Torsney, B. and Watson, J., 'Consultant Out-Patient Services: Provision at Health Centres in Scotland', *Health Bulletin* 50 (1992), 457–67.
48. SHHD, *Annual Report for 1975*, (Edinburgh, 1976), 656.
49. GGHB, HB/100/2/2/10, William W. Fulton to Denis Pereira Gray, 20 January 1992.

# Anne Crowther: List of Main Publications

## Books

Crowther, M.A., *Church Embattled: Religious Controversy in Mid-Victorian England* (Newton Abbot, 1970).

Crowther, M.A., *The Workhouse System, 1834–1929: The History of an English Social Institution* (Cambridge, [1981] 1983).

Crowther, M.A., *British Social Policy 1914–1939* (Basingstoke, 1988). Studies in Economic and Social History.

Crowther, M.A. and White, B., *On Soul and Conscience: The Medical Expert and Crime* (Aberdeen, 1988).

Crowther, M.A. and Dupree, M.W., *Medical Lives in the Age of Surgical Revolution* (Cambridge, 2007). Cambridge Studies in Population, Economy and Society in Past Time.

McGann, S., Crowther, A. and Dougall, R., *A History of the Royal College of Nursing 1916–90: A Voice for Nurses* (Manchester, 2009).

## Journal Articles

Crowther, M.A., 'Family Responsibility and State Responsibility in Britain before the Welfare State', *Historical Journal* 25 (1982), 131–45.

Crowther, M.A., 'Paupers or Patients? Obstacles to Professionalization in the Poor Law Medical Service before 1914', *Journal of the History of Medicine and Allied Sciences* 39 (1984), 33–55.

Crowther, M.A., ' "Savill's Disease": A Pauper Epidemic in Britain and Its Implications', *Bulletin of the History of Medicine* 60 (1986), 544–58.

Crowther, M.A. and White, B.M., 'Medicine, Property and the Law in Britain 1800–1914', *Historical Journal* 31 (1988), 853–70.

Crowther, M.A. and Dupree, M.W., 'A Profile of the Medical Profession in Scotland in the Early Twentieth Century: The *Medical Directory* as a Historical Source', *Bulletin of the History of Medicine* 65 (1991), 209–33.

Crowther, M.A., 'The Workhouse', *Proceedings of the British Academy* 78 (1992), 181–92.

Crowther, M.A., 'A Fermtoun Tragedy', *Scottish Local History* 29 (October 1993), 16–20.

Crowther, M.A., 'Criminal Precognitions and their Value for the Historian', *Scottish Archives* 1 (1995), 75–84.

Crowther, M.A. and Dupree, M.W., 'The Invisible General Practitioner: The Careers of Scottish Medical Students in the Late Nineteenth Century', *Bulletin of the History of Medicine* 70 (1996), 387–413.

Bradley, J., Crowther, M.A. and Dupree, M.W., 'Mobility and Selection in Scottish University Medical Education, 1858–1886', *Medical History* 40 (1996), 1–24.

## Chapters in Edited Collections

Crowther, M.A., 'The Last Years of the Workhouse', in P. Thane (ed.) *The Origins of British Social Policy* (London, [1978] 1985), 36–55.

Crowther, M.A., 'Church Problems and Church Parties', in G. Parsons (ed.), *Religion in Victorian Britain, Volume IV: Interpretations* (Manchester, 1988), 4–27.

Crowther, M.A., 'Poverty, Health and Welfare', in H. Fraser and R.J. Morris (eds), *People and Society in Scotland, II: 1830–1914* (Edinburgh, 1988), 265–89.

Crowther, M.A., 'The Tramp', in R. Porter (ed.), *Myths of the English* (Oxford, [1992] 1993), 90–113.

Crowther, M.A., 'Forensic Medicine and Medical Ethics in Nineteenth-Century Britain', in R. Baker (ed.), *The Codification of Medical Morality: Historical and Philosophical Studies of the Formalization of Western Medical Morality in the Eighteenth and Nineteenth Centuries, Volume II: Anglo-American Medical Ethics and Medical Jurisprudence in the Nineteenth Century* (Dordrecht, 1995), 173–89.

Dupree, M.W., Bradley, J. and Crowther, M.A., 'Micros and Medical Students: Sources and Methods for Exploring the Educational Careers and Completion Rates of Scottish Medical Students in the Late Nineteenth Century', in P. Denley (ed.), *Computing Techniques and the History of Universities* (St Katharinen, 1996), 155–74.

Crowther, M.A., 'Introduction', and 'Medicine and the Law in Nineteenth-Century Scotland', in Y. Otsuka and S. Sakai (eds), *Medicine and the Law: Proceedings of the 19th International Symposium on the Comparative History of Medicine – East and West* (Tokyo, 1998), ix–xiv, 63–82.

Crowther, M.A., 'Crime, Prosecution and Mercy: English Influences and Scottish Practice in the Early Nineteenth Century', in S.J. Connolly (ed.), *Kingdoms United? Great Britain and Ireland since 1500, Integration and Diversity* (Dublin, 1998), 225–38.

Crowther, M.A., 'From Workhouse to NHS Hospital in Britain 1929–1948', in C. Hillam and J.M. Bone (eds), *The Poor Law and After: Workhouse Hospitals and Public Welfare* (Liverpool, 1999), 38–49.

Crowther, M.A., 'Health Care and Poor Relief in Provincial England', in O. Grell, A. Cunningham and R. Jütte (eds), *Health Care and Poor Relief in 18th- and 19th-Century Northern Europe* (Aldershot, 2002), 203–20.

Crowther, M.A., 'The Toxicology of Robert Christison: European Influences and British Practice in the Early Nineteenth Century', in J.R. Bertomeu-Sánchez and A. Nieto-Galan (eds), *Chemistry, Medicine, and Crime: Mateu J.B. Orfila (1787–1853) and His Times* (Sagamore Beach, 2006), 125–52. Spanish edition published as *Entre la Ciencia y el Crimen: Mateu Orfila y la Toxicología en el Siglo XIX* (Barcelona, 2006).

# Index

Notes are indexed by page number followed by note number, e.g, 24n2